The Jury and Democracy

THE JURY AND DEMOCRACY

*How Jury Deliberation Promotes Civic Engagement
and Political Participation*

*John Gastil
E. Pierre Deess
Philip J. Weiser and
Cindy Simmons*

OXFORD
UNIVERSITY PRESS
2010

OXFORD

UNIVERSITY PRESS

Oxford University Press, Inc., publishes works that further
Oxford University's objective of excellence
in research, scholarship, and education.

Oxford   New York
Auckland   Cape Town   Dar es Salaam   Hong Kong   Karachi
Kuala Lumpur   Madrid   Melbourne   Mexico City   Nairobi
New Delhi   Shanghai   Taipei   Toronto

With offices in
Argentina   Austria   Brazil   Chile   Czech Republic   France   Greece
Guatemala   Hungary   Italy   Japan   Poland   Portugal   Singapore
South Korea   Switzerland   Thailand   Turkey   Ukraine   Vietnam

Copyright © 2010 by Oxford University Press, Inc.

Published by Oxford University Press, Inc.
198 Madison Avenue, New York, New York 10016

www.oup.com

Oxford is a registered trademark of Oxford University Press

Library of Congress Cataloging-in-Publication Data
The jury and democracy: how jury deliberation promotes civic engagement and
political participation/John Gastil ... [et al.].
   p. cm.
Includes bibliographical references and index.
ISBN 978-0-19-537730-9; 978-0-19-537731-6 (pbk.)
1. Political participation—United States.   2. Deliberative democracy—
United States.   3. Jury—United States—Decision making.   4. Jury duty—
United States.   I. Gastil, John.
JK1764.J87 2010
323'.042—dc22   2010001318

Printed in the United States of America
on acid-free paper

To the memory of Michael Fajans (1947–2006),
a public artist who glimpsed the jury's soul

Acknowledgments

The authors gratefully acknowledge that this material is based on work supported by the National Science Foundation Directorate for Social, Behavioral & Economic Sciences: Law and Social Science Program (Grant No. 0318513) and by the University of Washington Royalty Research Fund. Any opinions, findings, and conclusions or recommendations expressed in this material are those of the authors and do not necessarily reflect the views of the National Science Foundation or the University of Washington. We also thank the Helen Riaboff Whiteley Center at Friday Harbor Laboratories for providing us time to write portions of this book amidst deer, swallows, sailboats, and the occasional raven.

Assistance with the design of the study was offered by Valerie Hans, Reid Hastie, Dick Madsen, and Kay Schlozman. They helped work out the designs of the panel survey described herein, and each provided invaluable insights and encouragement that went far beyond the niceties of methodology. Additional suggestions that influenced the substance of our studies and the direction of our argument were provided by Don Braman, Leah Ceccarelli, Mark Forehand, Dan Kahan, Ron Kessler, Tom Munsterman, Gerry Philipsen, Ted Prosise, Nancy Rivenburgh, Mark Smith, Morgan Southwood, and numerous undergraduate and graduate students in John Gastil's courses on small group communication and political deliberation. We also received cover design advice from Phil Kovacevich and archival assistance from the librarian at the *Columbus Dispatch*.

Interviews with jurors and analyses of juries in popular culture were provided by a team of undergraduate research assistants, including Sarah Brisbin, Elysa Howard, Megan Koznek, Jordan Meade, Gabrielle Musser, Sarah Perez, Kayla Roark, Katie Schmidt, and Chelan Vukas. We also benefited from collaborative work that merited coauthorship in scholarly conference papers and publications from Kent Anderson, Laura Black, Stephanie Burkhalter, Hiroshi Fukurai, Tina Gall, Jay Leighter, Andrea Hickerson, Mark Nolan, Leah Sprain, and Mike Xenos. Literature searches and other preparatory tasks were completed with the assistance of Tamara Barnett, Kate Bell, Nick Cenak, Doug Clarke, Ted Coopman, Ameer Dixit, Rob Ewing, Traci Feller, Christian Gardner-Wood, Wenlin Liu, and Nafees Uddin. For editorial assistance with these and other writings along the way to this book, we thank Awanthi Vardaraj and Jamie Moshin, and the book itself received editorial attention from Angela Chnapko, Alexandra Dauler, David McBride, and Michael Philoantonie at Oxford University Press.

The national dataset presented in chapter 3 was collected, compiled, and coded by the authors and Laura Black, Stephanie Burkhalter, Rebecca Clark, Tom Cochran, Annabel Forbes, Tina Gall, Jay Leighter, and Mike Xenos. The following county staff and judges provided considerable assistance in identifying, preparing, and providing court and election records: Debra Crosser and Linda Bowers in the Boulder District Court and Patricia Stahl in Elections; Belinda Fernandez, Tamera Kato, Paul Manolopoulos, Irene Szczerba, Greg Wheeler, Judge Richard Eadie, Judge Ron Kessler, Judge J. Wesley Saint Clair, and the Members of the Jury Committee in the King County Court and Pam Floyd in Elections; Shannon Sims, Sandra Pena, and Judge Calvin Johnson in the Orleans Parish Civil Court, Michelle Rodney, Belinda Lassalle, and Dale Atkins in the Criminal Court, and Al Ater and Judy Outlaw at the Louisiana Secretary of State; Mike Havlick and Rudy Tesar in the Douglas County Criminal District Court and Justine Kessler in the Election Commission; Melissa Hernandez-Urbina at the El Paso County Court, Armando Balderrama and Chris Moreno at iDocket, and Jeff Smith at Opinion Analysts Inc.; Cliff Layman and Patrick Tamer at the North Carolina Office of the Courts, Tonia J. Clifton and Linda Priest at the Cumberland County Court, Helen Styles at the Swain County Court, and the North Carolina State Board of Elections; Andrew Bauer and Mary Lou Dougherty at the Summit County Common Pleas Court and Sean Gaffney at the Board of Elections; and, finally, where it all began, Linda Enlow at the Thurston County Clerk's office, Tillie Naputi at the auditor's office, and Election Systems & Software.

For assistance with collecting and processing the panel survey data reported in chapters 4 through 7, principal thanks go to Jay Leighter, who devoted a year of his graduate career to carrying out this survey. At the University of Washington and the New Jersey Institute of Technology, we also received assistance from Giorgia Aiello, Ray Calluori, Tina Gall, Irina Gendelman, Hillary Gillings, Sophia Liu, and Rachel Nez. Our research assistants would have had no work, however, were it not for the generosity and services of staff at the King County and Seattle courts. At the Seattle Municipal Court, we received helpful cooperation and oversight from Court Services Manager Kathleen Friedman and Judge Fred Bonner, assistance collecting survey data from Jury Administrators Kendra Lafayette and Juliet Dickens, and court records retrieval assistance from Sharon Petty. At the King County Court, those mentioned earlier, especially Jury Manager Greg Wheeler, were very helpful; assistance collecting survey data was also provided by Belinda Fernandez, Tamera Kato, and Irene Szczerba. Dorothy Paulsen at the University of Washington Human Subjects Division also helped shepherd the panel survey through a complex review process, which involved obtaining a Certificate of Confidentiality from the National Institutes of Health to ensure the security of our data.

We expect that few readers could bear the endless credits in the preceding paragraphs, so it may suffice to know this: There exist in our courts and public offices remarkably helpful, patient, and good-humored people who want to make government work for the betterment of all, even the poorly dressed, researchers who occasionally walk through their door. We are deeply grateful to them, because without their help, this study could never have been completed. And more important, these noble civil servants, through their daily work, facilitate the functioning of juries, a fundamental unit of American democracy.

Our final thanks go to all of those jurors who participated in this study. Conscientiously completing surveys time and again, these citizens collectively contributed thousands of hours to our research project. By the end of the study, many had become curious about what would come of their labors. One 50-year-old man from Bothell, Washington, wrote on his questionnaire, "Who will use the information collected on this survey?" The answer, we sincerely hope, is you.

Three Sets of Twelve, the mural by Michael Fajans that appears on the cover of this book, consists of three 9-by-80 foot panels, installed on three levels of the federal courthouse in Seattle, Washington. The work explores how the jury takes twelve people from their everyday work life and recasts them as jurors in a courtroom context. Reflecting on this piece, Fajans wrote, "A unique group of distinct individuals who make up a jury weigh the body of shared information and experience to deliver a joint decision, the verdict.... The jurors leave, transformed by the gravity of this service they have rendered. They carry that experience out of the courtroom into their daily lives, each in his or her own way."

Contents

Figures

Tables

Photos

The Jury and Democracy

Chapter 1

Freedom in Our Hands

In a 2007 speech, Federal Judge William G. Young, recalled an encounter with a juror:

> We are trying a short case, a three or four day case. We are on the second or third day. A juror is coming into Boston, her car breaks down on what we call the Southeast Expressway, a main artery clogged in the morning. Her fuel pump goes. She drifts off into the breakdown lane. She gets out of her car. This is Massachusetts. Nobody stops. Nobody helps her. Everyone just goes by. She's standing there in the rain. Eventually, our safety net kicks in. Here is a Massachusetts state trooper. He puts on the yellow flashing lights. He gets over into the breakdown lane, protective of her car. He is getting out of his cruiser, when she walks back to him and says, "I am a juror in federal court! Take me to the courthouse!" Mother of God! And you know what the trooper does? He puts her in the cruiser. He turns on the blue lights and he starts barreling up the Southeast Expressway. What's more, he has got a radio. He's patched through to us. We know the juror is coming in. I am ecstatic!...I am at the window, looking out into the rain. Then the cruiser comes up. It swoops in in front of the courthouse. She gets out. Very slow elevators in our courthouse....Very slow she comes up. She gets out of the elevator on our floor and she starts running along the hallway....She is out-of-breath and she says, "The trial...I tried." We've been down only about 17 minutes, you know. She's done it! And she says she wants to call AAA to get her car towed....She calls. They won't tow her car. They are afraid of liability. I go crazy. "Give me that phone. Do you know who this is? You get someone out there to tow that lady's car!" You know, respectfully, that violates about four judicial canons, but it captures the idea. And I honor that juror, because she, at least, has the vision.[1]

3

The "vision" Judge Young noted is the juror's sense of civic duty. Few of those who have served on juries have stories of rescue from the breakdown lane, but most of those Americans who have served on juries share this feeling of responsibility. Their concern is not with punctuality but with their charge to see justice done. As one person wrote about serving on a jury in 2005, "We deliberated thoughtfully and spoke about many details" of the trial. "It is no easy task to take someone's freedom into your own hands."[2]

Roughly seventeen million Americans have served on juries during the past five years. Estimates are that a full third of U.S. citizens are likely to serve on a jury at some point in their lives.[3] Yet there exists no Jury Veterans' meeting hall where former jurors can celebrate, critique, and compare their experiences. Instead, their time as jurors tends to get sealed up inside them, as though they were still following the instruction they received from the judge not to discuss the case while the trial was underway. All too often, their brief careers as jurors are ignored or trivialized as anomalous moments in their lives.

Their personal stories are overshadowed by the sensational narratives that come from a handful of famous cases, such as O. J. Simpson's trials. The mundane but memorable details of their visit to real court carry not a fraction of the candlepower of popular movies and books, such as *Twelve Angry Men* and *Runaway Jury*.[4] Exceptional cases and fictional tales shed little light on the typical jury experience, which more commonly involves a two-day trial on such matters as petty theft, drunken driving, medical malpractice, or breach of contract. Moreover, the most widely circulated accounts focus on the content and outcome of the trials themselves, not on the experiences of those who sat in the jury box.[5]

This book tells the story of *jurors*. In fact, we will share the experiences of the thousands of jurors we have surveyed and studied over the course of a decade. These individual stories have intrinsic value, but we collected them and now relate them with a larger purpose in mind. Simply put, we aim to demonstrate that jury service is more than a noble civic duty. Participating in the jury process can be an invigorating experience for jurors that changes their understanding of themselves and their sense of political power and broader civic responsibilities. The typical service experience *matters* to former jurors. Whether they served ten days ago or ten years ago, many can recount their brief time at the courthouse in vivid detail and draw important lessons from jury service. More generally, we hope to show that it is the experience of deliberating with fellow citizens that gives the jury much of its power, and that underscores the importance of understanding, appreciating, and promoting meaningful public deliberation in modern democratic institutions.

To clarify and amplify jurors' past experiences, we have taken three approaches in this book. We analyzed official county records of jury service (and voting history) from over ten thousand empanelled jurors from eight counties across the United States. With funding from the National Science Foundation, we then surveyed thousands of people called for jury service in King County, Washington. They filled out questionnaires when they reported for service, after they left the courthouse, and in a follow-up survey many months later. Finally, we conducted in-depth interviews—face-to-face and by phone—with a smaller number of jurors. Assembling and analyzing these data has taken many years and thousands of hours of work by a large team of investigators and research assistants. In the end, the effort has proven worthwhile, as we now have a much clearer understanding of precisely how often, to what degree, and in what ways the jury experience can promote positive civic attitudes and more frequent public engagement.

Jury Service as Educational Opportunity

But if juries really have this power, might we expect that the framers of the American constitution would have recognized it and established jury service not only as a civic duty but as the right of every citizen? That the jury serves the juror, as a student of democracy, was widely understood at one time. In his 1835 monograph *Democracy in America*, French political observer Alexis de Tocqueville wrote, "I do not know whether the jury is useful to those who are in litigation; but I am certain it is highly beneficial to those who decide the litigation; and I look upon it as one of the most efficacious means for the education of the people which society can employ."[6]

Though it took nearly two centuries for this view to take firm hold in American constitutional law, the U.S. Supreme Court now recognizes the right of qualified citizens to share in this powerful experience. In 1991, *Powers v. Ohio* completed a long line of cases stretching back to the post-Civil War Reconstruction era that established not simply the rights of defendants to stand before a jury drawn from the full community, but *also the rights of individuals to serve as jurors*. Before exploring our new data on the civic impact of jury service, it is important to review the legal story behind *Powers* to make clear where the modern jury stands—and what it stands for—in American democracy.

More than a century before *Powers*, the U.S. Supreme Court ruled in the 1880 case *Strauder v. West Virginia* that a state law excluding African Americans from juries violated the Fourteenth Amendment's equal protection clause.[7] Nonetheless, for a variety of reasons—not the least of them institutionalized racism—African Americans continued to be systematically excluded from American juries in many areas, not just the former Confederate states. The methods of this discrimination varied from the rules for summoning the jury pool to attorneys' routine objections to seating individual African American jurors.[8] (Similarly, institutionalized sexism prevented many women from serving on juries.[9])

Over time, the court came to see that the exclusion of African Americans from jury *pools* was unconstitutional,[10] but as recently as the mid-1980s, peremptory objections to *individual* African American jurors usually were upheld by the Supreme Court as constitutional.[11] (A peremptory challenge is a move during the jury selection process in which an attorney removes a potential juror, usually without having to give an explanation. It is a powerful tool, so courts limit the number of peremptories each side may make.[12])

A peremptory challenge allows an attorney to strike a juror based on intuition or a hunch, even assumptions based on the juror's appearance that the lawyer may not wish to say out loud. As Chief Justice Warren Burger said in 1986:

> The peremptory, made without giving any reason, avoids trafficking in the core of truth in most common stereotypes.... It is likely that certain classes of people statistically have predispositions that would make them inappropriate jurors for particular kinds of cases.... We have evolved in the peremptory challenge a system that allows the covert expression of what we dare not say, but know is true more often than not.[13]

The Chief Justice's quote reflected the belief, common among litigators until 1986, that peremptory challenges could be used to remove individual jurors based on their race.

For decades after *Strauder* struck down West Virginia's law against African Americans serving on juries, the U.S. Supreme Court let stand practices that effectively kept African Americans off juries.[14] Finally, in 1940, the court ruled in a Texas case that a grand jury had to be drawn from a pool that represented a fair cross-section of the community—including African Americans.[15] The case did not end racial bias in jury selection, but it pushed the locus of that discrimination from the formation of the jury pool to the selection of members for individual juries.

In 1965, the Supreme Court addressed the continued perception that African American defendants were harmed by having to appear before all-white juries, but it was a hollow victory for equality. In *Swain v. Alabama*,[16] the court ruled that a defendant could only demonstrate abuse of the peremptory challenge if it was found that the prosecutor systematically used those challenges to strike *all* African American jurors over a number of cases.[17] In practice, such a standard was almost impossible to meet.

All-white juries continued in many courts, deeply insulting many African Americans who were summoned but never empanelled on a jury. In 1984, an anonymous letter-writer who described himself as a "common laborer" complained to District Attorney Elizabeth Holtzman about his experience in the King's County, New York, court:

> There were a least sixty or seventy people sent to room 574 to pick a jury of twelve plus two alternates. The majority of the groups sent were Blacks.... After telling us what the law expected of us as possible

jurors, which, as the judge stated, was common sense and a promise from each of us to be fair and impartial, then the selection began; it made no difference to the judge, the district attorney or the defendant's lawyer that the majority of the prospective jurors were Black. They managed to pick thirteen whites and one black *second* alternate, making sure of an all-white jury....And so I ask you Mrs. Holtzman, if we Blacks don't have common sense and don't know how to be fair and impartial, why send these summonses to us? Why are we subject to fines of $250.00 if we don't appear and told it's our civic duty if we ask to be excused? Why bother to call us down to these courts and then overlook us like a bunch of naïve or better yet ignorant children? We could be on our jobs or in schools trying to help ourselves instead of in court house halls being made fools of.[18]

The Supreme Court finally changed its stance on peremptory challenges in 1986. In *Batson v. Kentucky*, the Justices ruled that an African American defendant's Fourteenth Amendment right to equal protection was violated when the prosecutor used peremptory strikes to remove all prospective jurors of his race. Thus, peremptory challenges based solely on race became illegal.[19]

In 1990, Daniel Holland, a white criminal defendant, claimed a violation of his Sixth Amendment right to be tried by a representative cross-section of the community when a Cook County, Illinois prosecutor used peremptory challenges to remove African Americans from his jury. The court ruled he had the legal right to object to their exclusion, but he would have to demonstrate his own membership in the same racial group that the prosecutor had systematically excluded. In an auspicious concurrence, however, Justice Anthony Kennedy wrote:

Exclusion of a juror on the basis of race, whether or not by use of a peremptory challenge, is a violation of the juror's constitutional rights. To bar the claim whenever the defendant's race is not the same as the juror's would be to concede that racial exclusion of citizens from the duty, and honor, of jury service will be tolerated, or even condoned. We cannot permit even the inference that this principle will be accepted, for it is inconsistent with the equal participation in civic life that the Fourteenth Amendment guarantees.[20]

Kennedy wrote that as far back as the *Carter v. Jury Commission of Greene County* decision in 1970, the court had recognized that jurors removed by a race-based peremptory challenge have the right to sue for that violation, but that as a practical matter they are extremely unlikely to do so. A "juror dismissed because of his race," Kennedy wrote, "will leave the courtroom with a lasting sense of exclusion from the experience of jury participation, but possessing little incentive or resources to...vindicate his own rights."[21]

And yet, to speak on behalf of these silent, aggrieved jurors, stood Larry Powers. Not every person whose name is associated with establishing a civil right is as likeable as Clarence Gideon, who penciled a letter to the U.S.

Supreme Court declaring that poor criminal defendants should be provided with attorneys. Before becoming the name behind *Powers v. Ohio*, Larry Powers was a Vietnam veteran and former carpenter, unable to work because of a back injury. The Hamilton County, Ohio prosecutor alleged that Powers might have been a hit man, hired to kill a man reputed to have had affairs with married women. Powers never denied killing Gary Golden and Thomas Kicas in the Columbus home of Golden's ex-wife in 1985. Powers said he shot Golden in self-defense, then killed Kicas to eliminate him as a witness. Powers was convicted of two counts of aggravated murder, plus attempted aggravated murder for shooting at Charlotte Golden as she fled her home.[22]

Powers was sentenced to life in prison for the crimes. But, perhaps because of Gideon before him, Powers got very good attorneys for his appeal. Robert Lane of the Ohio Public Defender Commission saw that the prosecutor had used seven of ten peremptory challenges to remove African Americans from Powers' jury. Although Powers' trial attorney had objected to the strikes, the judge had allowed them. Saying the *Batson* precedent did not apply because Powers was white and the removed jurors were African American, the judge did not require the prosecutor to provide a nonracial reason for the exclusions, despite a request from Powers' trial attorney that he do so.[23]

In looking for grounds on which to appeal, Lane saw that Powers' case was just what Justice Kennedy had asked for in his *Holland* concurrence. If Powers could win an appeal using the equal protection clause of the Fourteenth Amendment, he might get a new trial. "We needed to argue that Mr. Powers was denied a fair trial," Lane said in a 2009 interview. "The argument that we posited was that to have a fair jury, you need to have *all* those perspectives."[24]

The brief Lane wrote with Greg Ayers, the Chief Counsel of the legal division at the Ohio Public Defender Commission, argued that Powers had the legal right to assert the rights of the excluded African American jurors, that a defendant, "regardless of his race, has a personal interest in having his case tried before a jury that has been selected in a racially nondiscriminatory manner." Exclusions of African Americans from Powers' jury, they argued, violated the Fourteenth Amendment's equal protection clause and eroded public confidence in the fairness of the justice system.[25]

When the case was argued at the U.S. Supreme Court, the Justices asked Lane again and again how Powers had been harmed by the exclusion of African Americans. Lane turned the focus back on the excluded jurors, who had an equal protection right *not* to be pushed off the jury because of their race. He added that Powers himself was harmed because the racially biased jury selection process robbed his trial's verdict of the legitimacy a properly convened jury would confer.[26]

Seven Justices agreed that citizens have what Lane called "the juror's right to sit." Writing for the majority this time, Justice Kennedy identified jury service as a significant right of citizenship akin to voting[27] and described the important benefits jurors receive from performing this duty. The jury, he wrote, "postulates a conscious duty of participation in the machinery of justice."[28] Kennedy quoted Alexis de Tocqueville:

> The institution of the jury raises the people itself, or at least a class of citizens, to the bench of judicial authority [and] invests the people, or that class of citizens, with the direction of society.... The jury ... invests each citizen with a kind of magistracy; it makes them all feel the duties which they are bound to discharge towards society; and the part which they take in the Government.[29]

In that moment, Justice Kennedy explicitly affirmed not only the individual's right to serve on a jury but also the belief that jury service is an effective means of educating citizens. Justice Kennedy's majority opinion[30] asserted that the opportunity for jury service must be available to all citizens so that they might better understand and connect with the many other institutions of American democracy.[31]

An Overview of Our Argument

Though the Supreme Court claimed that the institution of the jury yields civic benefits, was it correct to do so? Is the jury system a quiet engine of democratic public engagement? Does it really influence—let alone *trans-form*—those who participate as jurors?

We begin to answer these questions by explaining in chapter 2 how the jury fits into a theoretical conception of democracy. We argue that members of a democratic society need to connect not just with each other but also with the state in ways that are inspiring, empowering, educational, and habit forming. This is what we call *political society*—a public sphere that stands apart from both the state (public officials and agencies) and civil society (primarily the private, individual, and community sphere). This perspective provides a new appreciation of the unique position of the jury, through which a state institution brings private citizens together to deliberate on a public problem. When viewed in this way, it is clear why we propose that the jury can help private citizens make new and lasting connections between their private lives, their communal associations, their public selves, and the state.

Chapter 3 presents our most simple and compelling finding—that deliberating on a jury causes previously infrequent voters to become more likely to vote in future elections. By merging voting and jury service records, we were able to see how jury service influenced the likelihood that a person would vote in later years. Like many other details about one's life, a person's voting history exists in the public domain and can be merged with other data using name-matching software. Our analysis of public records shows that the effect of jury service on voting applies only to criminal, not civil, trials and that it occurs for any jury that deliberates, including those that end as hung juries. The effect is amplified in those cases with multiple charges, where jurors have a more complex deliberative task.

How could just two or three days at the courthouse change a person's inclination to vote years into the future? To answer this, chapter 4 takes a careful look at the jury experience, exploring court records and surveys of jurors in Seattle, Washington, and the county that surrounds it. Our study draws out the *subjective* experience of deliberating with fellow jurors. Open-ended survey questions, complemented by transcripts from longer interviews, describe what it feels like to be a juror in the language of jurors themselves. Readers will find many surprises—such as the eagerness many prospective jurors have to be seated on a jury and the genuine admiration many jurors develop for judges and attorneys.

Chapter 5 focuses more narrowly on the experience of deliberating. We analyze spontaneous quotes from jurors to learn what deliberation *means* for jurors. We find that most citizens carry with them a shared understanding of this cultural practice, even if they have never previously set foot in a courtroom. One of the unique features of our data is that the King County judges permitted us to ask questions about the deliberation itself, something that only a handful of courts have ever allowed. This lets us describe which jurors draw on their personal experiences, how gender and ethnicity shape deliberation, how jurors judge their own performance, and what leads them to more—or sometimes less—satisfying verdicts. The evidence is encouraging, but this chapter also highlights the challenges that jurors face as strangers who must deliberate together on a complex case.

Having reached a better understanding of the jury service experience, we then return to the impact of that experience in chapter 6. We demonstrate that beyond the voting effects shown in chapter 3, serving on a jury can change many aspects of an individual's political and community life. We present narrative examples of people being changed by their jury experience with quantitative findings from a longitudinal survey that continued to track jurors several months after they completed their work at the courthouse. This investigation reveals general patterns, such as increased attention to news media and more frequent participation in conversations with neighbors about community issues. We also find more diffuse impacts, such as the tendency of jurors who reach guilty verdicts in criminal trials to become more active in charitable group activities after leaving the courtroom.

Chapter 7 shows how jury service changes not only behavior but also how people see the world. Using the same longitudinal survey data, we show that jury service often makes citizens more supportive of not only the jury system, but also of local judges and even the Supreme Court. Jurors can develop stronger faith in government and their fellow citizens, and they come to see themselves as more politically capable and virtuous. We also explore the complex relationships between civic attitudes and behaviors in this chapter, showing that the two have a mutually-reinforcing, reciprocal causal relationship.

Chapters 8 and 9, the last two chapters of the book, draw out the implications of our research for democratic theory and the practice of law. Over the past several decades, legislatures have whittled down the American jury system in the interest of expediency. Our research shows that those efficiencies have unintended consequences for our larger democratic society. Low voter turnout, political indifference, and a decline in civic involvement are all symptoms of a malaise for which reinvigorated citizenship is a good cure. Securing the jury as a special experience in citizen deliberation is essential. Though reforming the American jury system is appropriate and necessary over time, such changes must not harm its core features and functions, including its benefit to civic life.

Returning to the larger theoretical questions that frame our research, the final chapter considers how the civic impact of the jury experience can influence our thinking about deliberation and democracy. Our approach moves beyond an unrefined civil society and concern with free markets to an emphasis on engaging citizens and maintaining institutions capable of nurturing them. We show how this approach makes sense in efforts to introduce juries in countries as varied as Japan and Kazakhstan. We show how democracies could flourish by developing more deliberative institutions, such as Brazil's Participatory Budgeting process and Citizens' Assemblies in Canada. When structured appropriately, such bodies can provide even more powerful deliberative experiences that give citizens confidence in themselves and their state institutions, as well as the skills necessary to participate effectively as free citizens in a democratic society.

Chapter 2

Between State and Society

It is no coincidence that in establishing the right to serve on juries, the U.S. Supreme Court cited Tocqueville. His concern with "education of the people" reflected his belief that democratic citizenship cannot simply be *given* to free citizens. Rather, the democratic form of citizenship requires a practical and moral education that molds private citizens into politically engaged advocates and public-spirited, deliberative participants in collective decision making.

Political theorist Laura Janara draws out these themes in *Democracy Growing Up*—an analysis of Tocqueville's famous work as a theory of psychological and social development. Tocqueville repeatedly drew parallels between the young American nation and human adolescence. This metaphor, Janara explains, "captures the moment of world-historical change led by the American experiment; it captures the emergent democratic passion for the idea of equality and the proud separation from the smothering forces of England."[1] Just as the young nation was finding its way to becoming a mature democracy, so in every such society must each individual citizen leave the private home and step into the public sphere as a democratic citizen.

"In Tocqueville's mind," Janara writes, "the art of political liberty is learned through an apprenticeship in collective deliberation practices in political, judicial, and civil associations."[2] As an example, consider Tocqueville's analogy that local public institutions, such as town meetings, "are to liberty what primary schools are to science; they put it within the people's reach" and teach us "how to use and how to enjoy it." Political and civil associations teach their members "how order is maintained among a large number" and how "they are made to advance, harmoniously and

Photo 2.1 Alexis-Charles-Henri Clérel de Tocqueville (1805–1859), as portrayed by the French painter Théodore Chassériau

methodically, to the same object." In these small-scale collective endeavors, Tocqueville wrote, citizens (Photo 2.1):

> learn to surrender their own will to that of all the rest and to make their own exertions subordinate to the common impulse, things which it is not less necessary to know in civil than in political associations.

> Political associations may therefore be considered as large free schools,
> where all the members of the community go to learn the general theory
> of association.[3]

The institutions and activities Tocqueville had in mind include not only
the "citizen-driven jury" but also newspapers, town meetings, and a variety
of political and civil associations, which we shall discuss in more detail
shortly.

Tocqueville wrote about developing democratic citizens because he
believed that one must not simply assume that this process would occur
without designing appropriate civic educational institutions. Despite the
optimistic gloss put on Tocqueville by those who cite him, he frankly admitted, "I know it is difficult to point out with certainty the means of arousing a
sleeping population and of giving it passions and knowledge which it does
not possess....It would frequently be easier to interest them in the punc-
tilios of court etiquette than in the repairs of their common dwelling."[4]

Many writers since Tocqueville have expanded on the idea of democratic self-transformation,[5] and in recent years, considerable scholarship has
extolled the particular virtues of public deliberation as a means of cultivating democratic citizens.[6] For example, Indiana University education scholar
Donald Warren writes:

> Good citizens...are informed participants. They seek evidence, ana-
> lyze issues, devote time to civic duties, and demonstrate willing-
> ness to defer self and immediate interests to achieve common and
> long-term welfare. They are familiar with basic democratic concepts,
> endorse democratic ideals, and consent to be governed according to
> the ratified documents that organize and distribute political power.
> The traditional rationale for civic education in the United States has
> rested on the necessity of such citizens to the health and growth of the
> republic.[7]

This emphasis on the deliberative citizen returns our focus to the jury—the
only institution that can compel the average individual to step out of the
private sphere and into a brief but powerful role as a public official.

In *We, The Jury: The Jury System and the Ideal of Democracy*, legal scholar
Jeffrey Abramson celebrates this particular aspect of jury service:

> Deliberation is a lost virtue in modern democracies; only the jury still
> regularly calls upon ordinary citizens to engage each other in a face-
> to-face process of debate. No group can win that debate simply by out-
> voting others; under the traditional requirement of unanimity, power
> flows to arguments that persuade across group lines and speak to a
> justice common to persons drawn from different walks of life. By his-
> tory and design, the jury is centrally about getting persons to bracket
> or transcend starting loyalties. This is why, ideally, voting is a second-
> ary activity for jurors, deferred until persons can express a view of the
> evidence that is educated by how the evidence appears to others.[8]

To be sure, such deliberation has intrinsic value as a means of resolving legal disputes, but here we consider the power this deliberative exercise can have on the jurors. Just as Abramson hopes that "voting is a secondary activity for jurors," so have a team of British researchers found that jurors' satisfaction with jury service hinges not on their verdict but on *their perceptions of the process*.[9] Jurors, it would seem, understand that their job is to deliberate together, and as we will demonstrate, the different facets of that deliberative experience have a power that reaches beyond the close of a trial.

Locating the Jury in Democratic Society

To understand the many connections between jury service and wider democratic society, we now integrate Tocqueville with more modern theories of democracy. We begin by differentiating between three parts of democratic society, and we show how they interlace with one another. We then show how the jury situates itself at the center of democratic life.

Three Spheres of Public Life

Most accounts of democracy begin with an emphasis on political institutions. For instance, political scientist Robert Dahl likes to set aside the word "democracy" and instead refer to the key features of a "polyarchy"—a system of rule by many. A polyarchy benefits from a well-organized and accountable government, regular elections open to all citizens, freedom of expression and association, and non-governmental sources of information, all protected in a strong constitution.[10] Any who doubt the primacy of such state institutions need only consider the situation of people in countries like Zimbabwe and Iran, where criticisms of government officials during and between elections have resulted in severe repression.[11]

One key feature of healthy polyarchies stands outside the state apparatus. A *civil society* contains non-governmental, private, and communal activities. In Tocqueville's view, these are "not only commercial and manufacturing companies...but associations of a thousand other kinds, religious, moral, serious, futile, general or restricted, enormous or diminutive." Though Tocqueville notes that "civil associations...facilitate political association," they are important in their own right.[12] Non-political informal associations, private enterprises, and other activities play an important role in society, even helping to cultivate public deliberation and other forms of engaged democratic citizenship.[13]

The most popular conception of civil society and its importance comes from a pair of influential articles written by political scientist Robert Putnam in 1995.[14] Putnam warned that America was losing its stock of social capital—the social networks and mutual trust that hold civil society together. Over the past few decades, Putnam pointed out, membership in civic associations—from PTA clubs to bowling leagues—declined, social networks weakened, and citizens lost much of their trust in government and each other. Scholars have debated Putnam's thesis, but his work has foregrounded the importance of the civil sphere in democratic society.[15]

The simple distinction between state and civil society tends to blur important relationships between them. To articulate that relationship, Tocqueville posited that outside the state and beyond civil society lies a third sphere of public life—a *political society*. When acting within this sphere, we draw on the knowledge and interests we have developed as members of civil society. We use our civic skills to act on the state—to change laws, alter public budgets, or restructure political and civil regulations. Political society encompasses political parties, associations, and traditions, and it further develops citizens' capabilities as political actors.

It is popular to complain that government—or civil society—has become "too political" or "too partisan," but political life is *intrinsic* to democracy. In the United States, presidential elections—and even Congressional and special initiative elections—can awaken otherwise dormant groups and revitalize public life.[16] Competing with political parties for citizens' attention and energy are the wide array of other political organizations and advocacy groups, and these, along with explicitly political social movements, have also contributed to democracy because they are organizations in which people develop the skills and habits of effective citizen action.[17]

Sociologist Jeff Weintraub emphasizes this aspect of democracy by showing its similarity to other now commonplace terms, such as the "public realm" celebrated by philosopher Hannah Arendt and the "public sphere" scrutinized by theorist Jurgen Habermas. Weintraub explains that political society "coexists with both civil society and the state" but "is not reducible to either." When "private" citizens come together to act "as a public" on a political issue, there must be a conceptual space in which they act.[18]

Each of these three spheres—the state, civil society, and political society—have distinctive features, but we should not view them as separate. As political theorist Mark Warren points out, a strict delineation of these spheres distracts us "from the ways in which non-state arenas are characterized by power relations." Civil and political associations are not always strictly "voluntary," and we need to broaden our "conception of what counts as 'political'" to encompass some of the activities otherwise set aside as private affairs. Finally, many formerly private or professional associations have become "thoroughly entangled with states and markets." For instance, "public-private partnerships such as Community Development Corporations...bring together market forces, government regulators, and community groups."[19]

To take another example, social theorists Joshua Cohen and Joel Rogers argue for bolstering the "secondary associations" that are part of civil society. In their view, unions, neighborhood groups, and other local and community groups should become a more integral part of *political society*, thereby

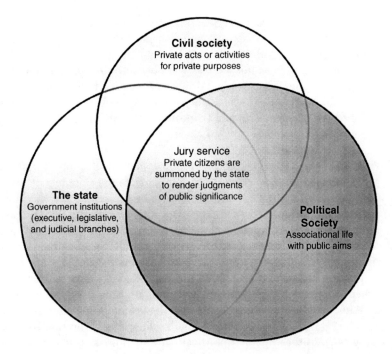

Figure 2.1 The interconnection of state, civil society, and political society in democracy

granting lay citizens more relevant opportunities to influence collective decisions that have immediate impacts on their lives.[20] Even short of adopting Cohen and Rogers' proposal, it is already the case that American political institutions play an important role in promoting civic engagement simply by virtue of the opportunities they create for political action.[21]

The Interconnected Jury

Reflecting this conceptual overlap, Figure 2.1 presents our basic theory of democracy by drawing three spheres that share considerable space. As succinctly defined by Weintraub, these include the state ("the more or less centralized apparatus of domination and administration"), civil society ("the modern sphere of individualistic relations centered above all on the market and private life"), and political society ("the sphere of collective action, conflict, and cooperation which mediates between the two").[22]

This figure also foregrounds the central subject of this book—the jury system—at the center of the three democratic spheres. Regarding civil society, the jury draws on private citizens, who come to the courthouse simply because the state happened to draw their names when it reached into the digital hat of registered voters and drivers. To a degree, fellow jurors still stand alone as individuals—without any political or civic ties, beyond a similar geographic residency, having brought them together in the first place. The jury implicates the state, as well, because the judicial branch of government convenes, oversees, and directs the jury as it carries out its function, which fits neatly into the large purposes of the court. The jury itself can thus be framed as a paradigmatic institution of political society, wherein individuals act collectively at the behest of the state to mediate between laws and the actions of civil society.

What does it mean to suggest that the jury is an institution of *political* society? Putnam's *Bowling Alone* fails to appreciate the significance of the jury and lumps it in with "other forms of civic involvement," such as "talking with neighbors" and "giving to charity," though Putnam also includes voting in this mix.[23] As legal scholar Vikram David Amar has argued, jury service is, indeed, closely related to voting. After all, the government uses a well-structured process to invite jurors to have their say on specific questions, just as it calls on citizens to fill out the ballots it prepares for regular elections. Moreover, it highlights the fact that jurors are involved in governance. After all, "Jurors *vote* to decide the winners and losers in cases—that is what they do." Amar sees even deeper connections: "The link between jury service and other rights of political participation such as voting is an important part of our overall constitutional structure, spanning three centuries and eight amendments." Underscoring this connection, constitutional questions about the right to participate, discriminatory policies, and equal protection pertain to both jury service and voting, and U.S. courts have offered similar rulings on both.[24]

Researchers have long recognized juries as political bodies. For instance, law professors Dan Kahan, Don Braman, and their colleagues have produced many examples of how our core values shape our judgments, even when making factual judgments about what constitutes reckless driving or self-defense.[25] The presumption that judges, in comparison to jurors, would somehow rise above such political bias ignores evidence to the contrary. Even many of the "plainest" facts often require political–cultural interpretation. As Judge Richard Posner mused after reflecting on the work of Kahan and Braman:

> Political preconceptions...are powerful in the case of educated people such as judges only when empirical claims cannot be verified or falsified by objective data. But the empirical claims made in judicial proceedings—for example, claims concerning the deterrent effect of capital punishment or the risk to national security of allowing suspected terrorists to obtain habeas corpus—often are unverified. So judges fall back on their intuitions.[26]

The conventional practice of electing judges in many local and state jurisdictions, as well as the pitched political battles over U.S. Supreme Court nominees, underscores that the judicial system remains tied to politics.[27]

More fundamentally, there exists the quiet tradition of jury nullification, which occurs when jurors willfully reach a verdict that ignores existing law. This practice is built directly into the American jury system and has been applied in real euthanasia cases, such as those involving the famous "Doctor Death," Jack Kevorkian. Though judges and attorneys may not explicitly inform jurors of their ability to exercise this power, Jeffrey Abramson explains that "jury nullification lives on, even when officially banished from the approved list of jury rights."[28]

The Citizen's Roles in Democracy

Whether taking the extraordinary action of nullification or simply making a decision by using its best judgment, the jury acts in a way that draws private citizens into political society to exercise official state power. By connecting each of the three spheres in democratic society, the jury provides an exceptional opportunity to educate jurors in the roles and responsibilities of democratic citizenship. To understand more precisely what civic and political connections the jury might stimulate, we consider several potential impacts, both on jurors' actions and their attitudes. We now review those by way of describing the complex roles citizens play in a democracy.

Figure 2.2 shows a wide range of relevant citizen actions and attitudes, and we explore almost all of those in this study, excepting actual service in elected office (because such service is statistically quite rare in any public survey sample). We do not mean to suggest that this is an exhaustive list of the activities democratic citizens might undertake. As we moved from theory to research, we eventually faced the practical matter of surveying jurors efficiently and without asking sensitive questions—say, about civil disobedience—that would cause judges to deny access to the jury pool. Instead, we aim only to touch on those aspects of democratic citizenship most plausibly influenced by a stint of jury service. We will say more shortly about how that effect takes place, but first, we review the behaviors and attitudes in Figure 2.2.

Public Confidence

We begin at the center, with the most likely immediate impacts of jury service. Provided that the jury system functions properly, we can ask people if they have some confidence in the jury verdicts rendered by their peers. One need not believe in the infallibility of democratic juries to believe that juries are a reasonable means of resolving criminal cases and civil disputes. Going a step further, the legitimacy of a democratic system hinges in part on the confidence citizens have in the judgmental competence of their duly-elected or appointed judges, as well as other public officials.

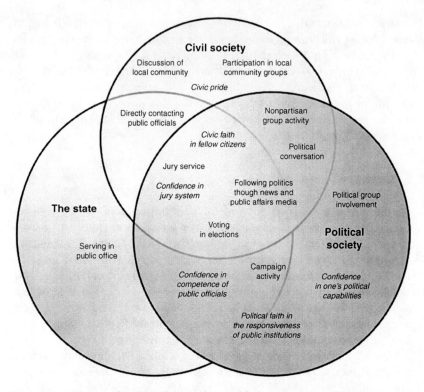

Figure 2.2 Civic and political attitudes and behaviors central to active democratic citizenship

Skepticism and vigilance against government corruption certainly have important roles, and blind trust in government would not serve democracy well. Conversely, deep doubts about the viability of democracy limit the effectiveness of democratic institutions. What a stable democracy requires is "warranted trust," that is, a confidence in state institutions and actors that comes from direct knowledge of its effective and just operation.[29] By providing a direct experience of deliberation within these, the justice system itself can promote a sense of the legitimacy of juries, judges, and perhaps, indirectly, even more distant state entities. As political theorist Jurgen Habermas has argued, a government's legitimacy hinges on our ability to collectively reason and debate the merits of its actions,[30] and the jury puts citizens right at the heart of a legal process and lets them not merely test its legitimacy but actually take responsibility for rendering its judgments.

Legal scholar Roger Mathews provides one of the few systematic investigations of how jurors perceive their attitudes toward juries and the justice system changing as a result of their service. In a study commissioned for the British government, Mathews found that 63 percent of English jurors "completed jury service with a more positive view of the process." This partly meant increased confidence in the jury system. But jurors were also favorably impressed by the judges. As one older male juror commented, "The lady judge, in the way she conducted the case, brought a huge amount of care and understanding.... [She] was absolutely fantastic and elevated my confidence in the system." A significant limitation of the Mathews study was that it had no pre-service baseline measure against which to assess the jurors' *perceptions* of attitude change, but the evidence nonetheless suggests such an effect.[31]

Returning to the United States, we found many similar firsthand accounts of jury service scattered across the blogosphere. Those jurors who took the trouble to reflect on their experience often came away with positive impressions. A librarian from Albany County, New York, offered this summary of his 2007 experience: "My feeling at the end of this long, tedious process, during which I got through five magazines, was that it made me more confident in the legal system, much to my surprise."[32] One could write a very long book cataloging such observations, but more systematic investigation requires hearing from a broad cross-section of jurors—not merely those who happen to be bloggers. After all, the experience of quieter jurors may differ markedly from those who choose to speak more openly about their service.

Faith and Future Deliberation

We not only theorize that jury service can build trust in fellow jurors and judges, but we also believe that the same experience can lead to a heightened sense of faith in fellow citizens and pride in one's own commitment to community and public service. We choose to use the word "faith" to emphasize that much of what we believe about one another is just that—a strong conviction that likely can never be tested directly.

Political philosopher Patrick Deneen, who directs the Tocqueville Forum on the Roots of American Democracy at Georgetown University, elaborated on this idea in his book *Democratic Faith*. "To the ears of many," he writes, "linking the words 'faith' and 'democracy' is strange, uncanny, bizarre, objectionable, and, for some, even sacrilegious." After all, "faith is belief in the unknown or the unknowable," whereas "democracy is a manifest and observable form of government." Modern democratic theory, however, "evinces considerable 'faith' in the capacities of ordinary people for self-governance."[33]

Jury service offers jurors a unique test of their faith in democracy, and in themselves. Many Americans harbor doubts about the critical capacities and civic responsibility of fellow citizens, and television and theatrical courtroom dramas often reinforce our sense that the average citizen can be manipulated by clever attorneys.[34] Others may carry a more optimistic view of fellow citizens and enter jury service expecting to see an eager and earnest public at work. In either case, serving on a jury gives individual jurors a rare opportunity to see how a random group of citizens behaves. Presuming that experience is, on balance, a positive and satisfying one, as earlier studies suggest,[35] it should reinforce citizens' faith in one another.

Returning to the study of British jurors, there is also reason to believe that a successful stint of jury service changes how we view ourselves—sparking a sense of civic pride in one's own civic instincts and acumen. As one juror serving for the first time said, "I've been approached after 35 years and this has now made me feel that I've been treated like a British citizen." Though this person had been a legal citizen for many years, he added that he now felt "far more a British citizen" through serving in the jury system."[36] That serving on a jury could give this individual a stronger civic identity—even a patriotic pride—suggests that a more modest impact could be likely for many other jurors.[37]

Both through these attitudinal pathways, and through other means, jury service might also lead to further exploration of one's opportunities for participating in civil society. Stephanie Burkhalter, John Gastil, and Todd Kelshaw developed a "self-reinforcing model of deliberation" that hypothesized many ways in which a deliberative experience might reinforce future deliberation. Figure 2.3 adapts that model to show some of the ways in which serving on a jury may increase participation in quasi-deliberative activities back in one's community and in political life.[38] Briefly, the range of effects include: creating or reinforcing habits of deliberation, whereby one comes to see deliberation as "normal"; bolstering civic faith and pride to make one optimistic about the potential for discovering common ground through future public discussion; developing the skills and knowledge that make one competent in deliberative activities; and, relatedly, gaining a political self-confidence that motivates one to deliberate again.[39]

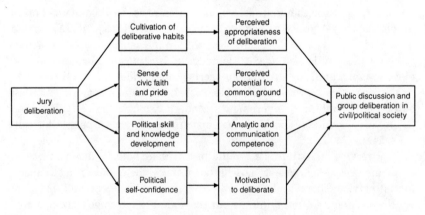

Figure 2.3 A model of how jury deliberation transforms jurors and leads them to take advantage of future opportunities for public discussion deliberation

These kinds of radiant effects of jury deliberation could plausibly reach outward to change the character and frequency of one's quasi-deliberative activities in civil and political society. Specifically, after a stint of rewarding, enlightening jury service, one might seek out more contact with fellow citizens through everyday conversations about community life—the same community, most often, to which the civil or criminal trial pertained. This might start as talking about the jury service experience, but it could also blossom into a more general interest in community and political affairs and a desire to have a smaller-scale deliberative conversation about such matters with fellow citizens.[40] For a closer approximation of the look and feel of jury service, ex-jurors might also increase their participation in small groups, ranging from community groups with educational, charitable, neighborhood, or religious purposes, as well as nonpartisan civic associations and more explicitly political groups. Each of these affords the citizen a chance to deliberate not within the state, as during their exceptional period of jury service, but instead within the civil or political society in which they operate day-to-day.

Political Attitudes and Actions

To better equip citizens to take direct action affecting the state, jury service might also reinforce what social scientists call "political efficacy." Extending social psychologist Albert Bandura's notion of self-efficacy, political psychologists have conceptualized efficacy as having two components—one *internal* and one *external*.[41] Internal efficacy is a sense of one's own ability to perform political behaviors competently, whereas external efficacy is one's perception that the political system will respond to one's actions. We refer to these concepts as *political self-confidence* and *political faith*, the latter invoking the idea that our convictions about the responsiveness of political institutions are, for all but the most well-read political scientists, matters of faith.

Past research on participation in more explicitly political activities, like voting and volunteering on campaigns, has complex reciprocal relationships with these attitudes.[42] Active membership in voluntary associations can increase political participation—whatever the intervening psychological mechanisms might be.[43] Surely, the jury experience could have similar effects on one's willingness to not only actively participate in political groups, but also contact public officials, take part in campaigns, and vote in elections.

All of these beneficial impacts of jury service presume that one has had a satisfying jury experience. The work on self-efficacy flowed out of the behaviorist tradition, which made a plausible case for the importance of *reinforcement*:[44] We seek to repeat behaviors when they are psychologically, socially, or materially rewarding. Our research will ultimately test the assumption that it is principally those jurors who have a stimulating, engaging, and satisfying service experience who show marked civic and political changes afterward. In the same sense, we expect a boost in one's political self-confidence only when a juror participates in what she considers a successful behavioral performance, such as a jury deliberation that reaches a suitable conclusion.

The key may be the character of the deliberation itself. Beyond the courtroom context, there grows an ever-expanding body of scholarship stressing the potential impact of democratic deliberation on citizens. Both theory and research provide reasons to believe that taking part in civic forums, public meetings, study circles, and other deliberative activities can transform disengaged private individuals into active, public-spirited citizens.[45] As one example among many, David Mathews, reflecting on his diverse experiences in democratic innovation as president of the Kettering Foundation, observed that citizens who have deliberated "have actually experienced a measure of the democratic ideal in practice" and come to believe that "if deliberation can happen in one meeting, it can happen in others." Mathews reasoned that "if citizens can claim responsibility and act in one community, they can become the 'solution' they are looking for in other communities."[46] Once again, the implicit key to deliberative impact is the *quality* of the experience—whether the participants were well-prepared, given clear guidelines and direction, and had adequate time for deliberation.[47] We expect the jury to be no different from other deliberative bodies in this respect.

Testing Tocqueville

We end this chapter with a conviction—a Tocquevillian *faith*—in the jury's power as an engine of civic education and the promotion of engaged democratic citizenship. If the jury really does function in this way, it has profound implications for both deliberative democracy generally and for the ongoing development and reform of the jury system in the United States and other nations. In 2004, for example, Japan rewrote its laws to develop a "quasi-jury" system based partly on the belief that the jury "promotes a more democratic society."[48] Japan moved forward with no direct evidence to that effect, just as the U.S. Supreme Court based its decisions on Tocqueville, a keen observer—but far from unimpeachable as an expert witness.[49]

To this point, however, we have presented only indirect evidence by reviewing theory and research on democracy, public engagement, and deliberation. In the chapters that follow, we will scrutinize the educational model of jury service by assessing more directly how jurors experience their period of service—and their deliberations with fellow jurors in particular. We will test the civic and political reach of the jury by seeing if the different nuances of jury service foster changes in the cluster of behaviors and attitudes characteristic of an engaged democratic citizen. This exploration begins, however, by focusing on a *single* connection—the link between jury service voting. Simply put, does serving on a jury make one more likely to vote in future elections? Chapter 3 provides an answer.

Chapter 3

From Jury Box to Ballot Box

Voting holds a special place among democratic responsibilities, for it is the means whereby citizens choose their representatives and hold public officials accountable. It is also a good place to begin examining the jury's impact because voting and jury service have a straightforward, plausible connection as civic acts. As legal scholar Vikram David Amar points out, "Jurors *vote....* That is what they do."[1] Electoral participation is also the lone public action for which we have comprehensive public records, which permits a unique form of longitudinal analysis. Thus, it is with voting that we begin to test the real power of the jury as a public body poised at the center of the state, civil, and political society.

Our investigation comes late in the research cycle, as it has been well over a century since Tocqueville first hypothesized a relationship between the institution of jury service and civic engagement, yet this claim has gone untested. In the mid-1970s, political theorist Carole Pateman restated Tocqueville's idea as a more general *participation effect*, whereby any form of civic engagement is likely to increase future civic participation.[2] In the years that followed, there emerged no compelling investigation of the proposition. Reflecting on this dearth of evidence, both Pateman and fellow political scientist Jane Mansbridge declared that the participation effect might remain untested in perpetuity, as they doubted anyone could design and implement a suitable test.[3] This chapter aims to provide one.

Begin by Asking

Social science cannot easily ignore the thoughts and understandings of its subjects. If jurors conceived their service as dispiriting rather than inspiring, any data showing how jury service promoted future electoral participation would be suspect, to both jurors and researchers alike. Thus, we began our study as ethnographers. We consulted directly with jurors to elicit their subjective experience of jury deliberation, in their own words. Toward this end, we enlisted University of Washington honors student Jordan Meade to conduct a series of detailed interviews with twelve randomly selected jurors from four trials held in the King County, Washington, Superior Court in downtown Seattle.[4]

The interviewees came from a representative set of trials, including a murder trial, a first-degree robbery case, a second-degree burglary trial, and a civil case in which the plaintiff sought $25,000 in damages for injuries suffered in an auto accident. The murder and robbery trials both resulted in guilty verdicts, but the jurors found the accused burglar not guilty. After deliberating on the civil case, the jury returned a mixed verdict, finding for the plaintiff but awarding only $8,000.

A First Glimpse at the Service Experience

In speaking with the twelve jurors who served during these trials, we began by asking about their overall impressions of their experience at the court-house. Almost all of the interviewees said they were satisfied, on the whole, with their experience of jury deliberation. Each of the jurors from criminal trials expressed satisfaction with their time in court, but one juror from a civil trial—though satisfied in the main—had some reservations, which we describe below.

Bonding was one positive experience several jurors reported: "I think everyone got a chance to have their say," one juror said. "We bonded really well as a jury. We're actually going to have a reunion in a couple of weeks. We jelled very well."[5] Another's satisfaction came specifically from the jury deliberation: "I guess I was satisfied with the deliberation part—not the entire process."

Even intermittent frustration with deliberation could, in the end, trans-late into a positive assessment. As one juror said, "I thought it was really good. It was frustrating, because everyone had different ideas and felt very strongly about it. I think the process worked. I think everybody was very serious about it."

Many of the interviewees' comments on their deliberation with fellow jurors expressed admiration for each other and their foreperson. Jurors emphasized the active and vocal role played by those with minority views. Even in the civil trial, which did not require consensus, a juror recalled that those in the minority "did most of the talking." She added:

> Our foreman was really good. He outlined what he thought the key points were and we talked about them and he polled everybody to find out who wasn't comfortable with it. And they got a chance to talk. There were a couple of times when it got heated and people were

trying to talk over each other, but most of the time people raised their hands and the foreman said, "So-and-so will be next."

Every juror said they would serve again if called back to jury duty. As one remarked after the burglary trial, "You always hear people saying [that jury service] is a pain, it's a nuisance, it's an inconvenience. Now that I've served on it, [I think] it's really good for people to go through it." Some were enthusiastic about serving, but others were concerned about the three-week duration of the murder trial.

Linking Jury Service and Voting

Chapters 4 and 5 will tell us more about how jurors experience their courtroom service, but for now, it is enough to say that these interviewees found that the experience met or exceeded their expectations for jury service. This fact made it reasonable to proceed to the second and more critical aim of the interviews: We hoped to learn whether and how jurors might make the cognitive leap from the experience of one type of civic engagement, jury service, to the only other institutionalized form of mass civic participation in the United States, voting.

That the two rarely come up together in regular conversation does not concern academics such as ourselves. Our model in chapter 2 made clear our belief that jury service and voting are closely related because they are two of the few instances where the state asks the citizen to take hold of the reins of government. Our interviews were designed to discover whether jurors, when asked a series of probing questions, would connect the dots between jury service and voting.

The interviews used a "funnel technique" to move from broad, general questions to narrow, specific inquiries.[6] The funnel approach was designed to determine the level of specificity necessary to elicit a comparison between voting and jury service. For instance, the interviewer obliquely started each interview by asking, "Does serving on a jury remind you of any other activities you have done in your life?" At the end of the sequence, if no previous question had brought up voting, she asked jurors directly, "Now that you have served on a jury, do you think differently about any [civic] duties or responsibilities?"[7]

As expected, the first question in the funnel-shaped series did not elicit any comparisons to voting. When asked whether serving on a jury reminded interviewees of "any other activities you have done in your life," most jurors thought of it as "a pretty unique situation" or as only somewhat comparable to other decision-making groups in their lives.

Two of the twelve jurors did draw the connection, however, in response to the second question, which asked whether they thought jury service had an important meaning to them. A civil juror replied, "I definitely think jury service is a responsibility. *It's like voting.* We're supposed to be by the people, of the people, and for people. Jury service is part of that. You're supposed to vote, pay attention to what goes on in politics, and supposed to have jury duty." A juror from the robbery trial "felt honored to be able to participate in the process.... It's a right that we have as an American citizen, and a lot of other countries do not have.... *It's like if you don't vote, don't complain about who's in office.*"[8]

Exactly half of the jurors made the first link between jury service and voting in response to the third question, which asked if jury service was a responsibility, and if so, whether it resembled any others. A juror from the murder trial replied that jury service reminded her of "the responsibility to vote, to do community service, those kinds of things. If everyone just does a little bit, then it's not so hard on people who are willing to give their time for community service, voting, all those sort of things." A juror from the robbery trial named voting as a similar responsibility, then added to the list "speaking out for causes I believe in." Finally, a juror from the burglary trial commented:

> Well, probably voting is a big thing. That's one big area where I can let my wishes and my preferences [be] known, as far as who has control in our country. To me, that would be somewhat of a similar thing, and I take my voting privileges very seriously. I would say voting to me is a big responsibility that is important.

The fourth question, which introduced the phrase "civic duty" for the first time, prompted one additional juror to make a connection to voting:

> There should be things that I'm willing to do as a citizen to help my community, my neighborhood, or city as it gets bigger. I have a responsibility to participate in a way that benefits not just me or my family, but my community. So whether it's voting, jury duty, [or] paying taxes, they are for the common good.

This small sample of interviews with jurors corresponds broadly to the expectations of Tocqueville and his admirers. Jurors fresh out of the courtroom did not view their experience solely as a function in the administration of justice. On the contrary, they conceptualized jury service as one of many similar *responsibilities*, including voting, paying taxes, "speaking out," volunteering in the community, and other "things that they don't necessarily get paid for."

The interviews also show that the link between voting and jury service was more than a theoretical one. Before introducing the phrase "civic duty" in the fourth question, three-quarters of the interviewees had already linked jury service and voting more directly than even Tocqueville might have expected. Not every juror made the connection; even after the final question in this series, three of the interviewees did not draw the link. Our job here, though, was not to estimate an exact frequency of connection, but simply to see if the connection *could be made*. As it turns out, it can.

It is also worth noting that many jurors found the deliberation with fellow jurors to be the key to their general sense of satisfaction and accomplishment. Folding this observation in with our main finding, these interviews suggest that many jurors do, indeed, view jury deliberation and voting as related responsibilities, both challenging and rewarding parts of what it means to be a citizen in a democracy.

Designing a Hard Test for the Participation Effect

These interviews themselves give no hint about the *strength* of the relationship between jury service and voting. They merely show the potential for a link between one rewarding experience and another that jurors perceive as related. Understanding the strength and character of the link requires a vastly larger sample of jurors and more objective measures of behavior. Fortunately, jury participation records and voting records can be compared to determine whether this theoretical possibility is realized in fact.

In moving away from in-person interviews and toward faceless archival records, we do not mean to diminish jurors' personal accounts of their experiences. Instead, we seek to find a research method that can provide a more objective test of the participation effect. Such a "hard test" should overcome many of the limitations common in social scientific research.

Studies on juries have often relied entirely on self-reported data (surveys) or a handful of in-depth interviews. In either case, the skeptic might doubt the truth of jurors' claims; after all, many addicted smokers assert that they can quit tomorrow. One could also doubt the veracity of our own interview study on the suspicion that the results are simply too good to be true. Respondents may have been reluctant to dampen the enthusiasm of a bright-eyed interviewer overcome by the sanctity of jury service. Or perhaps those who were dissatisfied felt guilty about their assessment and looked for the silver lining when anyone asked about it.

One might try to avoid these possible biases by using anonymous survey questionnaires. These come with their own problems, often including a low response rate. If only half—or even a quarter—of jurors agree to fill out a questionnaire, how confident can we be that its results are representative? The danger is that those least satisfied with their experience might systematically avoid further time processing their bleak days locked in the courthouse. Even with a good response rate, there are unavoidable problems of misinterpretation, as the survey writer and reader do not always understand words to have the same meaning. Investigators can fail to detect real but small effects in the midst of the distortion that inevitably accompanies human communication.

An ideal study would also test the impact of reluctant participation. Normally, when citizens choose to engage in a civic activity, they do just that—they *choose* to participate, either spontaneously and voluntarily[9] or in exchange for honoraria or other incentives.[10] Public deliberation might benefit those who seek it out, but an ideal study of the participation effect would determine whether a civic activity can spark future public engagement even when some participants would rather not be there.[11]

One more common problem in social scientific research is that effects are too often measured only hours, days, or a few weeks after the researcher's intervention. Short-term assessments of behavior change leave open the question of the how long an impact lasts, yet in the laboratory, researchers often have access to study participants only for a limited time. Even if there is a follow-up survey separate from the experimental manipulation, it usually comes promptly, lest too many of the study's participants drift out of the study's reach.

Our test of the civic impact of jury deliberation avoids all of these measurement problems by linking official jury records with the actual democratic act of voting as recorded by the registrar of voters. This is not the best way to understand the robust and varied nature of civic engagement, but it can demonstrate whether an effect exists under the most rigorous of testing conditions. Although subject to human error, the public records we gather do not depend on fragile human memory or anyone's desire to impress an interviewer. Given that the researchers and recording clerks only meet long after the court and voting documents have been produced, bias in the recording of the data is unlikely. In addition, this approach can yield as close to a perfect response rate as the archives will allow, with no chance that jurors' experience at the courtroom could influence the odds of their appearing in our final dataset. Because jury service is mandatory, it also brings into our study many people who embark on their public service journey at the county courthouse only reluctantly. Finally, our approach allows us to collect data spanning a period of years, such that we can measure the impact of jury service on voting in elections held months or even years after the study participants completed their service.

Making a Hard Test Fair

Though our research design provides a hard test of the participation effect, it is just as important to ensure that the test is *fair*. The rules of statistical inference are designed to encourage modesty. When one hears of a "margin of error," for instance, that is an acknowledgement that our estimates are not precise. If a survey finds that 15 percent of Hawaiians would like to take a holiday in Alaska, the more careful scholar might add that the correct estimate is really 10–20 percent. In this same way, when we make a comparison, such as whether more Hawaiians or Texans would like to travel to Alaska, we require that there be no significant overlap in the two estimates. If, in this case, we found that 15–25 percent of Texans hear Anchorage beckoning them, we would conclude that there was no statistically significant difference. The margins of error in these cases, overlap, and that makes a modest researcher reluctant to announce with confidence that a real difference exists in the vacation preferences of Texans and Hawaiians.

The smaller the differences one hopes to detect, the more likely it is that these margins of error will overlap. The same is true for our pursuit of the participation effect. We expect this effect to be relatively small, given the stability in people's voting behavior, the varied ways in which people respond to the jury experience, and the multitude of random factors influencing the likelihood of voting on any given day. Even expensive and much ballyhooed get-out-the-vote campaigns, for instance, have only minimal effects on voters (if any at all), with the most efficacious face-to-face canvassing yielding less (often far less) than a 10 percent increase in a citizen's likelihood of voting.[12]

Fortunately, one can counterbalance the difficulty of finding small effects by shrinking the margin of error. By the laws of statistical inference, the larger the sample, the smaller the error margin. To make our test fair, then, we sought to create a very large sample of jurors. We estimated the need for roughly a thousand jurors per group studied, meaning at least 1,000 criminal jurors and 1,000 civil jurors. If we met those targets and found no participation effect, it would be fair to say that our theory had undergone a strict test and failed.

The Olympia Project

The Olympia Project became our first hard test of the participation effect. We conducted this study in Thurston County, Washington, the county containing Washington's state capital, Olympia. In total, we gathered complete court records for 1,395 jurors who came from the 37 civil trials and 110 criminal trials conducted in Thurston County between September 8, 1994 and November 1, 1996.[13]

The case files did not include demographic information about the jurors, but the U.S. Census data for Thurston County paints a portrait of the community from which the jurors came.[14] Population in the county was rapidly growing, having increased nearly 25 percent in the seven years between 1990 and 1997. The median household income was $28,371 in 1994, somewhat below the national average, with 10 percent of the population living below the poverty line. The county was not a model of American diversity. The population was 92 percent white, the largest minority being Asian/Pacific Islander (4 percent).

All but 2 of the 149 case files our research team identified were available for the study. Juror names were merged with voter registration lists provided by the Thurston County Auditor's Office after the November 1997 general elections. Figure 3.1 illustrates the merging process.[15]

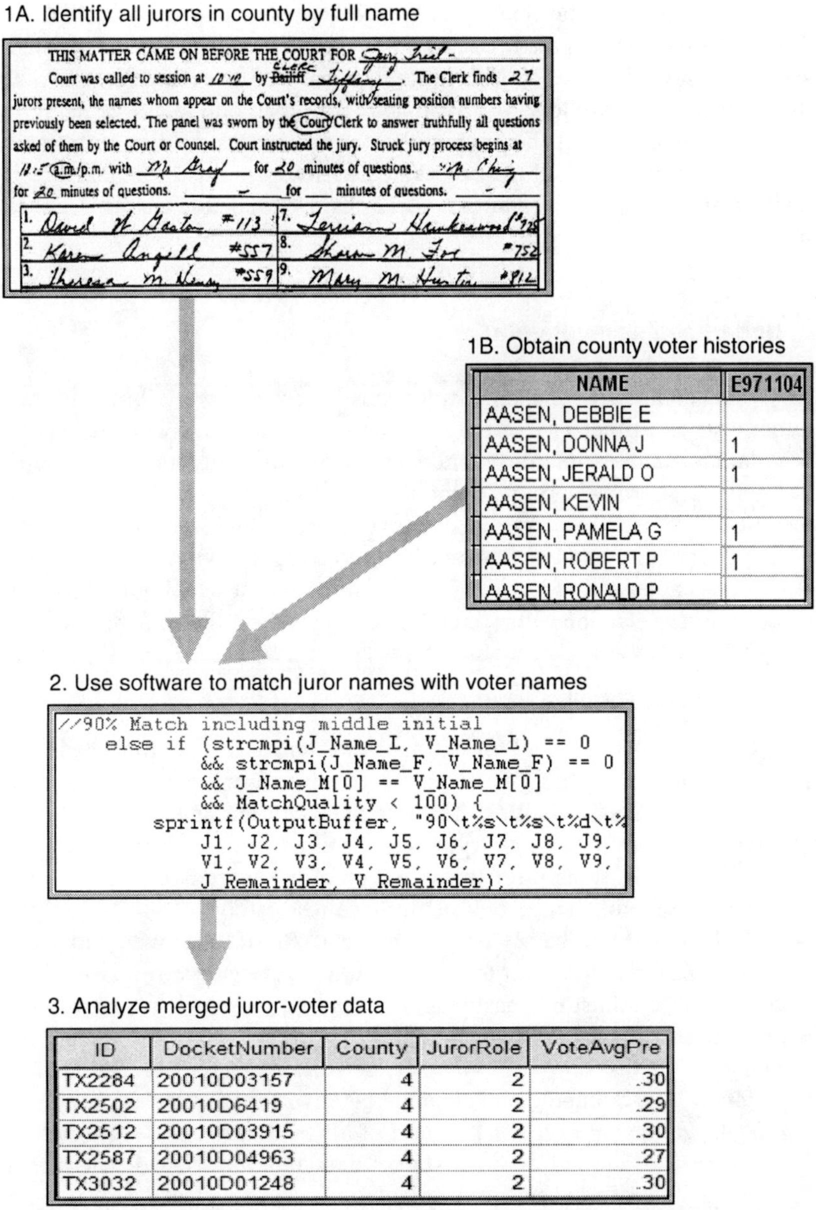
1A. Identify all jurors in county by full name
THIS MATTER CAME ON BEFORE THE COURT FOR
Court was called to session at by Bailiff . The Clerk finds
jurors present, the names whom appear on the Court's records, with seating position numbers having previously been selected. The panel was sworn by the Court/Clerk to answer truthfully all questions asked of them by the Court or Counsel. Court instructed the jury. Struck jury process begins at
a.m./p.m. with for minutes of questions.
for minutes of questions. for minutes of questions.
1B. Obtain county voter histories
NAME
E971104
AASEN, DEBBIE E
AASEN, DONNA J 1
AASEN, JERALD O 1
AASEN, KEVIN
AASEN, PAMELA G 1
AASEN, ROBERT P 1
AASEN, RONALD P
2. Use software to match juror names with voter names
//90% Match including middle initial
else if (strcmpi(J_Name_L, V_Name_L) == 0
&& strcmpi(J_Name_F, V_Name_F) == 0
&& J_Name_M[0] == V_Name_M[0]
&& MatchQuality < 100) {
sprintf(OutputBuffer, "90\t%s\t%s\t%d\t%
J1, J2, J3, J4, J5, J6, J7, J8, J9,
V1, V2, V3, V4, V5, V6, V7, V8, V9,
J_Remainder, V_Remainder);
3. Analyze merged juror-voter data
ID DocketNumber County JurorRole VoteAvgPre
TX2284 20010D03157 4 2 .30
TX2502 20010D6419 4 2 .29
TX2512 20010D03915 4 2 .30
TX2587 20010D04963 4 2 .27
TX3032 20010D01248 4 2 .30

Figure 3.1 Three-step process for creating a dataset of jurors with complete voting histories

After the merger, the final sample size was large enough to detect the small effect we anticipated, but only for criminal trials.[16] As anticipated, some jurors' names could not be uniquely matched to voting records (i.e., the juror name "Toby Johnson" matched more than one identical name in the voter database), but the more serious problem was the low proportion of civil trials conducted during our study period. Even with the hamstrung civil sample, however, we forged ahead, as a partial test was better than none.

Understanding the Results

Analyzing complex data can be stultifying, but we will walk through it one hypothesis at a time. The activity we looked at was voting. In the general population, some people do it, and some people do not. Our main interest was *post-jury service* voting. To understand linear regression, the statistical technique we used to carry out our investigation, imagine that we paired each aspect of jury service that we measured with post-service voting to see which ones appeared to have an impact on the rate at which jurors participated in future elections after finishing their service at the courthouse.

Reviewing the Possible Causes

In the case of the Olympia Project, there was a manageable number of variables possibly contributing to increased post-jury service voting. The first, no surprise, is *pre-jury* voting. The rate at which one voted prior to jury service surely predicts post-jury service voting.[17] Indeed, jurors who had voted in most elections prior to serving on a jury were likely to continue to do so after serving, and likewise for those who rarely voted. This finding was so obvious it was barely worth looking at. But if those who had voted in nearly every election prior to service suddenly *stopped* voting, we would have needed to adjust our basic model of voting (or matched jury records with those at the coroner's office).

Our real interest lay with what we called the "conclusive deliberative experience." We defined conclusive deliberative experiences as participating in jury deliberation and being part of a jury that reached a verdict. In other words, jurors had a conclusive deliberative experience when their final judgment prevailed and contributed to a verdict that had a clear impact. *Inconclusive* experiences, by contrast, occurred when a juror did one of the following: (a) remained an alternate (i.e., the person watched the trial but did not join in jury deliberations); (b) observed a trial that was not completed (because a mistrial was declared, the parties settled, or the defendant changed his or her plea to guilty); (c) took part in deliberation that failed to produce a verdict (i.e., a hung jury); or (d) cast a dissenting vote on a civil jury that used majority rule.[18] In these cases, the juror had no clear impact on the decision or might have experienced the frustration of deadlocking with fellow citizens. If the jurors with a conclusive deliberative experience increased their post-jury service voting rate, while those with inconclusive experiences remained unchanged, we would have the first strong evidence of a relationship between jury service and future civic engagement.[19]

The case files also included the number of charges against criminal defendants, and we thought this might serve as an indirect indicator of the complexity of a criminal trial and the ensuing jury deliberation. One might reasonably suspect that the number of charges could influence how jurors experienced a trial, as those cases with more charges required more delicate weighing of evidence and multiple decisions during the deliberation phase.

The fourth factor was trial duration—the number of hours jurors spent at trial. In spite of the variety of activities happening during the course of a trial, we expected trial duration to have an effect similar to number of charges, as total duration was likely another indirect measure of the complexity of the trial.

Finally, we looked at the duration of the deliberation. Deliberation duration was the number of hours jurors spent in deliberation, which, like number of charges and trial duration, likely was linked to the complexity of the trial. In addition, this factor could be an indicator of the *social* complexity of the jury deliberations themselves, with more hours suggesting a more challenging experience working through different juror perspectives on a case, regardless of how complex the case itself had proven.

Presenting the Evidence

We begin our analysis with the larger of our two Olympia jury samples—those jurors who were seated on *criminal* trials. When we regressed the five factors described above on the criminal jurors' post-jury service voting, we found that pre-jury service voting clearly had the strongest individual effect. More than anything else, this association represents the overall stability of voting behavior over time. If two jurors served on the same trial, the one who had voted steadily in the previous election would be 43.7 percent more likely to vote in the next election than the one who had not cast a ballot. This surprised no one on the research team, but it reassured us that our data were behaving as one would expect.

More importantly, the results showed that *having a conclusive deliberative experience in a criminal trial was a statistically significant influence on post-service voting*. If two jurors had the same pre-jury service voting rate, the one who had a conclusive deliberative experience would be 9.6 percent more likely to vote in the next election. This is a powerful effect if you consider that the turnout boost for a nonpartisan, face-to-face get-out-the-vote drive is about 9 percent, and a nonpartisan voter mobilization telephone campaign call yields roughly 4.5 percent.[20]

The number of criminal charges also had an independent impact, regardless of whether the juror had a conclusive deliberative experience. A more complicated criminal case with more charges raised the likelihood of voting by an average of 2.1 percent per charge. This suggests that the experience of participating in a complex criminal trial itself brings a juror into the democratic process and underscores the relevance of voting.

Figure 3.2 juxtaposes these first three findings with more direct efforts to increase voter turnout. It seems that if a political candidate could get all her supporters to serve on criminal juries in the year prior to the election, she would effectively counter any opponent's more conventional get-out-the-vote campaign. Of course, she would also have some explaining to do about her unconventional campaign tactics.

The other two predictors—the total days spent in trial and hours spent deliberating—had no significant impact on post-jury service voting. This means that the length of time reviewing evidence in the courtroom or time spent in the jury room have no measurable influence on jurors' future voting habits after taking the aforementioned factors into account.

Table 3.1 shows the technical details of the linear regression results for criminal jurors. (No need to panic if the table looks daunting. Asterisks beside a number in the last column indicate that a factor had a significant influence on post-service voting rates.) The first column of numbers tells the

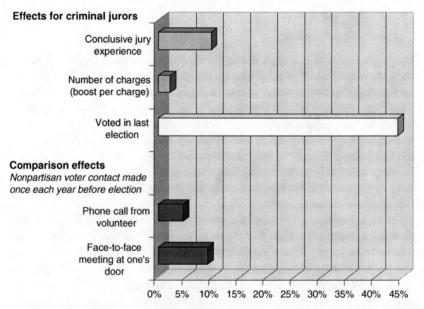

Figure 3.2 Comparison of estimated effects from the Olympia Project and voter turnout efforts on the likelihood of voting in future elections

Table 3.1.   Linear regression measuring the effect of criminal jury experience on post-jury voting rate in Thurston County, Wash

Predictor	Unstandardized coefficient (B) and standard error (SE)		Standardized coefficient (b)
Conclusive jury experience	.096 (.037)		.077***
Number of charges	.021 (.007)		.095***
Trial duration (hours)	.002 (.001)		−.057
Deliberation duration (hours)	.004 (.005)		.022
Pre-jury voting rate	.437 (.023)		.562***
R^2		.334*	
N		794	

Note: * $p < .10$, ** $p < .05$, *** $p < .01$. Conclusive jury experience is a dichotomous variable: 1 = juror deliberated and reached a verdict; 0 = any other outcome for empanelled juror.

effect expressed as the change in voting rate. The .096, for instance, means that one conclusive jury experience accounts for a 9.6 percent increase in the likelihood of voting in the next election.

When we repeated this analysis on our smaller sample of civil jurors, however, it yielded no significant service effects. Pre-jury voting had a powerful predictive value for civil jurors, just as it did for criminal jurors, but the other factors we measured did not reach statistical significance. Table 3.2 summarizes these results. For civil jurors, nothing other than the pre-jury service voting rate appears to predict voting rates after jury service.

In retrospect, the absence of a civil jury effect fits with the interviews recounted at the beginning of this chapter: In the course of those interviews, a juror from a civil case was the only one to express reservations about her jury experience. At the same time, it is important to recall the earlier discussion of margins of error. It is possible that the sample of civil jurors was

Table 3.2.   Linear regression measuring the effect of civil jury experience on post-jury voting rate in Thurston County, Wash

Predictor	Unstandardized coefficient (B) and standard error (SE)		Standardized coefficient (b)
Conclusive experience	−.041 (.058)		−.040
Trial duration (hours)	.001 (.002)		.022
Deliberation duration (hours)	.001 (.008)		−.012
Pre-jury voting rate	.411 (.047)		.494***
R^2		.250*	
N		243	

Note: * $p < .10$, ** $p < .05$, *** $p < .01$. Conclusive jury experience is a dichotomous variable: 1 = juror deliberated and reached a verdict; 0 = any other outcome for empanelled juror.

simply too small to detect a participation effect that does, in fact, exist. Thus, without a larger sample, one should be cautious to avoid over-interpreting these earliest findings.

Debriefing after the Trial

The Olympia Project found clear evidence of a causal relationship between jury service and future voting rates, and that single finding is the most significant result. Nonetheless, as so often happens in empirical research, the findings suggest a more complicated reality than was predicted. In particular, we came away from this study wondering whether the civil jury experience has what it takes to inspire citizens to greater levels of civic engagement after their courthouse service. A larger sample of jurors from civil trials is necessary to test the efficacy of the civil jury, and we will present such a sample shortly. The Olympia results, however, led us to ponder why criminal juries might have more impact than their civil cousins.

Criminal trials may have a better chance of demonstrating the participation effect because of their significance in the minds of jurors. As Joseph Bessette writes, "Jurors in criminal cases...are made keenly aware of how profoundly their judgments can affect the life of the defendant. The vesting of such weighty matters in the hands of average citizens can...promote serious deliberation."[21] By contrast, attitudes toward civil trials are often mixed, with some citizens believing many civil suits are frivolous, civil litigants are corrupt, and civil judgments excessive.[22]

Another distinction between civil and criminal jury trials is that civil trials are more likely to involve complex factual and technical issues that jurors either do not fully understand or do not find engaging. Studies show that expert witness testimony plays a key role in over 85 percent of civil jury cases.[23] This high percentage of cases involving expert witnesses suggests that complex business disputes such as antitrust violations and patent infringement may be far more intimidating and less accessible to ordinary jurors than most criminal trials. In emphasizing this aspect of civil trials, we are not suggesting that jurors do a bad job of sorting through the relevant information.[24] We are only pointing out that deliberating on the average civil jury may be less satisfying and inspiring than in criminal trials.

A final explanation for the significance of criminal trials concerns the decision rules employed during jury deliberation. In Thurston County, Washington, as in most jurisdictions, criminal juries must reach unanimous verdicts, but civil juries can use a supermajority or two-thirds majority rule. Small group research suggests that the consensus decision rule promotes more thorough discussion and a stronger commitment to group decisions,[25] particularly in a cooperative group setting.[26] With consensus decision-making rules, therefore, criminal juries may engage in more thorough and memorable deliberation than civil juries do, and this could explain why the deliberation-voting link only applies to jurors in criminal cases.

Taken together, the civil trial's private function, lower societal esteem, greater degree of complexity, lower juror engagement, and majoritarian decision rule lead us to expect that the civic impact of jury deliberation may be weaker for civil cases than for criminal trials. In chapters 4 and 5, we will look more closely and directly at these aspects of jury trials by moving to survey data. For now, we only make the crude differentiations permitted by public court records, which clearly distinguish between civil and criminal trials.

The civil versus criminal trial contrast also squares with a surprising finding that appeared in the Olympia Project. Just as criminal cases may have more pull on the juror, those criminal trials involving more charges appear to have a deeper impact than single-charge cases. The jurors in these relatively complex cases may be more involved in the discussion, or perhaps more personally attached to the outcome. This involvement may stimulate more vigorous deliberation among jurors and give a sense of personal accomplishment. This explanation is consistent with other research, which has shown that careful analysis of arguments (i.e., deliberation) is most likely to occur when people have a high level of involvement in the discussion.[27] Before saying more about this finding, however, caution takes hold, as it was not an effect we expected to find. Reproducing this same result in a larger dataset would be necessary to warrant more in-depth analysis.

The Olympia Project provides seductively compelling results about the link between jury service and voting, but there are limitations. Thurston County does not have a sufficiently diverse population, and it represents a single jurisdiction, which might have a unique approach to jury service. Like any other state-level court, it also employs particular rules for criminal and civil trials that make it somewhat distinctive. In addition, the Olympia Project had a limited sample size, which made for an inadequate test of civil trials and required conflating a variety of jury service outcomes—treating mistrials, hung juries, and all other "inconclusive" outcomes as a single category. Thus, a critic would be warranted in asking that the Olympia Project be augmented by a larger, more diverse sample of jurors.

The National Jury Sample

In 2004 and 2005, a team of researchers set off to broaden our study to include counties from diverse regions across the United States.[28] This undertaking required not only a large travel budget, but also resilient optimism. After all, it was entirely possible that this larger national investigation would, in the end, disconfirm the more tentative findings yielded by the initial study.

A Refined Test

The principal objective of the National Jury Sample was to determine whether the jury–voting link would persist across a diverse sample of jurors and jurisdictions with varied trial rules, jury facilities, and court practices. Going out of our way to gather a disproportionate number of civil jurors, the national study would also test whether this participation effect appeared equally strong for criminal and civil juries.

Collecting records on thousands of jurors across a broader range of trials also permitted the creation of a more precise comparison group consisting solely of "cancelled trials," in which the juror is empanelled, the trial begins, and then the trial ends prematurely—even before the jury can begin its deliberations. This includes mistrials, dismissals, withdrawn cases, cases settled out of court, or cases in which the right to a jury was waived after the trial began. The study works as a natural experiment where cancelled trials are the control group against which we compare four distinct jury experiences: serving as an alternate, defendant pleading guilty after the trial begins, hung jury (in part or full), and complete verdicts.

Based on the Olympia Project, we expected that reaching a verdict would have a positive effect on future voting relative to the experience of merely sitting in the jury box for what would end up as a cancelled trial. In addition, we anticipated that hung juries would have a net positive effect compared to cancelled trials.

The hung jury prediction puts the focus squarely on experiencing *deliberation*, rather than the personal satisfaction of convicting a defendant or setting one free. A review of contemporary data on hung juries found that they typically result from a complex case for which neither side can predict the trial outcome; juries typically hang only after intensive, prolonged jury deliberation.[29] Moreover, a hung jury often results in a decisive finding for the defendant (or respondent), so it serves as a final jury verdict in that sense. In any case, the hung jury constitutes an unambiguous experience of deliberation, regardless of outcome, and a core claim in this study is that participation in deliberation *itself* is the most critical component of the jury experience. To presume otherwise would require all deliberative forums to yield conclusive group decisions or fail to inspire their participants.[30]

The other two outcomes—sitting in the jury box as an alternate or witnessing a guilty plea before beginning jury deliberation—were less clearly distinct from a cancelled trial. Alternates do not participate in deliberation, therefore when their jury reaches a verdict, they play no direct role, but they did listen to the presentations of both sides in the trial. If the act of witnessing a trial plays a role in promoting civic engagement, then it should apply to alternates as well. Similarly, a guilty plea yields a final verdict for all jurors, akin to a "conclusive" outcome, but it involves no jury deliberation. To test our expectations, these two outcomes were also compared to cancelled trials to test whether either would produce the same positive effect predicted for hung and full-verdict juries.

In addition, consistent with the Olympia Project, we predicted that the number of charges against the defendant in criminal trials would provide an additional boost in post-jury voting rates. More charges are one indicator of the complexity of the decision task, with multiple counts against the defendant requiring the jury to reach multiple verdicts. Deliberative theorists and practitioners alike have stressed the importance of the *depth* of deliberation when considering its potential benefits for participants.[31] In the context of the jury, the number of charges provides one glimpse of such depth.

A Closer Look at Voting History

The National Jury Sample was further refined by distinguishing between historically frequent and infrequent voters, based on pre-jury voting behavior. A commonsense consideration of the participation effect is that it can draw into public life those citizens who are relatively less engaged, rather than merely reinvigorating those who are already regular participants. For instance, in his study on campaign participation, political scientist John Freie writes, "The popular panacea offered by some to reduce alienation is often participation itself. Political participation, it is hypothesized, will alleviate feelings of alienation and result in future political involvement."[32]

To test the jury effect for less versus more electorally active citizens, we split the National Jury Sample between habitually infrequent and frequent voters, based on their pre-trial voting rates. The study still controlled for variation in voting rates *within* these two groups, but we separated low- from high-turnout juror groups to determine whether the participation effect is visible across both populations.[33]

Our expectation was that less active citizens would be more likely to experience a cognitive and behavioral shift toward greater future public engagement than those who had already caught the civic spark. For infrequent voters, jury service offers entrée to a largely unexplored world—that of citizen participation in self-government. If jury service makes citizens, in Tocqueville's language, "feel the duties which they are bound to discharge towards society,"[34] this feeling is newer for those previously less inclined to recognize and fulfill such duties. Regular voters may still experience the participation effect, but its impact should be stronger for infrequent voters than their steady-voting counterparts.

Building the National Sample

Collecting a large and diverse sample of jurors required identifying a variety of counties in different parts of the country that had publicly accessible court archives, legible and complete jury records, and cooperative administrative staff. The eventual merger with electoral data also required access to complete and digitally archived voter histories dating back to at least 1994. To test the generalizability of the Olympia Project findings, we also aimed to assemble a set of counties that were demographically and politically diverse.

It was not possible to construct a fully representative national random sample of jurors for technical and logistical reasons. Chief among these was that only some courts make their jury records readily available for public inspection, and among those, many do not consistently record jurors' full names, which are necessary for matching jury lists with voting records. In addition, counties above a modest size (e.g., those hosting a city larger than Seattle) would produce too few unique matches between full juror names and the corresponding county list of registered voter names. (After all, there is more than one person named *James Bond* in Los Angeles.) With these limitations in mind, the goal was, once again, to create a broad and diverse sample—not a perfectly representative one. Following these guidelines, the final set of data collection included Boulder County (Colorado), Cumberland and Swain Counties (North Carolina), Douglas County (Nebraska) El Paso County (Texas), Orleans Parish (Louisiana.), Summit County (Ohio), and Thurston County (Washington).[35] Figure 3.3 shows the geographic distribution of the counties contributing to the National Jury Sample.

For each of the eight counties studied, we employed the same general procedures developed in the Olympia Project. All told, the collection, entry, assembly, and merging of these data required roughly 1,100 hours of labor from the research team, plus additional support from county court and election staff, for which we are more grateful than this book's acknowledgements can adequately convey.

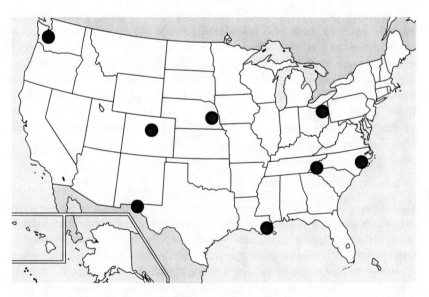

Figure 3.3 Map of the United States showing the research sites where jury and voting data were collected

The final result was a dataset with 13,237 empanelled jurors, including 8,573 who were seated in the jury box for a criminal trial and 4,664 who sat for a civil trial. Of these jurors, 10,300 served on juries that reached complete verdicts, 554 were hung on some or all charges or claims, 818 were excused from the jury box after the defendant changed their plea to guilty, 904 were dismissed for various other reasons (mistrial, withdrawn charges, out-of-court settlement, etc.), and 576 served only as alternates, never joining in jury deliberation.[36] Of these jurors, 65 percent matched voter files to produce 8,614 jury records with matching voter histories (see Appendix Section 3a). A sample of this size was necessary because we were pursuing a relatively small effect size and breaking the sample down into smaller subsamples for comparisons.[37]

A National Investigation

Comparing the Olympia Project to the National Jury Sample is like comparing a burglary investigation to an FBI probe of an organized crime syndicate. For the National Jury Sample, we used the same statistical regression analysis as before, but we looked at more variables and variables of a different nature than those analyzed in the Olympia Project. Compared to the Olympia Project, the National Jury Sample measured pre- and post-jury service voting histories over an even longer period of years: Voting histories included all regular countywide elections, from the 1994 primary to the 2004 general, with information reaching all the way back to 1992 in North Carolina and 1987 in Nebraska. For the full sample, the average pre-jury voter turnout was 52.3 percent, but pre-jury service turnout varied considerably across counties, from a low of 33.7 percent in Swain County to a high of 71.1 percent in Thurston County.[38] (Appendix Section 3b provides details on the national sample.) (Photo 3.1)

With the larger overall sample in the national investigation we were able to divide our sample further to look separately at two broad groups of voters. There are the already dutiful, self-assured frequent voters, who cast a ballot in at least half the elections held before reporting for jury service. Then there are the infrequent voters, who have a history of passing up at least half their chances to punch out chads or pull a lever.

We also were able to more carefully distinguish between two different places where the participation effect may have come into play. One area of interest was the criminal trial, where we investigated a number of factors in the Olympia Project. In the national study, we had enough jurors to carry out a proper investigation of the participation effect on jurors in both criminal *and civil* trials.[39]

The national study allowed us to analyze the effect of some new variables. Thanks to the success of the Olympia Project, we could predict a large effect from conclusive deliberative experience, but now we could break down the

Photo 3.1. Exterior photos of courthouses in the National Jury Sample. Clockwise from top left: courthouses in Thurston County (Washington), Swain County (North Carolina), Boulder County (Colorado), Cumberland County (North Carolina), Summit County (Ohio), Douglas County (Nebraska), Orleans Parish criminal courthouse (Louisiana), and El Paso County (Texas)

other trial outcomes and look at them separately. We could, for instance, look at hung jurors, who deliberated but failed to return a verdict. Their experience was not conclusive, but unlike the other "inconclusive" jury experiences, theirs at least involved deliberation—quite intensive deliberation at that. Those who had the experience of being named alternate were also analyzed independently, as were jurors who served on a criminal case in which the defendant changed his plea to guilty, stopping the trial cold.[40]

We also looked again at the number of charges. Cognizant of the possibility that this unexpected effect was simply a freak chance occurrence, we were curious to see whether it would again prove significant.[41] Finally, we included in our equation the pre-jury service voting rate as nothing more than a reality check.

Presenting the Findings

Just as in the Olympia investigation, we conducted regression analyses to judge which of our predictors explained changes in jurors' voting behaviors. In this national study, it meant conducting a total of four analyses. For persons with a history of infrequent voting, we ran separate analyses for criminal versus civil jurors. We then ran the same analyses for more steady voters.

The left-hand column in Table 3.3 shows which variables in the regression analysis predicted increased election turnout among infrequent voters

Table 3.3.   Linear regression measuring the effect of jury experience on infrequent voters in the National Jury Sample

Predictor	Served on a criminal trial		Served on a civil jury	
	B (SE)	b	B (SE)	b
Jury verdict	.043 (.03)	.076*	.020 (.02)	.029
Hung jury	.068 (.04)	.063**	−.111 (.17)	−.019
Alternate	.022 (.04)	.022	.000 (.05)	.000
Guilty plea	.019 (.04)	.021	–	–
Number of charges	.013 (.01)	.061**	–	–
Pre-jury vote	.640 (.06)	.273***	.769 (.07)	.322***
R^2	.128		.156	
N	1,397		997	

Note: * $p < .10$, ** $p < .05$, *** $p < .01$. Both R^2 were significant at $p < .001$. The reference group for the Jury Verdict, Hung Jury, Alternate, and Guilty Plea dummy codes was Cancelled Trial (mistrials, dismissals, withdrawn cases, settling out of court, or waiving the right to a jury after the trial began). The other variables entered in the regression equations were the dummy variables representing county and oversample; they are omitted for economy of presentation. B denotes unstandardized regression coefficient, SE denotes standard error of estimate, and b denotes standardized coefficient.

serving on criminal trials. Criminal jurors reaching a verdict were more likely to vote in later elections: In the National Jury Sample, the likelihood of voting in a future election rose by an average of 4.3 percent over the span of several years.

Those previously infrequent voters who had the intense deliberative experience of a hung jury showed the largest effect. These jurors did not reach a conclusive verdict, but they did all have the opportunity to deliberate at length about the trial with their fellow jurors. On average, a participant in a hung criminal trial experienced a 6.8 percent increase in their voting rate in the years after completing their jury service.

Consistent with this emphasis on the intensity of the deliberative experience, the number of charges against the defendant again proved a significant contributor to post-service voting. Each additional charge added a 1.3 percent increase in the likelihood of voting. For a complex criminal trial with, say, four charges against the defendant, this would amount to an average increase in voting of roughly 4 percent.

Figure 3.4 puts these findings in comparative terms. For previously infrequent voters, the effect of deliberating on a criminal jury is comparable to the civic boost a high-school student gets from taking a mandatory civics course for a semester, and it exceeds the impact of service on

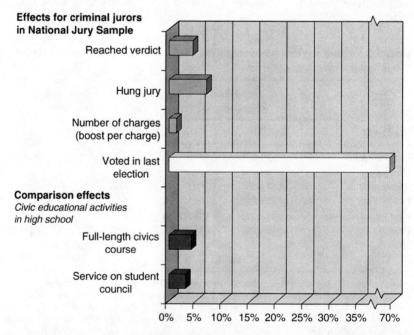

Figure 3.4 Comparison of estimated effects from National Jury Sample and high-school civic education on the likelihood of voting in future elections

student council. Thus, the civic lessons gleaned from jury service compare quite favorably with more familiar means of instruction and experiential learning.

The other results in Table 3.3 are unremarkable. As expected, neither of the other trial outcomes—serving as an alternate or having a defendant plead guilty before deliberation began—had any significant effect on the likelihood of voting. Also, in the National Jury Sample, the effect of a better-estimated pre-jury voting history (i.e., measured over more elections) was even greater than in the Olympia Project, but again, this was to be expected and simply reinforces the widely-held belief that voting is, indeed, habitual behavior.

In fact, the rest of the analyses in this investigation are *all* non-findings. The results confirmed suspicions from interview data and the Olympia project: civil trials really are different. In the National Sample (as shown in the right-hand column of Table 3.3), no significant participation effect was found for the civil jury experience among infrequent voters. The same column in Table 3.4 shows that civil jurors with a history of regular voting also experienced no civic benefit from their civil jury service. More generally, Table 3.4 shows that there were no participation effects for either civil *or criminal* trials among frequent voters. Aside from the obvious impact of pre-jury voting service, the likelihood of voting after jury service was not significantly related to any feature of that service experience.

Table 3.4.   Linear regression measuring the effect of jury experience for frequent voters in the National Jury Sample

Predictor	Served on a criminal trial		Served on a civil jury	
	B (*SE*)	*b*	B (*SE*)	*b*
Jury verdict	−.007 (.03)	−.012	.000 (.02)	.000
Hung jury	.036 (.03)	.037	−.013 (.13)	−.003
Alternate	.030 (.03)	.026	−.042 (.04)	−.035
Guilty plea	−.002 (.03)	−.003	–	–
Number of charges	−.008 (.01)	−.036	–	–
Pre-jury vote	.751 (.04)	.382***	.737 (.05)	.394***
R^2	.209		.195	
N	1,950		1,193	

Note: * $p < .10$, ** $p < .05$, *** $p < .01$. Both R^2 were significant at $p < .001$. The reference group for the Jury Verdict, Hung Jury, Alternate, and Guilty Plea dummy codes was Cancelled Trial (mistrials, dismissals, withdrawn cases, settling out of court, or waiving the right to a jury after the trial began). The other variables entered in the regression equations were the dummy variables representing county and oversample; they are omitted for economy of presentation. B denotes unstandardized regression coefficient, *SE* denotes standard error of estimate, and *b* denotes standardized coefficient.

Summarizing the Evidence

We bring our investigation to a close by revealing the results of the National Jury Sample inquiry. The replication of the effects found in the Olympia Project provides strong evidence for a pervasive and enduring effect of criminal jury deliberation on civic engagement, at least for those entering jury service with a relatively spotty voting record. The effect amounts to a 4–7 percent increase in average turnout. On top of that, we found a participation effect that increased more than 1 percent per additional charge against the defendant. These effects were present even with the post-jury voting rate being measured over roughly five years, versus just one in the Olympia Project.[42] The National Jury Sample also yielded these results with a diverse sampling of courts and jury pools.

These results qualify the Olympia Project's conclusions in many important respects. First, the effect of criminal jury deliberation on voting does not hold for those voters who are already active. We had expected this population to experience *less* voting change, but the data make it clear that the jury does not affect these individuals' voting behavior. Chapters 6 and 7 will consider the possibility that jury service affects these individuals in other ways beyond voting, but in the meantime, this finding substantially qualifies the extent to which one should expect the participation effect to occur in juries.

Second, the National Jury Sample made clear that the participation effect comes from *all* deliberating jurors, not just those who reach verdicts. We anticipated that hung jurors would experience the participation effect, and as it turned out, it had an effect slightly greater than that obtained for jurors who agreed on verdicts. Again, the nature of the deliberation may be a factor. Analysis of the court records showed that hung jurors, on average, were more likely to have asked a judge for assistance during deliberation (79 percent of those on hung juries did so, compared to just 28 percent of jurors reaching verdicts). Also, hung juries deliberated for a considerably longer time—roughly nine hours—than did their verdict-reaching counterparts, who were usually done in four.[43] For many jurors, long and challenging deliberations that end in a contested deadlock can leave a stronger impression than does reaching a comfortable verdict with one's peers.

In addition, the point for jurors was not simply whether the trial they served on reached a verdict: There was no voting effect for those individuals serving as alternates or at criminal trials that ended because the defendant switched to a guilty plea. A spontaneous guilty plea in the courtroom may feel, to the juror, more like a cancelled trial than a conclusive experience. Serving as an alternate also appears to leave no strong impression on jurors, regardless of their prior voting history or the type of trial to which they were assigned.

Finally, the clear impact of the number of criminal charges reinforced the significance of jury deliberation, but in a complex way. In the pilot study, we speculated that the number of criminal charges reflected the *seriousness* of the charges, but a post hoc analysis of the severity of the charges did not bear out this interpretation. (Appendix Section 5b describes how we measured the severity of charges.) Perhaps the best alternative interpretation is that juries weighing more charges simply face a more complex deliberative task as they make *more* decisions often involving interlocking judgments and mixed verdicts. (We will revisit this issue in chapter 6.)

Notice, however, that the number of charges had this effect *independent of whether the jury was sent away to deliberate.* As we explained before, statistical regression analyses separate out the effects of each independent variable, and the number of charges has its own heft as a predictor of future voting. This implies that jurors begin processing a case before they sit down face-to-face to discuss it. We will investigate this idea of "reflective deliberation"[44] in more detail in chapter 5, but for now it is enough to note that jury service *can* influence participants in ways other than through jury room deliberation.

Looking beyond the Archives

We have now marshaled sufficient evidence to show that jury service can, indeed, contribute to an increase in civic engagement, at least in the form of voting. But we have also learned many other lessons along the way.

Talking to jurors through in-depth interviews yielded four ideas that guided our analysis throughout the study. These structured conversations showed jurors are, on the whole, quite impressed by their jury experience. Jury deliberation is central to that experience, and jurors can conceptualize jury service and voting as related civic responsibilities. These comments from the twelve jurors weighed in as only the lightest form of evidence, but without them, the analysis of immense datasets might have missed important findings lurking in the statistical shadows.

Seeing farther than any study before it, the Olympia Project showed a measurable causal link between jury deliberation and voting behavior. In Thurston County, jurors who reached conclusive verdicts in criminal cases were more likely to vote compared to those who did not reach conclusive verdicts. The study also underscored the importance of deliberation by showing that the complexity of the case, as represented by the number of charges brought against the defendant, contributed to an increase in jurors' post-service voting rates.

The National Jury Sample then deployed a geographically and ethnically diverse sample ten times the size of the Olympia Project. This permitted a more definitive and fine-grained investigation of the link between jury service and voting. The national study produced three main findings. First, the main increase in voting rates results from the experience of jury *delibera-*

tion, not merely from trials in which jurors reach a verdict. Second, cases involving multiple charges have an additional, positive participation effect, which suggests the need to consider the complexity of a case and other features that might make jurors' deliberative task more challenging or engaging. Third, none of these effects occur for jurors who are already frequent voters or who sit in the jury box for civil cases.

The National Jury Sample also gave a more refined estimate of the participation effect. The study suggests that one can expect an increase of roughly 4–7 percent, at least in the case of criminal jurors' post-service voting rates. Figures 3.3 and 3.5 showed that this effect is comparable to nonpartisan get-out-the-vote campaigns and likely exceeds the average impact of a full length civics course or a stint on the student council.[45]

The National Jury Sample made these insights possible through its unusual design. Merging public jury and voting records allowed a compelling test of our predictions without many of the biases that can be present in survey data. None of the data we used in this chapter (other than Meade's interview sample) were anything other than formal, objective records from public archives and databases. The records themselves were made by public employees with no personal stake in the data, let alone foreknowledge of our research objectives. These features made for a rigorous test.

Relying on archival data, however, meant that we could not probe the subjective experiences of jurors or look at civic behaviors not recorded by public officials. To address these limitations, chapters 4 through 7 will elaborate on the National Jury Sample by presenting survey data that take us far beyond objective trial features and voting histories. These survey data will come with their own limitations, but they permit us to study aspects of the jury experience that one cannot access through archival data.

Before moving on to these other subjects, though, we wish to close by drawing out one of the broader implications of the data presented thus far. Our study suggests that other meaningful deliberative events, beyond jury service, may also yield a participation effect. A recent national survey found that Americans deliberate in a variety of ways in the course of their public lives, from attending public meetings to taking part in online discussions.[46] Our research suggests that the strength of the participation effect at such deliberative events probably depends on the quality of the deliberation and the gravity or complexity of the issue under discussion. We will explore this question more in the final chapter of the book, but for now, it is enough to simply recognize that deliberation's effect on voting may well appear in other venues beyond the courthouse.

Undoubtedly, the main finding is simply that, as the U.S. Supreme Court assumed in *Powers v. Ohio*, there is wisdom in Tocqueville's claim that juries serve as a school for democratic citizenship. The objective measures in the

Olympia Project and the National Jury Sample demonstrate that, consistent with a broad range of theories on democracy, different forms of civic engagement are linked. Moreover, they show that the link carries a participation effect, whereby an intense—preferably deliberative—experience in one civic arena can spur increases in another.

Chapter 4

Answering the Summons

With most written communication now arriving electronically, a jury summons in the mailbox stands out as an important, if quaint document. Prospective jurors in Washington D.C., for instance, have received a summons that reads:

> By order of the Chief Judge of the Superior Court of the District of Columbia, you are hereby summoned to serve as a juror as indicated below. Please complete the enclosed juror qualification form and return it within five (5) days. Failure to appear as directed by this summons may result in a fine of not more than three hundred dollars ($300) or imprisonment for not more than seven (7) days or both.[1]

In the 1995 comedy *Jury Duty*, the underemployed Tommy Collins cringes when his jury summons arrives in the mail. He tosses it into the garbage. Many otherwise upstanding citizens share Collins' repulsion toward jury duty because they cannot imagine taking time away from work and family to sit in a courtroom and listen to self-important lawyers argue for days on end. Collins, however, becomes desperate to serve when he realizes a sequestered high-profile case will mean free room and board at a hotel and a modest honorarium. He digs the summons out of the trash, strides off to the courthouse, and manipulates his way into a murder trial. Hilarity ensues.

In reality, the experience of jury service is very different from what onlookers imagine. Consider the comments of a juror from Redding, California, who was interviewed after he had participated in his *sixth* criminal trial.[2] Though his service is a matter of public record, we will call him by the pseudonym Jeff.[3] Nearing his sixties, this small business owner admitted to hesitancy every time the court has called on him to serve. "The first thing you think about is, 'Oh my goodness. I don't *really* want to do this.' I think everybody goes through that." It is normal to not "really want to serve on jury duty," he said. But serve he did.

And the experience? Jeff did not say it was pleasant spending all those days at the courthouse. The challenge, he found, was that you have to "judge your fellow man.... I just hate to have to do it." Having said that, he admitted that in even one stint of jury duty, "you really do get an opportunity to learn the system." Then "the next thing that goes through your mind is that [it's] a civil responsibility and that you really kind of owe it to the community."

In spite of his discomfort with passing judgment, Jeff said that in the end, he "never really felt uncomfortable with the result. I felt that society asked you to do this as part of the system." It may be challenging for the jurors, but "to have a jury of your peers, that's the American way." Jeff even saw a larger value in his service: "I think that my experience on the jury has made me a better community civilian [sic]," he said. "I think being part of the community, it's been an education."

Entering a Northwestern Courthouse

This, of course, was just the experience of one juror. To get a sense for whether Jeff's experience was typical and to learn the other reactions people have to jury service, we shifted our attention away from the archives described in chapter 3. We focused instead on a single locale, the county and city courthouses in King County, Washington. This county holds nearly two million residents, who live in cities such as Seattle, Bellevue, and Redmond (of Microsoft fame); in suburbs like Shoreline and Mercer Island; and in smaller communities across the Cascade Mountains, such as Snoqualmie and Carnation. From February to July, 2004, we tracked every person who reported for jury duty at the Kent Regional Justice Center, the King County Courthouse, or the Seattle Municipal Court.[4]

Each venue provided jurors with a different first impression. In the heart of downtown Seattle, the King County Courthouse provided the most prototypical setting for jury service. Our study tracked 3,380 jurors who passed through the building's busy security screening station and into a marbled lobby with banks of elevators and a modest sign telling them to ascend to the jury waiting area. Once there, they would stand in a long line to check in with the jury administrator. The courthouse was undergoing construction, and jurors would be sent to wait in empty courtrooms or seated in serviceable plastic chairs. Their orientation would consist of a script read by the administrator—and sometimes a motivational speech by a judge, along with an instructional video narrated by Raymond Burr, the star of the mid-century courtroom drama, *Perry Mason*.[5]

The sheer volume of cases in King County necessitated the construction of a second courthouse, the Kent Regional Justice Center. This newer building provided a more spacious setting, with a wide open central lobby topped by a rotunda and lined with large windows. The 2,530 jurors we tracked through this building gathered each morning in a nondescript waiting area, and the Justice Center staff provided this slightly smaller jury pool with a comfortable space and a predictable routine.

Photo 4.1 King County downtown courthouse (top) and the Kent Regional Justice Center (bottom)

Those who received a summons from the City of Seattle, however, enjoyed a more pampered experience. The 710 jurors who rode the elevator to the top floor of the Seattle Justice Center received panoramic views of the city and Puget Sound from the two-story windows and open-air balcony. This elegant Jury Assembly Room featured a well-stocked break area, a computer lounge, and sculptures by Tacoma glass artist Dale Chihuly.[6]

Whether charmed or appalled by their facilities, those who carried the jury summons into their respective courthouses came prepared to serve—and to be surveyed. After their orientation, our team of research assistants introduced each prospective juror to our study and invited their participation.[7] To put the jurors at ease, we joked that they would find they had plenty of time on their hands to complete the surveys, and we offered to supplement their meager daily earnings ($10 each day, plus mileage) by providing them with ball-point pens from the University of Washington and Washington State University, the cross-state rival in Pullman, where many King County residents went to college.

With just the right mix of politeness, patience, and begging, we elicited responses from more than 80 percent of jurors, an unusually high response-rate for any survey.[8] This is all the more remarkable when considering that jurors knew from the outset that they were stepping into a *three-wave panel survey*. This meant that there would be three survey waves—one done with pen-and-paper in the Jury Assembly Room at the beginning of their service, a second done in response to a mailed (or e-mailed) survey after completing their courthouse service, and a final follow-up survey done electronically or through the mail after the 2004 presidential election.[9] In each of these three waves, more than three-quarters of the individuals we contacted completed their surveys. In retrospect, our good fortune likely came from the fact that these persons were, after all, the very same people who chose to respond (often reluctantly) to a jury summons in the first place.[10]

On Becoming Empanelled

Showing up for jury duty, however, is no guarantee that one will serve on a jury: Only 39 percent of those who sat in a King County or Seattle jury assembly room were "hopeful" that they would "be required to serve on a jury today," and nearly a quarter confessed to wanting to leave without serving. In the end, only 27 percent of prospective jurors actually became empanelled—sworn in as a juror and seated in the jury box. Just weeks after the study ended, the first author of this book received his summons and sat for the required two days of service in the waiting area, reading the newspaper, doing paperwork for his job, and never getting called to a courtroom—let alone seated on a jury. Of those who answer the summons but never serve on a jury, a third share this brief purgatory. The rest march off to courtrooms but are not chosen for a panel.

Ducking Out

For some prospective jurors, however, going home without serving on a jury represents a kind of victory, not a failure. Judges and attorneys can dismiss prospectives for a range of reasons, and many of us have heard stories about how to avoid jury service. A few of the participants in our study commented on this issue in the open-ended portion of their survey. One highly educated man serving at the Kent Regional Justice Center said he was "disappointed some of the other jurors were obviously scamming...to keep from getting on a jury." A juror with a graduate degree who served at the downtown King County courthouse concluded that jury selection is "a game" in which people "lie and say just about anything to get out of service."

The idea of misbehaving at court to get dismissed from jury duty has currency in contemporary comedy. Likely inspired by the juror who served briefly during the 1996 Whitewater trial in a red and black Star Trek commander's uniform, the writers of NBC's *30 Rock* showed Liz Lemon dodging jury duty by dressing up as Princess Leia from *Star Wars* and explaining to the judge, "I don't think it's fair for me to be on a jury, because I can read thoughts." The next scene showed Liz Lemon being served champagne in her first class airplane seat, relieved of her courthouse obligations.

Occasionally, real jurors behave no better. When Senator Ted Stevens (R-Alaska) was tried on corruption charges in 2008, one juror was excused owing to her father's untimely death. As it turned out, she had actually departed to attend the Breeders' Cup horse race. When asked to explain herself, the *Washington Post* recounted that she offered "a rambling statement that involved wiretaps, horses and drugs in Kentucky." Later, she simply admitted to the press that she had to leave because she had already purchased her tickets to the race.[11]

Even before performing theatrics to seek release, those hoping to avoid jury service may plead their case to jury administrators or otherwise try to make themselves scarce, but as Figure 4.1 shows, the likelihood of getting called to a courtroom and temporarily seated as a possible juror fell randomly across the entire jury pool. At the same time, the most reluctant prospectives became sworn in as jurors only 16 percent of the time—half the rate attained by those with an interest in serving.[12]

Like the fictional jurors Liz Lemon and Thomas Collins, the reluctant juror has a chance to be dismissed during *voir dire* (pronounced "vwahr deer"). This jury selection procedure, which varies considerably across jurisdictions, removes prospective jurors based on the judge's discretion or the wishes of the prosecution or defense attorneys, who can generally remove any juror "for cause" (such as a personal relationship with the defendant or pleading that service on the particular jury would represent a "hardship" for the juror due to the expected length of the trial). Typically, attorneys can also exercise a limited number of "peremptory challenges,"

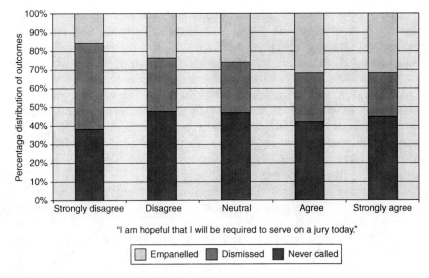

Figure 4.1 The relationship between desire to serve and outcomes at jury service

which require no rationale for removal. (Even with these more arbitrary dismissals, however, it is illegal for an attorney to exercise them in a discriminatory manner.[13])

Which of these causes removal varies with a juror's disposition toward serving. Only 22 percent of those enthusiastic prospectives who were removed were sent away "for cause," with the majority (57 percent) exiting due to the exercise of a peremptory challenge from the prosecution. A third of all others were dismissed for cause/hardship, with the rest receiving peremptory challenges as likely to come from the defense as from the prosecution.[14] The surprising finding here is that prosecution attorneys appear suspicious of the most eager jurors. This characteristic has never surfaced in the vast scholarly literature on jury selection, and in our dataset, willingness to serve on a jury bore no relationship to the verdicts that jurors ultimately reached.[15]

Why might the prosecution target the most eager jurors? One potential explanation draws on the idea that jury service represents a special civic-political activity imbued with a democratic spirit of citizen empowerment. In this view, those citizens eager to serve, relative to their more reluctant peers, have stronger convictions about their rightful place in government. A perceptive prosecutor might sense in these individuals a greater skepticism toward official authority, such as that held by the police, who often prove critical witnesses for the prosecution.

Skeptics, however, might argue instead that the association is spurious—that willingness to serve simply correlates with other demographic characteristics. To check for this possibility, we tested the predictiveness of willingness to serve against an array of other demographics, including age, sex, ethnicity, employment status, and education. As in chapter 3, we employed regression analysis, this time using a binary logistic method because the dependent variable was a dichotomy between dismissal at the hands of the defense versus prosecution. The only significant predictors in this model proved to be willingness to serve and, marginally, level of education. Essentially, prospective jurors were equally likely to be dismissed by one side versus the other if they had no graduate degree and no particular eagerness to serve. Having either one, though, made it twice as likely that the prosecution made the dismissal. The eager jurors who held advanced degrees were four times as likely to be dismissed by prosecution versus defense.[16]

The education effect is consistent with some prosecutors' conviction that highly educated jurors tend to overthink cases, which helps the defense. After all, the defense aims only to raise doubt, whereas the prosecutor or plaintiff must prove their case. Legal analyst and former prosecutor Jeffrey Toobin put it this way: Federal prosecutors "sought jurors smart enough to understand the evidence but not so clever that they would overanalyze it; educated, but not to excess."[17] Perhaps the eagerness of civic-spirited prospective jurors comes across in the same way as advanced education, leading prosecutors to eschew them.

Systematic Exclusion

Aside from which side offers the dismissal, a larger issue concerns what kind of person will be selected for a jury *at all*. Recall that the U.S. Supreme Court affirmed the constitutional right to jury service lest one or another social group be denied this unique civic educational opportunity.[18]

Some of the jurors in our study expressed precisely this concern. A young, college-educated white woman who served on a downtown jury found her *voir dire* session to be very interesting: "Any person who was a minority was quickly eliminated. The nature of the system makes it such that only housewives, retirees, or upper-middle class people with good jobs can participate." In the end, she felt "less positive about the idea of a 'jury of your peers' after witnessing this process." Other jurors pointed to two specific bases for elimination—loquacity and intelligence. For instance, a Kent woman who got dismissed without serving on a jury said, "My experience of voir dire was that it is a process of eliminating those who have opinions and ideas and are able to communicate them. Many of those who ended up on the jury were able to walk the thin line between prosecution and defense without raising a red flag by knowing or saying nothing. I'm curious as to how this results in a well-formed jury." One prospective juror believed that he got caught in precisely this net. A college-educated, middle-aged male working a full-time job wrote, "The fact that I spoke up was the reason I did not get chosen as a juror. The people who had nothing to say were chosen."

To test the general veracity of these perceptions, we conducted another binary logistic regression—this time to distinguish those who became sworn jurors from those who were considered but then individually dismissed by either the judge or attorneys. To the set of predictor variables included earlier, we added two new variables to reflect the aforementioned concerns about the makeup of the jury pool. First, we combined survey items (discussed at length in chapter 6) to create a *public talkativeness* index. This index averaged three questions assessing the frequency with which survey respondents talked with others to "change their mind about a political issue, a candidate, or a ballot initiative," to "learn more about a political issue, a candidate, or a ballot initiative," or simply to "discuss local community affairs."[19] Using the semantic scaling of these items, the mean response averages to speaking slightly more than once-a-month, a figure slightly lower than average, based on national research on the frequency of political conversation in the United States.[20]

Second, to test whether *voir dire* excludes those who are more knowledgeable of public affairs and current events, we measured respondents' awareness of federal, state, and county political information, such as which party had more members in the U.S. Senate, how State Supreme Court justices are chosen in Washington (they are elected), and the identity of the King County executive.[21] Modestly exceeding the political knowledge levels found in national surveys, our average respondent got three to four of these questions correct.[22]

Taking these new factors into account, along with the standard demographic measures, Figure 4.2 shows the factors that influence whether

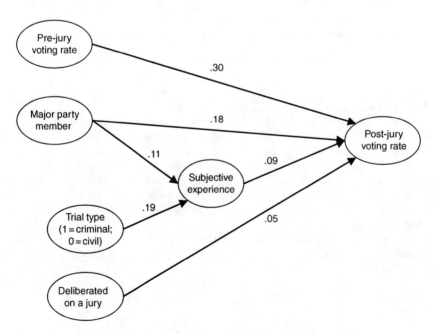

Note: All paths shown are significant standardized coefficients.

Figure 4.2   Simplified path analysis of hypothesized predictors of post-jury service voting in King County for pre-service infrequent voters

reluctant, indifferent, and hopeful prospectives end up as empanelled jurors, once they get considered for that role in a specific case. As it turns out, only a handful of these predictors reach significance for any of the three juror groups. First, the left-hand columns show women who seek to avoid jury service have greater success in that regard than do men. Using the conventions of logistic regression, Table 4.1 shows an "odds ratio"—the statistic exp(B) in the table, which means that reluctant female prospective jurors are 36 percent less likely to end up sworn into a jury than are reluctant male prospectives.[23]

The next significant effect is work status. Being retired had no effect, but those who worked full time were 40–45 percent *more* likely to end up as jurors relative to their non-retired peers. This effect was consistent across all three levels of juror enthusiasm for serving, though it did not reach statistical significance for reluctant jurors.

A prospective juror's level of education *did* have a significant effect for all types of prospective jurors. Whether reluctant, indifferent, or eager, each additional step on the educational ladder reduced a juror's odds of serving by roughly 10 percent. Relative to a prospective juror with no high-school education, one with a college degree was 40 percent less likely to end up empanelled and a graduate degree reduced one's odds by twice that figure.

One clear finding in Table 4.2 speaks to the concern expressed by some of the jurors in our study. The third set of columns shows that jurors who are

Table 4.1.   Predictors of whether prospective jurors become empanelled once considered

Predictor	Reluctant to serve		Indifferent		Hoping to serve	
	B (SE)	exp(B)	B (SE)	exp(B)	B (SE)	exp(B)
Female	−0.44 (0.21)	0.64**	0.12 (0.18)	1.12	−0.01 (0.17)	0.99
Age	0.00 (0.01)	1.00	0.00 (0.01)	1.00	0.00 (0.01)	1.00
White	−0.06 0.31)	0.94	−0.26 (0.25)	0.77	0.06 (0.25)	1.07
Retired	0.83 (0.51)	2.29	0.23 (0.35)	1.26	0.37 (0.32)	1.45
Full time	0.32 (0.24)	1.37	0.37 (0.21)	1.45*	0.34 (0.2)	1.40*
Education	−0.11 (0.07)	0.89*	−0.11 (0.05)	0.90*	−0.13 (0.05)	0.88**
Political knowledge	−0.08 (0.08)	0.92	−0.02 (0.07)	0.98	−0.08 (0.07)	0.93
Talkative	0.18 (0.12)	1.20	−0.02 (0.09)	0.98	−0.26 (0.09)	0.77***
Constant	1.13 (0.59)	3.10*	1.25 (0.48)	3.50***	2.48 (0.53)	11.91***
Nagerlkerke R²	.040		.020		.046	
X2 (8 df)	13.47*		10.21		27.76***	
% Predicted correctly	70%		72%		77%	
N	457		739		895	

Note: * *p*<.10, ** *p*<.05, *** *p*<.01. Education is entered as a continuous variable from 0 (no high-school diploma) to 8 (doctoral degree).

more talkative about public issues have a reduced chance of being selected for a jury, though *only when they are also hoping to serve on one.* Again using the language of odds, these results refer to a five-point talkativeness measure, and movement up each point of this scale decreases the odds of being empanelled by 23 percent. Expressed in the exact terms of the talk-ativeness scale, those hoping to serve on juries who *never* talk about local and political affairs are more than twice as likely to end up empanelled than their eager counterparts who talk about public issues more than once a week. It seems safe to presume that these same talkative (or reticent) ten-dencies manifested themselves in the courtroom—with those who spoke up (and out) during *voir dire* expressing too much enthusiasm and perhaps too much information to make prosecutors, defense attorneys, or even judges comfortable with leaving them in a jury panel.

It is also important what these results do *not* show. Specifically, the array of other demographics included in this survey end up having no bearing on a person's likelihood of being dismissed during *voir dire.* A juror's level of political knowledge, age, ethnicity, and retiree status did not matter for this particular sample of jurors in King County, Washington. Discrimination against prospective jurors led to rulings like *Powers v. Ohio*, which recog-nized that court procedures had unfairly excluded some groups from service. Strong evidence suggests systematic racial bias persists in many jurisdic-tions, but in our study of King County, those most likely to be dismissed were those with the highest levels of formal education.[24]

Table 4.2.   Comparison of demographics from U.S. Census and survey respondents for King County and Seattle

Statistic	King County			Seattle		
	County census	Appeared at court	Sworn in juror	City census	Appeared at court	Sworn in juror
Median age (yrs)	46	48	48	46	50	49
In labor force	71%	75%	76%	67%	76%	76%
HSgrad (25 and up)	91%	91%	92%	84%	95%	95%
BA/BS (25 and up)	43%	69%	70%	27%	59%	58%
Female	51%	54%	53%	51%	52%	51%
White	74%	86%	88%	76%	82%	84%
Black	6%	3%	3%	12%	5%	4%
Asian	13%	7%	6%	4%	10%	9%
Hispanic	7%	2%	1%	14%	2%	2%
N. Amer/ Pacific	1%	2%	2%	< 1%	1%	2%

A Jury of Peers

At this juncture, it is useful to step back and assess precisely how different jurors are from the rest of those eligible for jury service. We address this question only in reference to our particular sample—and the King County and Seattle jurisdictions in this survey. Table 4.2 shows that those *reporting* for jury service had more years of formal education than did the general population of King County or the city of Seattle. Roughly two-thirds of prospective jurors age twenty-five and older (69 percent in King County, 59 percent in Seattle) were college graduates, compared to just 43 percent and 27 percent in the general county and city populations, respectively. In addition, 86 percent of prospective King County jurors and 82 percent of those in Seattle identified themselves as White, compared to just 74 percent of the county-wide population and 76 percent of Seattleites. The most under-represented ethnic group among prospective jurors, particularly in Seattle, was Hispanic residents, making up just 2 percent of the jury pools despite comprising 7 percent of the county population and 14 percent of the Seattle population. Contrary to conventional wisdom, juries were not made up principally of retirees. Median ages only two to three years higher than those of the general population, with jurors being slightly more active in the labor force.

Jurors differ very little—if at all—from the wider *jury pool*. The demographic differences between the juries empanelled in King County and Seattle relative to the corresponding census figures result from distortions in who responds to the jury summons. The challenge this poses for courts with similar statistics lies in the summoning, not in the *voir dire* process. Less educated, unemployed, and Hispanic King County residents are less likely to return their summons and more likely to request to be excused or have their service deferred—a result consistent with past research on summons responses.[25] What exactly causes this skew—and how to remedy it— lies outside the scope of this survey, which focuses on those who do report to jury service.

Finally, there exist no census figures on the general population's interest in serving on juries, but we have strong indirect evidence that most people are willing to serve, given that roughly four-fifths of the population responds to the court when summoned.[26] Thus, the jury pool skews strongly toward those interested in becoming jurors. When looked at in relation to the general population, perhaps the most overrepresented groups on juries are those persons who *want* to serve on juries. Given this fact, it seems less pressing a concern that attorneys and judges should trim back this group, at least when their eagerness is mixed with a strong disposition to make their views (and enthusiasm) known to all who care to listen.

How Jurors Assess Their Experience

It is useful to consider how the average juror perceives the *voir dire* process. As it turns out, most of the prospective jurors dismissed during *voir dire* still

Photo 4.2 Photos of the Seattle Justice Center and Municipal Court.
Clockwise from top-left: street-level exterior view, seated six-person jury,
room reserved for jury deliberation, and view of downtown from Jury
Assembly Room

gave it good marks. When asked about "the process that was used to select
who got to sit in the jury box during the trial," 30 percent rated it as "very
good" or "excellent," one-third rated it as "good," and only 7 percent gave
it a "less than satisfactory" rating. Seventy-two percent of those who sat as
mere bystanders, never called into the jury box even for questioning, rated
voir dire as "satisfactory" or "good." Empanelled jurors gave the highest
marks, with 41 percent rating it as "very good" or "excellent," with another
34 percent rating it as "good."[27]

Beyond the assessment of *voir dire*, what do jurors make of their time
in court? Much of the anecdotal information we hear about jury service
concerns its tedium. Former U.S. Western District Judge William Dwyer
conceded that many trials are guilty of "the sin of fecklessness," providing
jurors with aimless, meandering, and plodding exchanges of objections, procedural disputes, side-bars, and delays.[28] Some of the reluctance to serve on
juries surely stems from such concerns.

If our study had only collected anecdotal and open-ended responses, we might well have concluded that, for the most part, jurors regretted their time spent at the courthouse. The last question in our survey asked jurors to write whatever they wished, and many of those comments expressed regrets and frustration. One who sat in the jury administration room for two days said that his "biggest disappointment was not even being called for consideration for a jury." A Hispanic woman working part-time who could have added more diversity to a downtown King County jury wrote, "Although I had reservations about jury duty when I was first summoned, I was disappointed that I didn't have the opportunity to actually serve on a jury." On a more positive note, she added, "I surprised myself with these feelings, and I hope I'll have another chance someday."

Comments from those seated on juries sometimes turned bitter. One male juror serving downtown wrote, "I hope I never have to be judged by 'a jury of my peers.' That sincerely scares me! I am stunned by the level of incompetence displayed in the jury room." Two related comments came from jurors who were nearly identical demographically to this first one. One of these men wrote that jury service was "a waste of time and money." The third man in this set pointed his finger at the courtroom actors: "I think judges, court staff, and attorneys 'talk down' to juries. The people on juries aren't given enough evidence [to know] what is going on with the process." He asked the research team to "tell judges to stop being so condescending."

Overall Satisfaction

Of the 3,149 respondents in our post-jury service survey, fewer than one in six offered further open-ended comments at the end of the survey. Fortunately, we do not have to rely on those few written notes to estimate the distribution of juror experiences. We addressed the topic directly in a series of questions.

Knowing that for every juror we would have three non-jurors, we chose to continue our study with only a fraction of those who showed up at the courthouse but never became empanelled. This resulted in a post-service dataset consisting of 1,721 non-jurors and 1,428 jurors. In the analyses below, we keep these groups distinct, because their experiences differed markedly, as we have already gleaned from jurors' open-ended comments.

The first question we posed to respondents simply asked, "Overall, how would you rate your experience at jury duty?" Table 4.3 shows a modest difference between the experience of non-jurors across the three courthouses but *dramatic* differences between jurors and non-jurors in all three cases. The first of these effects clearly reflects the uniquely pleasant facility and setting of the Seattle Municipal Courthouse's jury administration room, not to mention that the assembled jurors on a given day numbered forty to fifty, rather than the crowds twice that size at the King County courthouses. For all its charm, the superior amenities and comforts of the Seattle courthouse made no difference in jurors' assessments if they served on a jury—an experience that overwhelmed more trivial first-impressions.

The clear difference in Table 4.3 is between jurors and non-jurors. Combining the data for all non-jurors, 24.5 percent of non-jurors rated their overall experience as "very good" or "excellent," whereas one-third said it was merely "satisfactory" and 13.8 percent rated it as "less than satisfactory." Fewer than one in twenty jurors shared the latter sentiment, with nearly two-thirds (61.3 percent) rating their experience as being very good or excellent. Clearly, what one takes away from the courthouse depends principally on whether one ever gets promoted from bystander to juror. Moreover, though some empanelled jurors clearly ended up disappointed with their experience, the vast majority—a relatively silent majority in the open-ended comments—had a very positive overall assessment of their time at the courthouse.

This general sense of satisfaction (or disappointment) only provides a general overview of jurors' subjective experience at the courthouse. It is useful to consider the reasons that jurors gave for their satisfaction ratings, more or less in their own words. We say "more or less" because when we posed an

Table 4.3.   Overall satisfaction with jury service by courthouse and whether empanelled

	Rating	Downtown King County	Kent Regional Justice Center	Seattle Municipal Court	Total
Did *not* serve as a sworn juror	1 Less than satisfactory	15%	12.5%	14.3%	13.8%
	2 Satisfactory	34%	35.3%	27.0%	33.3%
	3 Good	29%	28.2%	27.7%	28.5%
	4 Very good	18%	17.7%	16.3%	17.4%
	5 Excellent	5%	6.2%	14.7%	7.1%
	Total	100%	100%	100%	100%
	n	752	662	307	1,721
Served as a sworn juror	1 Less than satisfactory	3.3%	4.1%	3.6%	3.6%
	2 Satisfactory	13.2%	10.6%	10.9%	12.1%
	3 Good	24.6%	22.4%	18.6%	23.0%
	4 Very good	35.1%	37.4%	42.1%	36.9%
	5 Excellent	23.8%	25.5%	24.7%	24.4%
	Total	100%	100%	100%	100%
	n	793	388	247	1,428
	Total N	1,545	1,050	554	3,149

Note: Chi-square tests showed that satisfaction responses varied among the three courthouses only for non-jurors (X2 = 37.4, *df* = 8, p <.001) but not for empanelled jurors. When the ordering of analyses was reversed, the difference in satisfaction ratings was tremendous within each courthouse, including downtown King County (X2 = 271.5), Kent (X2 = 185.4), and Seattle (X2 = 79.0), all *df* = 4, p<.001.

open-ended question requesting the main reason for jurors' satisfaction rating, we got replies from 87 percent of our respondents. To summarize these 2,750 different responses, we employed four data coders to perform a content analysis—a systematic method whereby one can reduce massive amounts of qualitative data into manageable statistical summaries. The first coder went through every reply, identified the range of responses, then created twenty-five "response categories"—roomy conceptual boxes into which one could place sets of similar responses. Afterward, each of the four coders independently combed back through the thousands of responses and attempted to place each into one or more categories, with some lengthy comments falling into two, three, or even four of our different boxes. In the end, these four codings were integrated into summary statistics showing how frequently the average respondent gave a particular reason for their jury experience.

Table 4.4 shows the main results of our content analysis, with the results broken down by whether prospective jurors ever became empanelled and by how they rated their overall experience at the courthouse.[29] After removing general categories (undifferentiated "general satisfaction" and "disappointment"), the vague catch-all "other/unclear," and the rarest rationales (i.e., those given by fewer than 5 percent of our sample), there were ten common justifications for rating the jury experience positively or negatively.

For disgruntled non-jurors, who rated their experience as only "satisfactory" or even "less than satisfactory," the main complaints were that they perceived their time to have been wasted. Nearly a third said the sheer amount of time spent at the courthouse was excessive (32 percent) and/or complained that they showed up to serve but never were seated on a jury (29 percent). These were also the main justifications given by those non-jurors who rated their experience as simply being "good." Those who rated their experience as "very good" or better in spite of never being empanelled, most often cited their satisfaction with the court itself: 30 percent praised the personnel, 19 percent liked their accommodations, and 17 percent thought the court organization was efficient. An additional 13 percent cited the educational value of jury service as a reason to be pleased with their time spent at the courthouse. One Seattle woman attending college wrote that she found the overall experience "very educational." She "wanted to learn about the justice system but was nervous about getting put on an actual case," so serving two days and not being placed on a jury suited her just fine.

Those few empanelled jurors who gave low satisfaction ratings also cited excessive time spent at the courthouse (31 percent). To explore this result further, we conducted a quick check of official court records, which we had merged with the survey data. Those less satisfied jurors who complained about time were, indeed, serving longer than their other empanelled peers—though not much longer (an average of 6.5 versus 5.5 days). For some jurors, this probably reflects the difference between serving one week and having one's service extend into a second one.

Table 4.4. Reasons given by jurors and non-jurors for their overall satisfaction (or dissatisfaction) with jury service

Rating of overall service experience	Setting and personnel			Personal time use		Jury deliberation			Civic education	
	Quality of court personnel	Quality of court organization	Venue and accommodation	Amount of time spent at court	Did not get to serve on a jury	Feelings/ thoughts on case assigned	Quality of jury decision made	Fellow jurors' actions	Educational value of service	Importance of civic duty
Not empanelled										
Satisfactory or less	5%	9%	7%	32%	29%	1%	N/A	1%	2%	3%
Good	11%	9%	9%	18%	22%	1%	N/A	2%	8%	3%
Very good/ excellent	30%	17%	19%	9%	9%	1%	N/A	2%	13%	4%
Served as juror										
Satisfactory or less	5%	8%	5%	31%	2%*	7%	7%	10%	4%	2%
Good	12%	7%	7%	18%	0%	5%	4%	9%	15%	8%
Very good/ excellent	24%	12%	8%	7%	0%	4%	4%	13%	21%	8%

Notes: 2,750 total comments were received. What was the main reason for the rating you gave?"

* indicates jurors who were empanelled but then served only as alternates.

It is also noteworthy that 2 percent of the sworn-in jurors nonetheless complained that they did not get to "serve on a jury." These unlucky few were designated by judges as alternates, and that fact alone colored their reflections on their overall experience. Checking this finding against our larger database, however, seventy alternates in our database completed the post-service questionnaire, and the average satisfaction rating for those jurors was not significantly lower than for the other empanelled jurors.

One key experience cited by both 10 percent of less satisfied jurors and 13 percent of pleased jurors was the behavior of fellow jurors. Those unhappy with their experience often pointed to jurors who failed to fulfill their responsibility to serve thoughtfully and carefully. A retired male juror serving downtown regretted that his fellow jurors "would not follow the judge's instructions." Other complaints often concerned impartiality toward defendants and witnesses, such as one female juror who worried that "a member of the jury I was serving on discounted all testimony from any witness who might have been of a non-conforming sexual preference." Jurors who rated their experience favorably, by contrast, *praised* the performance of their peers. A juror at the Kent Regional Justice Center who worked full time and had graduate education remarked that he "served on a jury with many good, sound-thinking people, which was encouraging and enjoyable."

Those jurors most satisfied with their experience gave a wider variety of other reasons for their positive overall assessment. Some mentioned the court personnel (24 percent), court organization (12 percent), and accommodations (8 percent), but more than one in five (21 percent) also pointed to the educational value of the experience. The same Kent juror quoted in the previous paragraph wrote that "it was interesting to see the judicial system at work for the first time." A small but important subset of the jurors also commented on their service as a chance to fulfill a responsibility of democratic citizenship. Three different jurors at the Seattle Municipal Courthouse, for instance, commented that their service was satisfying because "it's an honor to perform my civic duty," it provided the "feeling of performing a civic duty," and that service "was citizenship affirming."

Such comments refer back to themes in chapter 3, where we saw how during in-depth interviews, many jurors spontaneously connected jury service with other civic responsibilities. These passing comments provide additional evidence of such a linkage, but they also underscore that the civic impact of jury service surely impacts some citizens more than others. Educational benefits were cited by a fifth of all empanelled jurors who had a favorable experience but at lower rates by less satisfied jurors.

Expectations and Engagement

These findings suggest that the civic impact of juries may hinge not merely on whether jurors deliberate but also on their subjective experience of serving. Chapter 5 will explore the nuances of jurors' deliberations, but we now consider just two survey questions to learn which jurors became more engaged during the course of a trial and which, in the end, had their expectations met or exceeded.

A convention we used to glean jurors' impressions of their service was to present a statement and ask jurors to respond by saying whether they would "strongly agree," "agree," be "neutral" toward, "disagree," or "strongly disagree" with the statement as a descriptor of their experience. In this case, jurors responded to the sentence, "The trial was very interesting to think about." The most common response was the fourth scale point, with 54 percent agreeing with the statement, and an additional 23 percent strongly agreeing. In other words, the trial was interesting to 77 percent of jurors, with the rest finding the trial less than fully engaging.

The results from chapter 3 suggest two factors influencing juror engagement—whether the empanelled jurors got to deliberate (versus being designated as an alternate, having their trial cancelled after getting underway, etc.) and whether they sat on a criminal or civil trial. Both of these factors were helpful in tracing the influence of jury deliberation on voting, but in this survey, only the type of trial correlated significantly with interest in the trial: 70 percent of civil jurors found their trial interesting to think about, compared to 79 percent of criminal jurors.[30]

Though jurors generally became cognitively engaged in their trials, it is important to consider not only whether jurors found their service interesting but how it felt relative to their initial expectations. To set up this question, our survey read, "People usually have expectations that come with them when they show up for jury service," then asked, "Overall, how would you rate your experience as a juror *in relation to your initial expectations?*" Responses were generally positive but widely distributed: 1 percent marked "much worse than I expected," 4 percent circled the "below expectations" option, 31 percent said their experience was "about what I expected," 42 percent reported it was "better than expected," and 22 percent said that jury service was "much better than expected."[31] Neither the type of trial nor the deliberation were keys to the variation in this assessment, with roughly two-thirds of empanelled jurors reporting that their experience exceeded expectations for both civil and criminal cases, whether deliberating or not.

Revisiting the Jury–Voting Connection

With so many jurors having positive experiences at the courthouse, it is important to remember that, nonetheless, respondents' assessments *did* vary. Roughly two-thirds of empanelled jurors reported very favorable, engaging experiences that exceeded their expectations, but the other third did not. All too often, we look for and find a population's central tendency—the majority view or experience. It is a majoritarian impulse, but it obscures real variation, and the variety of subjective assessments might prove important in understanding the central question of this study—the civic impact of jury service.

Thus, having established the positive impact of criminal jury deliberation on electoral participation via the National Jury Sample in chapter 3, it is useful to retest this effect with this new population—the sample of empanelled King County jurors introduced in this chapter. By using survey data, we can look more closely at the *mechanism* through which the jury–voting effect occurs. Specifically, does the critical path to changing voting patterns follow the objective fact of participating in jury deliberation, or is the key path the *subjective* experience of jury service?

To address this question, we developed research hypotheses matching the general structure and findings of chapter 3, but with a few important differences. The central hypothesis was that for previously inactive voters empanelled as jurors in King County, deliberating on a jury would have a positive impact on post-jury service voting rates relative to the experience of serving on a jury that did not deliberate. The simple contrast between deliberation and no deliberation was used for two reasons: There were too few hung juries in the King County sample to examine them in their own right in this study, and the National Jury Sample also showed that hung juries and verdict-reaching juries had essentially similar effects. In addition, we assumed this effect would persist even after controlling for previously unmeasured variables traditionally associated with voter turnout, including age, education, and major party membership.[32]

We also went a step beyond the regression methods used thus far and conducted the first of the path analyses presented in this book. Path analysis allowed us to estimate the strength and direction of relationships among a chain of interconnected variables. Using this approach, we hypothesized that jury deliberation would have two causal paths to post-service voting—both a direct effect and an indirect effect mediated by jurors' subjective experience at jury service. Individuals likely vary in how they experience the same deliberative event, and it is well-established that how one experiences an activity influences that activity's behavioral impact.[33] Therefore, survey data were collected to learn how jurors assessed their experience, and we expected that this subjective experience variable would account for a significant portion (but not all) of the effect of deliberation on voting.

Finally, consistent with the correlational results mentioned earlier, we expected that jurors' subjective accounts of jury service would be shaped by the differential experience of criminal versus civil trial. Chapter 3 found changes in voting behavior for criminal trials but not for civil ones, and we reasoned that this reflected the public's different estimation of the value of the two types of trial.[34] Thus, in the present data we expected that the contrast between criminal versus civil trials would have an indirect effect on post-service voting through its impact on jurors' subjective assessments of their experience.

Figure 4.2 shows a direct effect of jury deliberation on post-service voting for infrequent voters, a finding consistent with chapter 3. The net effect was even of roughly equivalent size, showing an average increase of 4–5 percent in turnout during the elections following jury service. The absence of a significant path from deliberation to jurors' subjective experience, however, suggests that how jurors experience deliberation does not explain deliberation's effect on voting. At the same time, subjective experience *did* play a significant role in the model. Criminal trials (relative to civil ones) were associated with a more positive experience, and that experience, in turn, had a significant direct effect on post-service voting. Thus, trial-type may appear to influence the civic impact of jury service owing to its effect on jurors' subjective experiences at the courthouse.[35] (The full results of this analysis are shown in Appendix Section 4b.)

Moving Forward

These results provide additional evidence that jury service provides not only civic education but also civic *inspiration*. Criminal jurors who deliberate become more likely to vote after their period of service than do their peers who become empanelled but do not get to retire to the jury room and seek to return a verdict. We can now also see more clearly that the *subjective* experience of jurors connects the *objective* experience of jury deliberation with that of voting. In other words, those whose jury experience was relatively engaging and better than expected became more likely to vote in the future relative to those who had a less satisfactory experience. Along these same lines, the relatively strong impact of criminal trials versus civil cases seen in chapter 3 appears to reflect the difference in jurors' subjective experiences in those different trials.

Beyond the impact of jury service on voting, these survey data provide a clearer portrait of jurors' experiences at the courthouse. Just over a quarter of those answering the summons actually became empanelled, and the winnowing that occurred during *voir dire* disproportionately rejected those gregarious jurors who were most eager to serve. With few other factors substantially distinguishing sworn jurors from the larger jury pool, we found that in King County and Seattle, juries bore considerable resemblance to the larger communities from which they were drawn, though residents who were Hispanic, unemployed, or who had less formal education were slightly less responsive to the courts' summoning than were their peers.

Jurors generally left satisfied with their experience overall, though satisfaction ratings were dramatically higher for those serving on juries. Though some of those in the jury pool believed that their time was wasted, particularly when never assigned to a jury, jurors more often heaped praise on court staff and the legal and administrative processes they witnessed than did the non-jurors. Many jurors had low expectations of what would happen during their period of service, and some hoped not to be seated on a jury. In the end, however, nearly two-thirds found the experience better—or even much better—than their initial expectations, and even more jurors found their trials to be interesting and engaging.

These broad statements about jury service press us to consider in more detail what exactly happens when empanelled jurors sit through trials and deliberate together. What do jurors experience when sworn in and asked to determine other people's freedom or finances? What do jurors think? What do they feel? How do they behave? What do jurors think of the decisions they reach, their fellow jurors, and their judge? Chapter 5 moves the King County study forward to answer these questions in detail.

Chapter 5

Citizen Judges

The critical stage of jury service for many jurors begins when they enter the deliberation room. They sit together through the trial, through lunches, through long delays and breaks, never discussing the case itself, and unsure of what to think about what they have heard in court. At that point, many jurors have an experience like that of Ted, who discovered quickly that his King County jury was already unanimous. As sometimes happens, the foreperson "did do a preliminary vote," and "we all voted he had done it."[1]

The criminal charge in this case was violating parole by carrying a concealed weapon into court. Having looked around the room and seen that all were in agreement, the jurors, nonetheless, opted to pick apart the prosecution's case. As Ted explained:

> We did not want to just come back with that opinion. Everyone agreed that we should talk about it and see if there was any way we could be wrong....And I remember feeling very good that we did that....Everyone wanted to discuss it, even though we all had other things to do in life. We all kind of wanted to make sure that we weren't missing something.

The coat of the accused was found in the courtroom with a gun in it, and Ted and the jurors began to speculate about possible explanations, beyond the one they had first accepted:

> Either maybe it was his coat and he sold it or lost it. Maybe there were many of that model that had the same pattern, or I think it actually was a stain rather than a [distinctive] pattern....We wondered if the police had put the gun in the coat, if there was any chance of that. We thought that was pretty far out. But maybe they had it in for him. Maybe he had

been bad to them and they were trying to nail him. And we tried all these angles to see what was reasonable and of course you can never really *prove* it. It's not like a mathematical formula.

Try as they might, Ted and his fellow jurors could not come up with any reasonable doubt about the defendant's guilt. They recognized, as Ted said, that you cannot "really *prove* it"—not beyond a *shadow of a doubt*, but the prosecutor had succeeded in convincing Ted's jury beyond a *reasonable* doubt. As Ted and his fellow jurors understood, that was good enough, and they left the deliberation room with the same verdict they had expected when they entered it.

We believe it is important to note that Ted offered these recollections *two years* after serving at the King County courthouse. Surely, his recollections are not crystal clear, but when he spoke of the trial and the deliberations, it was clear that these experiences had left their mark, certainly when compared to the other day-to-day details of his life those two years back.

For others, though, jury service has burned an even brighter image in their memory. Before turning to the patterns and correlations of a large jury population, we offer the recollections of Maude, a White homemaker who served at the Kent Regional Justice Center and had an experience quite unlike Ted's. Maude found herself "fascinated by the process" and "how everything comes together [as] story-lines." In her case, the story would turn out to be more about the jury itself than the trial.[2]

When the two-month trial began, Maude remembered that her "main concern was this man who was going on trial for murder." She admonished herself to "pay attention, remember everything to the best of my knowledge, keep a clear open mind. My decision is going to affect this person for the rest of their life. It was nerve-wracking. I was scared I might miss something. I took it very seriously."

The twelve jurors composed "an amazing group" that found itself "cramped" inside a small deliberation room. She noticed the jury's lone African American member, who "when she sat down, turned her back to all of us and faced the wall." This juror had been designated foreperson through random assignment.

As the jury deliberations wore on, it became clear that the foreperson was holding out for a verdict of second-degree murder, whereas the rest of the jury had become convinced that the defendant was guilty of premeditated murder in the first degree, which carries a much stiffer sentence. Driving home after the first day of deliberation, Maude remembered that she "burst into tears" and "cried all the way home" from the stress and frustration of the deliberations.

The next morning, she and the foreperson had a pointed disagreement about the murder charges, and then, Maude recalled, "another juror stepped in and said this is 'about deliberating,' [and] we all have to come to a consensus together." Maude asked the foreperson to "come up with a good reason to convince us" that only the second-degree charge was warranted. At that point, the foreperson stood up and left the jury room, never to return. After a brief delay, an alternate juror joined the jury, and before long, they returned a verdict of murder in the first degree.

As Maude would later learn, the foreperson who left the room went to the judge and alleged that the jury was guilty of racism, and the judge held a hearing to weigh whether there existed grounds for a mistrial. In the end, the verdict stood, and the jurors got back together after the fact to discuss the case and their reactions to it. Maude found that once through the crucible of jury service, she had changed.

INTERVIEWER: How was your life different after the trial?

MAUDE: I realized after it was over...how much I liked the law...and just how personally I took this, how much it meant to me to put all the pieces of the puzzle together, and how important it was to get my verdict in.

INTERVIEWER: Did being on a jury change your role in society? Do you feel like you want to be more involved?

MAUDE: Oh yeah, I volunteer with this organization involving my daughter...I'm more politically involved. It just became very clear to me that I wanted to go back to work. After this experience, it gave me a purpose. I just didn't want to get a job to get a job and then be miserable and hate it, I wanted something with passion and purpose.

Juror recollections such as these can offer considerable insight into the jury experience and its lasting impact. Direct interviews and detailed surveys, however, have not been the default research method in jury investigations. Over the past half century, researchers and trial consultants have devoted far more energy to assembling thousands of mock juries, and these fictional juries have taught us much about how people think about arguments, witnesses, and evidence.[3] Few studies, however, have examined *actual* deliberation among real jurors serving on empanelled juries. In large part, this is due to restrictions on access to juries. In all federal courts and in almost all states and municipalities, field observation of decision making in the jury room is illegal. The secrecy of jury deliberation is so sacred that most judges refuse to grant social scientists systematic access to jurors.

For the purpose of this study, mock juries did not suffice because our core argument is that the experience of sitting as a citizen judge has a real power and significance that a mock trial cannot possibly generate. Thus, we aimed to learn more about how citizens experience civil and criminal trials and their time in the jury deliberation room by *asking* them directly. Do jurors themselves believe that they have deliberated? What individual and group-level factors make actual jurors more or less likely to report a deliberative experience? Is the quality of their deliberative experience related to their satisfaction with the process and outcome of their labors?

We also continued to rely on the large sample survey to get past the limitations of individual interviews, such as those reported above.[4] We began by continuing the examination of the more than one thousand King County jurors' trial experiences begun in chapter 4, and we then turned to their thoughts about the deliberation room and their final verdict.[5] When we looked at details of deliberation, we narrowed our focus on the Seattle Municipal Court, whose judges were less anxious about the problems that could arise by asking jurors about the details of their deliberation experience. In the end, we pulled together jurors' different experiences and perceptions to create a composite portrait of their service, but first, we needed to work through the discrete details of jurors' sojourn through the courthouse.

The Context of Jury Trials

The jurors in our study represent a snapshot of the range of experiences typical of most jurors. The National Center for State Courts estimates that there are more than 150,000 jury trials annually, with 31 percent of those being civil cases, 47 percent addressing felonies, and 19 percent on misdemeanor charges. Over 96 percent of those trials occur in state courts—typically, in county or municipal jurisdictions, with just a few thousand juries forming in federal courts each year.[6]

Eighty percent of the jurors in our study served on criminal trials, with the remainder assigned to civil trials. Jurors weighed a vast range of different charges and claims. The most frequent criminal charge was assault, which accounted for 15 percent of trials. Robbery (12 percent) and domestic violence (11 percent) were the next most frequent, and only 4 percent of cases involved murder. Civil trials most often concerned vehicular injury (40 percent), followed by breach of contract (11 percent) and malpractice (9 percent).

Using official court records, we also estimated the duration of the trials on which jurors served, and every such metric showed a significant difference between civil and criminal trials. Table 5.1 shows that the average civil juror spent over eight days in the courtroom—from *voir dire* through verdict, including six and a half hours in the deliberation room discussing the case with fellow jurors. That average reflects the impact of a few particularly lengthy trials (with the longest going for 40 days) because the median trial was only six days long (including four hours of deliberation). The most common duration was a four-day trial, coupled with roughly three hours in the deliberation room (and three hours of deliberation) being most common. Criminal trials took less time, and their deliberation period was briefer.

A final bit of information in Table 5.1 could prove useful for those holding a summons in their hand: Two-thirds of those seated on a civil jury will end up in a courtroom for anywhere from 3 to 14 days, whereas the similar subset of criminal jurors will be on trials ranging from 2 to 7 days in length.

Table 5.1.   Duration of civil and criminal trials for the average juror in King County/Seattle

	Statistic	Civil jurors	Criminal jurors
Total days in courtroom (from *voir dire* to verdict)	Mean (average)	8.7 days	4.9 days
	Median (midpoint)	6 days	3 days
	Mode (most frequent)	4 days	2 days
	Range for middle two-thirds of jurors	3–14 days	2–7 days
Total time spent discussing trial in the deliberation room	Mean (average)	6.5 hours	4.4 hours
	Median (midpoint)	4 hours	4 hours
	Mode (most frequent)	3 hours	1 hour
	Range for middle two-thirds of jurors	2–10 hours	1–7 hours

Note: With unequal variances not assumed, mean comparisons were significant for both days in courtroom ($t = 6.68$, $p < .001$) and duration of deliberation ($t = 3.74$, $p < .001$).

In other words, if seated on a civil jury in King County or a comparable jurisdiction, it is a good bet that your trial will take roughly twice as long as a criminal trial would have, and though it will probably take just a few days, it just might span two weeks.

On a subjective level, however, a juror serving on a longer trial was not necessarily inclined to criticize the court for excessive delay. When asked, 63 percent of jurors believed that their "time was well used by the court," and only 16 percent disputed that statement. These ratings bore no significant relationship to the duration of a juror's service. Although those jurors who gave the King County and Seattle courts lower marks for effective time use spent, on average, a few hours longer at the courthouse (and a few more minutes in deliberation) than did their peers, these minute differences did not reach statistical significance.[7]

Jury Diversity

Moving beyond the trial's topic and duration, we return to examining how jurors experience their trial. Recall from chapter 4 that the makeup of the typical King County or Seattle jury differed little, in the end, from the larger jury pool but that those juries were not a mirror image of the larger community. Did jurors themselves come to view their fellow deliberators as a diverse group? Seventy percent of sworn jurors agreed that their "fellow jurors…came from very different backgrounds," and only 11 percent disputed that characterization. After all, the random selection process means that jurors must work closely with people they might otherwise never even have a conversation with in daily life.

One might expect that such diversity is in the eye of the beholder. To test this, we conducted a linear regression to see whether juror characteristics predicted diversity perceptions. Given the political culture of King County and Seattle,[8] we included a measure of political party membership, along with a seven-point scale assessing one's self-described "political ideology," ranging from "strongly liberal" (1) to "strongly conservative" (7). Consistent with our expectations, the famously left-leaning Seattle had a higher proportion of Democratic jurors than did King County (68 percent versus 52 percent), as well as more jurors self-identifying as "liberal/strongly liberal" (50 percent versus 31 percent).

Of these factors, left-right self-identification was the most significant predictor in Table 5.2, with political conservatives tending to see their juries as somewhat more diverse than did their more liberal peers. Women also tended to see the juries as more diverse than did men. Both of these effects are quite weak—with neither factor able to move average responses from even one scale point to the next on our diversity measure.[9]

Later in this chapter, we return to the question of diversity to see the degree to which jurors' experiences of deliberation are shaped by their own backgrounds. For now, the point is simply that King County jurors believed that they were sworn onto diverse juries.

Table 5.2. Predictors of perceived jury diversity

Predictor	(B) (*SE*)	*b*
Ethnicity (White = 1, Other = 0)	−.160 (.096)	−.060*
Respondent sex	.197 (.061)	−.110***
Age	−.004 (.003)	−.057
Education	−.004 (.019)	−.007
Retired	.106 (.118)	.041
Full time	.005 (.076)	.003
Conservative	.081 (.028)	.145***
Party affiliation	.003 (.027)	.005
R^2	.043***	
N	902	

Note: * $p < .10$, ** $p < .05$, *** $p < .01$. B denotes unstandardized regression coefficient, *SE* denotes standard error of estimate, and *b* denotes standardized coefficient.

How Jurors Get Treated

However diverse the juries may be, we have seen that jurors certainly had varied overall assessments of their jury experience. Some of these stemmed from the treatment they received by judges, attorneys, and courtroom staff. For some jurors, these courtroom actors triggered frustration, as in the case of the young Redmond woman who reported that "the attorneys were badly prepared, so the case was frustratingly slow." Another woman complained, "I felt that one of the lawyers wasted days of our time. It seemed like we received lots of irrelevant information and spent hours listening to details which had nothing to do with the case." One Seattle woman serving at the Kent Regional Justice Center was downright angry: "I felt that the process was about one side winning and not about finding the truth," she wrote. "Information was withheld by both sides that would have helped us to make a more informed decision. We were not provided information on how to deliberate and I think we were at a loss as to how that should be done."

Then there were jurors who left brief notes of praise for the courts. A woman who drove downtown each day from the suburb of Issaquah wrote, "The case we were involved in was very interesting, the judge and attorneys involved in the case were extremely professional and courteous towards the jurors." One juror noted that she especially appreciated "the efforts made by the courthouse staff including the judge to see to our welfare and answer questions." These positive comments raise the question again, What is the more representative experience—frustration with or appreciation of the treatment jurors received from attorneys and court staff and judges?

To hear from the larger sample, our survey directly asked jurors how they were treated by attorneys, court staff, and judges. Figure 5.1 shows that nearly two-thirds (62 percent) received what they considered "excellent" treatment by the judges, with a majority (55 percent) reporting excellent treatment by court staff, as well. Only 3 percent reported merely "satisfactory" or worse treatment by either judges or court administrators and other personnel.

To appreciate the last result in Figure 5.1, step back from these data momentarily for an anecdote. In February 2006, the lead author of this book, John Gastil, presented preliminary findings from our research at the U.S. Federal Courthouse in Seattle—the first time one of us had seen the larger-than-life portrait of jurors that appears at the courthouse and on this book's cover. Gastil had been invited to share our research with Pacific Northwest attorneys at the 9th Circuit Judicial Conference. In doing so, Gastil asked the hundred or so attendees to raise their hands if they expected to hear that the jurors in our survey felt well-treated by the courthouse staff. About ninety hands went up. When asked if they expected to hear that jurors felt respected by the judges, about 50 hands went up. Finally, Gastil asked, "Knowing all that you know about how people talk about *lawyers*, how many of you expect to hear that jurors felt that the attorneys treated them well?" About ten hands rose sheepishly, and even a couple of those went

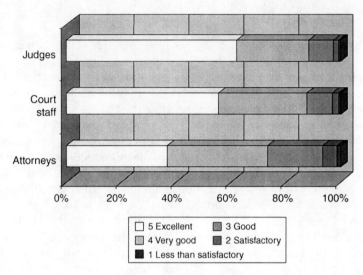

Figure 5.1 How empanelled jurors felt treated by judges, court staff, and attorneys

down when they looked around the room. (Attorneys are also subject to peer pressure, it would seem.)

When Gastil showed the result in Figure 5.1, the attorneys in the audience gasped and laughed in relief. Lawyer jokes notwithstanding, fully 37 percent of jurors rated attorneys' behavior toward them as "excellent," with the same proportion rating attorneys as "very good." Fewer than 2 percent of empanelled jurors said that attorneys' treatment of them was "less than satisfactory." If this result surprises the reader as much as it did these attorneys, one must remember that even the surliest attorneys know to show considerable grace, tact, and charm when in the presence of a jury, which, after all, controls the fate of the lawyer's client.

In addition to these strong ratings, we also found that staff, judges, and attorneys did not wear out their welcome, even as longer cases wore on the patience and stamina of jurors. In fact, the number of days a juror served was *positively correlated* with the treatment they received. A simple statistical correlation can range anywhere from −1.0 to +1.0, with a zero representing no association, and small, medium, and large correlations having an absolute value of roughly .10, .30, and .50.[10] In this case, treatment by judges, staff, and attorneys had correlations of .10, .08, and .05, respectively—all small effect sizes, to be sure. Nonetheless, jury administrators might feel some relief from these findings, as they suggest that when it is necessary to press jurors into longer periods of service, there are no hard feelings.

As a point of comparison, consider a variable introduced in chapter 4—a prospective juror's initial eagerness (or reluctance) to serve on a jury. This variable has similarly small significant associations, with willingness to serve correlating at .08, .06, and .10 with judge, staff, and lawyer treatment ratings. Thus, how jurors felt they were treated in King County proved largely independent of both whether they hoped to be seated on a jury and how long they ended up staying at the courthouse. Moreover, these findings did not vary depending on whether jurors served at a criminal or civil trial.

It is still possible, however, that extra days at the courthouse—or long hours in the deliberation room—take their toll in another way, through making the jurors weary of *each other*. Across all trials, 45 percent of jurors reported excellent treatment by "fellow jurors," with another 40 percent rating their peers' behavior as very good. That left only 16 percent of jurors giving a rating of "good" or lower, with just 1 percent giving fellow jurors the lowest score.[11] A juror's initial enthusiasm for service colored this rating only lightly ($r = .08$), but the number of days spent at the courthouse, as well as the number of hours spent in deliberation, made no difference one way or the other.

Each of these treatment perceptions, however, did have one strong set of covariates in the data: each other. Correlations among these items ranged from .44 to .61, which suggest that they measure a single overarching concept—general perceptions of treatment during jury service (see Appendix Section 5a). Thus, we averaged these items into a single index—a technique we will use extensively in chapters 5 and 6.

Jurors at Trial

Even when jurors sat on objectively similar trials and had consistent perceptions of external treatment, jurors had widely ranging *internal* experiences. Here, we consider the emotions that jurors reported during the course of their service, and we look at how engaged—and occasionally confused— jurors became during trials.

Private Deliberation

As we move the focus into the heart of jury service—the act of deliberating and deciding—it is important to recognize that for jurors, a meaningful kind of "private deliberation" takes place before the jurors talk with each other about the case in the deliberation room. Imagine yourself sitting on a civil trial in which you hear evidence for and against the contention that the defendant committed medical malpractice, causing the plaintiff to suffer avoidable complications after receiving cosmetic plastic surgery. During the course of the trial, you hear from experts who explain what can reasonably be expected from such surgeries, what routine risks they involve, and how often serious complications occur. You also see documents—legal contracts between doctor and patient, perhaps an e-mail exchange after the surgery. Both parties testify, along with other character and ancillary witnesses, and the attorneys point you to relevant laws and precedents that support their arguments. How could you possibly absorb all that information without processing it? Could you somehow hold all these facts, claims, and arguments at once, without turning a single one over in your mind before formally deliberating as a jury?

The evidence suggests that jurors process information as it comes up during trial. Communication researcher Ann Pettus interviewed jurors who completed trials and concluded that for the average juror,

> the decision-making process begins early in the trial. Points in the trial when the jurors make their decisions include: when they see the defendant for the first time, when the information is read, during opening statements, and during the presentation of prosecution witnesses. While some jurors might form their opinions at specific points during the trial, others begin the process with the "sense" or intuition that the defendant is guilty or not guilty. As the trial proceeds, that decision becomes more certain. Thus, although jurors are instructed to wait to form an opinion until after all the evidence has been presented, this study indicates that they do not wait.[12]

Larger samples of juries have confirmed that jurors routinely make up their mind about a case *before* leaving the courtroom to deliberate. Jurors are ready to vote by the first straw poll (a nonbinding vote by ballot or raised hands to see where the balance of opinion lies), and in nine out of ten cases, the initial vote a jury takes predicts the ultimate outcome.[13]

In our King County database, nearly a quarter of all juries (22 percent) spend less than two hours in the deliberation room, a finding that supports the view that jurors already have been doing a kind of private deliberation during the trial. In fact, there were a half dozen trials where deliberation took less than one hour after a trial that had spanned four or more days. Such cases notwithstanding, there is a strong correlation between the length of a trial and the duration of deliberation ($r = .54$), such that longer trials tend to result in longer periods in the jury room. Figure 5.2 shows not just the average time in deliberation but also the 90 percent confidence interval around those averages. This represents the time range within which we can expect nine out of ten deliberation periods to fall.

Some King County jurors felt an urge to deliberate during the trial phase.[14] A few jurors mentioned that they were "not supposed" to form a judgment until after the close of the trial. Yet one juror admitted, "I felt I knew how to vote before all the facts were in." Another expressed "frustration at not being able to discuss the process with the other jurors" during the trial, and a third admitted to "feelings of isolation" because of this.

Emotional Processing

Is feeling isolated before the jury retires to deliberate a common experience? What other feelings did jurors have as they sat silently watching their trials? Media accounts of juries often emphasize the traumatic effects of jury service in grizzly criminal trials. An article in the *Austin American-Statesman* described

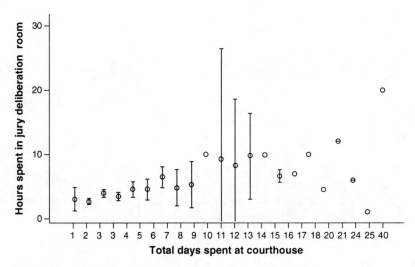

Note: Circles represent means and bars show standard errors thereof.

Figure 5.2 Average hours spent in deliberation room broken down by total days at courthouse

a jury that viewed photos of crash victims during an intoxicated vehicular man-slaughter trial: "Some look down or clamp their hands over their mouths. Some turn pale and look away. Some refuse to look at them at all." As a result of such experiences, jurors serving on gruesome trials often report having "disturbing memories" or feeling "numb and detached" even after their service ends.[15]

But as we saw in Figure 5.1, most King County trials are of a more brief duration, and it would be a mistake to generalize from these headline-grabbing trials to the broader juror experience. To get a rough handle on this question, we began by asking jurors the following question: "Some jurors report that they have strong emotional reactions in relation to the trial they witnessed. Thinking back on the trial, *what emotions did you feel during the trial?*" Nearly two-thirds of jurors (64 percent) reported feeling "both positive and negative emotions," whereas only 21 percent felt "no emotions during the trial." Of the remaining 14 percent of jurors with strongly one-sided feelings, three experienced "negative emotions" for every one who felt uncomplicated, "positive emotions."

To better understand the nature of these emotions, we followed this question with a small space and the instruction, "If you did feel emotions, in just a few words, what were the strongest of those?" As described in chapter 4, a team of content analysts coded the open-ended responses to these items, and Table 5.3 shows how often two or more coders detected the same emotion when scanning those written comments. The table breaks down the comments in relation to the closed-ended responses, so we can see what jurors meant when they described their emotions as positive, negative, or mixed.

Table 5.3. Jurors' descriptions of their positive, negative, and mixed emotions and cognitions

Category	Specific emotion or cognition	Positive	Negative	Mixed
	Satisfaction with the process	32%		8%
	Dissatisfaction with trial, deliberation, jurors, etc.		24%	16%
General satisfaction/ expectation violations	Disappointment at the trial, jurors, case, etc.		10%	6%
	Surprise at testimony, proceedings, jurors, etc.		10%	5%
	A sense of civic duty as a juror	20%		15%
	Pride in fellow jurors, quality of trial, or verdict	12%		6%
Strong positive emotions	Appreciation of each other and/or legal process	8%		7%
	Humor at the situation, trial, jurors, etc.			3%
	Sadness about the case itself		52%	32%
	Frustration with the process, jurors, etc.		52%	37%
	Anger at the city/county, the jurors, etc.		14%	18%
Strong negative emotions	Horrified at the trial testimony, evidence, etc.		2%	5%
	Fear of witnesses, defendant, prosecution, etc.		2%	9%

	Sympathy for the defendant, victim, others	4%	31%	53%
	Stress/tension about the deliberation, trail, etc.	4%	7%	12%
Empathy and complex feelings	Conflicted feelings about the trial, decision, etc.			10%
	Indifference toward defendants, the case, jurors		12%	4%
	Anticipation of the verdict, deliberations, etc.	16%	2%	
	Curiosity about the trial, fellow jurors, etc.	4%	2%	6%
Thoughts and reflections	Confusion about the trial, deliberation, etc.	4%	5%	6%
	Certainty about the verdict, process, etc.	4%		1%
	Skepticism about the case, process, decision, etc.		7%	4%
	Total number of respondents	52	142	871
	Number of comments written	25	42	246

Note: Percentages reflect the proportion of total written comments that two or more (of four) coders categorized as containing the corresponding emotion/cognition. By design, many responses received multiple codes, so columns total more than 100 percent each. Empty cells reflect a category that no two coders agreed applied to a respondent in the corresponding column.

Only twenty-five of the jurors who reported feeling good during the trial elaborated on that sentiment, and nearly a third of those (32 percent) reported a general satisfaction with the trial. One-fifth felt a sense of civic duty, along with 12 percent who felt pride in their fellow jurors or the trial and verdict. This group also listed various cognitions when trying to capture their positive emotional experience, ranging from anticipation to curiosity (or even confusion).

Forty-two of those who recalled a strong negative emotional reaction gave a written explanation for their response, and a majority of these responses included at least one reference to sadness about the case and/or an expression of frustration with the legal process (52 percent in each case). Along with general dissatisfaction (24 percent), there was also a noteworthy contrast between sympathy for the defendant, victim, or others (31 percent) versus a sense of indifference (12 percent). Rounding out the negative emotion list were disappointment and surprise, at 10 percent each, both of which relate back to the idea in chapter 4 of a service experience meeting, exceeding, or not living up to jurors' prior expectations about what happens in a courtroom trial.

Most jurors, though, reported strong and *conflicting* feelings, both positive and negative, and roughly a quarter of these jurors tried to put those sentiments into words. This group's emotional stew included sympathy (53 percent of written responses), sadness and frustration (32 percent and 37 percent, respectively), anger at the city/county or the case itself (18 percent), and overall dissatisfaction (16 percent). The bright side of these jurors' mixed feelings were not mentioned as frequently in written comments, but these positive references included a sense of civic duty (15 percent), appreciation or pride (7 percent and 6 percent, respectively), and even, occasionally, amusement with the proceedings (3 percent).

Much could be written about the specifics of these juror comments, but we will elaborate only on indifference versus empathy and civic duty, which have special significance for our study. First, there is the case of juror indifference as an emotional state. The category name was inspired by a part-time Seattle worker who served as a juror in the Municipal Court for an assault case. He wrote that he felt a "lack of empathy for both the plaintiff and defendant!" A Seattle woman serving at the King County courthouse expressed a similar sentiment: "All parties," she wrote, "were not very bright and none of the accounts supported each other—on defense or prosecution. I suppose I was a bit disdainful." As an example of the mixed feelings jurors most often reported, she then added, "But [I was] also concerned that our decision would affect someone's future."

The conflicting emotions of jury empathy and indifference—or even disdain—are particularly interesting because prior to this study, scholars concerned with democratic deliberation have stressed the importance of mutual respect, perhaps even as a *precondition* for genuine deliberation that takes diverse views into consideration.[16] Our findings suggest that jurors run on a complex fuel that may more consistently contain respect and regard for the process than for the individuals appearing at trial.

Again, public deliberation scholars prize a degree of empathy, such as when a group discussing welfare reform listens to and empathizes with a mother currently receiving federal assistance.[17] For the jurors in our study, there may often be a kind of empathy related to but distinct from this variety—a generalized sense of identification that does not necessarily bias judgment. One juror noted on a DUI case, for instance, that she felt "empathy for the defendant even though we fairly delivered a guilty verdict." In cases such as these, the complex emotions jurors feel may well propel thoughtful deliberation, rather than derail it.[18]

Next, a positive emotional reaction of special significance is the jurors' sense of civic duty, a sentiment present in a significant portion of both positive comments and mixed emotions. This idea of jury duty as a special civic responsibility is at the heart of our argument, and it is helpful to comb through the juror comments to get a better sense for how jurors *feel* this sense of duty, in all its complexity.

To begin, there were those jurors who framed even the emotions of jury service in the terms of public service, justice, and democratic citizenship. Jurors described their experience as a "common goal of service to our county" and as giving "the feeling we, as a jury, were working towards justice." Still another said:

> Serving as a juror is an American right, and there is nothing negative about that. However, I have a hard time with, "Who am I to have a say if one is innocent/guilty?" Then I go back to the positive thought [that] "serving as a juror is an American right." Hope that makes sense. :) (smile emoticon)

The last comment is particularly telling because it shows a juror working through the connection between jury service and citizen responsibility. In the end, this young Seattle juror is still unsure of how to explain the unique character of jury service and hopes that she "makes sense" to us. (She does.)

Other jurors expressed a similar sentiment—that their role and responsibility was of paramount importance, not just to society but to the specific individuals involved in each trial. Even at the relatively low-stakes municipal court, a Seattle woman who took two days off from her full-time job to serve on an assault trial wrote that she had an "intense sense of duty and importance" about the "impact" of the jury's decision on the parties. Other comments shared similar sentiments, a strong sense of responsibility owing to the gravity of the task:

> I became keenly aware of the power that the jury has...it was both frightening and impressive.

> It could have been me or any member of my family. I need to listen closely so I don't get the outcome wrong. Someone's life has been

changed and someone's life still can change based on my input or lack of.

[I felt]...the emotional investment in light of the fact that we were making a decision that affected the lives of two human beings, as well as their family and friends. I felt strongly that it was paramount that we reach a fair verdict based on the evidence.

Finally, some of the shorter comments that indicated a sense of civic duty made clearer the emotional toll that responsibility could take and how it mixed with sadness and other strong emotions. Different jurors said they felt a "conflict between sympathy and duty," "pity mixed with a sense of duty," "Civil responsibility [but also] isolation, sadness/distress." One felt "fright" at the "awesome responsibility to decide another man's fate," and another said that the "responsibility to place someone in jail or worse is very emotional." Comments such as these make clearer that the sense of civic duty—the civic *spark* that jury service can provide—is not simply a cognitive connection but, at least for some jurors, a palpable sense that one has taken on the grave responsibility of self-government. Administering justice is not simply a civic educational exercise, but rather a demanding, sometimes frustrating, and often stressful task that jurors will not soon forget.

Gravity and Confusion

One other aspect of Table 5.3 that stands out is the set of comments grouped together as "thoughts and reflections." These were not the most prominent accounts of jurors' emotions, but they helped jurors explain positive, negative, and mixed emotions. We had assumed that active cognitive engagement would be an important part of jurors' experience, and in chapter 4, we already indicated that 77 percent of jurors reported that "the trial was very interesting to think about." To this finding we now add two more related survey items.

The theme running through the jurors' comments was not one of detached interest in a given trial so much as a sense of the *gravity* of the proceedings. To get a sense for whether the wider sample of jurors shared this perception, we asked jurors to react to the statement, "The case discussed during the trial was important enough to take up the time of a full jury." Responses to this item correlated positively with how interesting jurors found the trial ($r = .43$), and Figure 5.3 gives a graphic impression of the strength of this relationship. The shift is quite dramatic: 86 percent of those who found their trials altogether uninteresting also believed that the case did not merit the attention of a full jury, whereas 79 percent of those most stimulated by the trial thought it appropriate for jury deliberation. Clearly, for King County jurors, a trial worthy of a jury's attention does precisely that—it *holds* their attention and interest.

What kind of trial struck jurors as more important? Consistent with findings in chapter 3, criminal trials were more captivating than were civil ones,

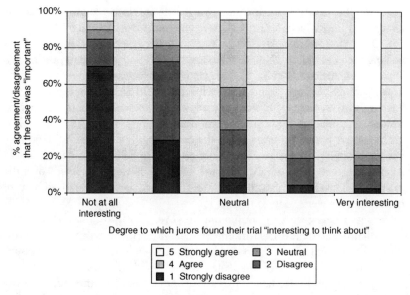

Figure 5.3 The relationship between how interesting and how important jurors found their trials

though only modestly so ($r = .15$). The number of charges in criminal trials likewise increased jurors' perceptions of a trial's importance ($r = .11$).

A slightly larger predictor of perceived trial importance was found when we introduced a new variable—the seriousness of charges. (Appendix Section 5b describes how we measured this variable.) Using these indices to measure seriousness of charges, the correlation between jurors' perceptions of trial importance and the index of charge seriousness was roughly the same for the criminal trials ($r = .27$) as it was for civil cases ($r = .25$). Expressed in percentages, the trials with the lowest seriousness index struck 43 percent of jurors as having sufficient importance to warrant a jury trial, with almost as many (41 percent) doubting that the trial was that important. For trials with the highest index rating, 81 percent thought it sufficiently important, with 10 percent undecided, and the remaining 9 percent questioning the trial's significance.

Regardless of whether jurors' viewed the case as important or found it mentally engaging, some jurors found their trials to be *confusing*. To make this judgment, we asked jurors to respond to the statement, "Some important aspects of the trial were difficult for me to understand." Over a quarter of jurors (28 percent) strongly disagreed with that statement, and another 50 percent simply disagreed. This left only 22 percent of jurors willing to admit to a degree of confusion.

That figure is higher than the roughly 5 percent who spontaneously mentioned "confusion" when asked to describe their emotional response to the trial.

Those comments gave some texture to the nature of this experience, which was reported by jurors feeling positive, negative, and mixed emotions during the trial. One White woman serving in Kent said she felt "confusion because of the language and cultural barriers between myself" and persons appearing at a domestic violence trial, which spilled over into "embarrassment and pity for the alleged victim" and her "frustration" with the "multiple side bars and delays." A young man serving at the same courthouse on a telephone harassment case expressed "confusion regarding the truthfulness of testimony," and he linked this to "stress" when thinking about the charges and "penalty for the crime." A woman serving nine days of jury duty on a motor vehicle accident case had pleaded to be excused initially, and she then found herself "confused" over the course of the trial, complaining that she "did not like the limited amount of information we were allowed to hear."

These various forms of confusion, however, bore no relation to jurors' level of interest in the case or the perceived seriousness of the charges. Jurors on criminal trials reported a bit less confusion than their civil counterparts ($r = -.06$), but we suspected that individual differences between jurors would better help us identify those experiencing confusion.

In addition to standard demographic measures, we introduced a new variable—whether jurors had served previously. At the end of the first survey jurors completed, we asked them if they had been summoned previously and, if so, how many times they had become a sworn juror. As it turns out, 32 percent of the jurors in our sample reported that they had served previously. We expected that those jurors with extra practice would be less likely to find their trial confusing.

Conducting another regression equation to test this expectation, we found that we were wrong: Confusion at trial bore no connection to one's prior jury service record. Non-White jurors and those with less education, however, did have statistically greater difficulty understanding the trial, but it is important to recognize the small size of those differences. Table 5.4 shows the combined effects of all difference in the summary statistic R^2, which indicates the proportion in the dependent variable (confusion at trial) predicted by the full set of individual difference variables in this equation (including education and ethnicity). The R^2 value of .03 means that our combined set of predictors can explain only 3 percent of the variation in jurors' ability to understand the case without confusion—a low percentage, indeed. Put in percentages, 83 percent of White college graduates did not believe the trial confused them, compared to 74 percent of non-White jurors without a college degree.

In the Deliberation Room

When the public trial phase concluded, the jurors moved from the stage of privately processing the trial to doing so in face-to-face discussions with their fellow jurors. Though their deliberations did not typically last more

Table 5.4.   Predictors of juror confusion about the trial

Predictor	B (SE)	b
Previous service	−.069 (.059)	−.034
Respondent sex	−.046 (.054)	−.024
Race	−.204 (.085)	−.067**
Education	−.078 (.017)	−.129***
Full time	−.098 (.068)	−.049
Age	.002 (.003)	.032
Retired	.063 (.107)	.023
R^2	.030***	
N	1267	

Note: * $p < .10$, ** $p < .05$, *** $p < .01$. B denotes unstandardized regression coefficient, SE denotes standard error of estimate, and b denotes standardized coefficient.

than a few hours, this was a critical phase of the service experience for many jurors. To address this critical aspect of the jury experience, we begin by looking more closely at the *meaning* of jury deliberation—both theoretically and in jurors' own words. After briefly reviewing past research, we look at how jurors experienced deliberation in the King County courts, where we used broad survey questions on a wide range of issues and a large sample of juries, and in the Municipal courthouse, where we had a smaller sample but the freedom to ask more specific questions on juror deliberation.

Legal Constraints on Deliberation

In the vernacular meaning of the term, all juries "deliberate." When a judge sends a jury out of the courtroom "to deliberate," the jury retires to the "deliberation room" and begins "deliberations" on the case. In this book, though, we work with a more precise meaning of the word. To understand this definition, one might ask whether a given jury deliberation was of the highest *quality*. Figure 5.4 presents a definition of "high-quality jury deliberation." The basic question is, what kind of talk does a jury engage in when it conducts a high-quality discussion of a case?

Starting at the top of Figure 5.4, jurors receive an "information base" through the argument, evidence, and testimony that attorneys and witnesses present to them. In fact, judges admonish jurors to consider *only* the evidence presented during the trial. In the 1957 movie *12 Angry Men*, the character played by Henry Fonda stabs a knife into the jury room table. He uses the knife, which he bought at a store during the trial, to show that the murder weapon was not unique—that it could have been someone else's. In actual practice, such behavior would be grounds for a mistrial, as the juror expanded the information base set by the judge during the trial.[19] Thus, as written in Figure 5.4, the carefully deliberating jury is only to "consider all

Analytic process	
Create a solid information base	Consider all of the facts and testimony provided during the trial. Avoid adding personal experiences and biases.
Prioritize the key values at stake	The paramount values are ensuring justice and the rule of law.
Identify a broad range of solutions	The judge specifies a range of verdicts and/or sentences or judgment the jury can give. No others are available.
Weigh the pros, cons, and tradeoffs among solutions	Consider whether each possible verdict or sentence upholds the relevant laws identified by the judge and serves the larger cause of justice.
Make the best decision possible	Follow standards for reasonable doubt and other guidelines to render the appropriate verdict and/or judgment.
Social process	
Adequately distribute speaking opportunities	The foreperson and others should ensure a balanced discussion by drawing out quiet jurors and welcoming dissenting jurors to speak up.
Ensure mutual comprehension	Speak plainly to each other, and ask for clarification when confused. Ensure understanding of technical evidence or finer points of law.
Consider other ideas and experiences	Listen carefully to what others say, especially when you disagree with their view of the case. Try to understand their unique perspective on the case.
Respect other participants	Presume that each juror is honest and well-intentioned. Remember that cases go to trial because the parties involved see the case differently.

Figure 5.4 Key features of high-quality jury deliberation

of the facts and testimony provided during the trial" and must "avoid adding personal experiences and biases" into their discussion.

High-quality jury deliberation also does not venture beyond the values of justice and the rule of law when weighing the case. One might think that values do not come into play at all in the best deliberation, with the jury merely applying the facts to the case and taking the law as given. As one justice typically instructed his jurors, they must apply to the facts of the case "the law as the court will give it to you. You must follow that law whether you agree with it or not."[20]

In fact, as mentioned earlier, American juries have the right to "nullify" existing law when they believe that following the law is an unforgivable miscarriage of justice. Until 1894, this fact was well-known to juries, who knew they were free to exercise their independent judgment, though asked to remain mindful of the law. In that year, the U.S. Supreme Court declared that the jury no longer had "the right to determine questions of law," yet it affirmed that juries still had the final say on cases.[21] In other words, juries retained their right to independence but lost the right to be *informed* of that authority. This paradoxical state of affairs has resulted in the occasional jury defying what they consider as unjust applications of the law. Unaware of this power, and likely reluctant to disregard the law in any case, jury nullification is exceedingly rare.[22] Nonetheless, it is because of the authority of nullification that Figure 5.4 stipulates that juries are to consider the law itself *and ensuring justice* as the key values in judging a case.

As for the "range of solutions" a jury can consider, there are none but those provided by the court—often nothing more than a choice between guilty and not guilty or finding for the plaintiff or defendant. The evidence either supports or refutes these alternative verdicts or findings, and the jury ultimately must reach a decision that best upholds the law and justice in relation to the facts of the case.

Whereas the jury's discussion procedures and rules are highly structured, the social aspect of high-quality jury deliberation is more flexible but generally follows democratic principles. In a high-quality process, jurors take turns speaking, address each other in terms they can understand, and consider carefully what each juror has to say about the case. The jurors presume one another's honesty and good intentions, even when honestly disagreeing about the facts of a case or the interpretation or application of the relevant legal statutes. Though within the narrow parameters of a legal proceeding, these are essentially the relational qualities of any deliberative discussion.

In Jurors' Own Words

This provides a theoretical account of ideal deliberation, but we can learn more about jurors' own sense of deliberative norms by turning back to their written comments in our King County survey. Though we never asked them an open-ended question about deliberation, some jurors spontaneously commented on that aspect of their experience. One foreperson serving on a breach of contract trial in Kent, for instance, suggested that the judge provided her and fellow jurors with a framework but no guidelines for deliberation:[23]

> Though we were given instructions from the court on the law and on the claims made by both parties, we were not given suggestions on how best to handle jury deliberations. As presiding juror I felt a huge burden of responsibility to ensure a fair trial for all involved. It would have been helpful to have some suggested protocols or procedures to follow to ensure a fair and non-confrontational deliberation process.

The juror's basic notion is that deliberation should be respectful and non-confrontational, but did jurors require politeness at the expense of free expression of disagreement? A review of juror comments on the subject suggests otherwise. For instance, a White woman empanelled for an arson trial wrote, "It surprised me that the jury members, although from different backgrounds, mindsets, etc., were very considerate of others' feelings and fair in their dealings in deliberating to change others' opinions in the outcome of the deliberations."

Many other juror comments shared this sentiment, but other times, juries got stuck. A juror from an assault trial at the Municipal Courthouse wrote that she "generally understood the other views but was a bit frustrated in that neither side really was able to move the other closer to their side for a verdict. The more we discussed, the more we agreed to disagree amiably." A young man serving downtown went a step farther: "I was picked for a jury and it went longer than expected, during deliberation, we had a pig-headed juror who refused to listen to reason or see the obvious, so we couldn't convict on certain counts…this left me and several of the other jurors very frustrated."

The sense of frustration is telling because it reveals this juror's sense of how deliberation *ought* to proceed. That is, we began this section by simply recounting how jurors understood their task, and the general sense one gets from these jurors' spontaneous recollections of deliberation is that there was a broadly-shared sense of how it *should* unfold, even if it did not always happen that way.

This should hearten deliberative theorists, for jurors' intuitive norms of how they should behave match up well with abstract definitions of deliberation like the one presented in Figure 5.4. In particular, the jurors' comments revealed a belief that jury deliberation involves both a careful analysis of evidence but also a set of democratic social relations among the participants. Jurors need to give each other relatively equal speaking opportunities, then listen respectfully and with an open mind to what is said.

As to the practical significance of this finding, consider former Vice President Al Gore's book, *The Assault on Reason*, which argues that demagoguery and manipulation have overtaken American politics. "American democracy is now in danger," he asserts, because of its eroding public sphere.[24] Our data suggest—and the findings below will continue to show—that beneath the corroding discourse of American campaigns lies a broader commitment to the principles of deliberative democracy that transcends partisan and cultural divides.[25]

Prior Research in the Deliberation Room

Though jurors may *aspire* to deliberate thoughtfully and respectfully, do they, in fact, do so? Past research on real and simulated ("mock") juries has found that most jury decision making is "verdict-driven," meaning that most jurors enter the jury room with a preliminary decision on the verdict and the goal of quickly making a decision.[26] It has been estimated that the ideal of making full consideration of facts and evidence with an open mind and respect for others' positions may occur in only 35 percent of cases and that in only one in ten cases does discussion in the jury room result in a reversal of the initial majority's verdict preferences.[27]

Prior research presents mixed findings regarding how deliberative jury decision making works in actual practice.[28] On the one hand, there is evidence that many juries do *not* engage in high-quality deliberation. As indirect evidence, many studies have shown that jurors' initial verdict preferences are a strong predictor of the jury's final verdict. In fact, about 90 percent of the time the jury's final verdict is the same as the majority of jurors' pre-deliberation positions. This result has been found in field studies of actual juries, as well as mock juries.[29] This finding does not prove that juries did not engage in rigorous face-to-face deliberation; rather, it points to the power the initial majority has over the final decision. A crude majoritarian bias could forestall deliberation, which requires thoughtful case analysis and consideration of each juror's point of view. If the final outcomes are routinely consistent with initial opinions, there is little motivation for jurors to review carefully the facts of the case and the judge's instructions.[30]

On the other hand, some studies indicate that many juries *do* engage in thorough, respectful, and egalitarian deliberation. Rejecting the common misperception that most juries start their deliberations with a preliminary vote, social psychologist Shari Diamond and her colleagues found that preliminary votes are often suggested, but typically not employed, as juries instead begin discussing evidence.[31] Additional research using post-trial interviews has found that a quarter or fewer juries hold early votes.[32]

From another perspective, it is remarkable that 10 percent of trials *do* result in a verdict that is the opposite of the jury's initial preferences.[33] One potential explanation for why some juries reverse their verdict is the deliberation style: Research has shown a major difference between juries that use a verdict-driven style of decision making and those that use an evidence-driven style.[34] Verdict-driven juries tend to start with an initial vote and then spend the bulk of their time discussing verdict options. Evidence-driven juries, on the other hand, structure their discussion around the various pieces of evidence and do not vote until a great deal of discussion has taken place. An evidence-driven style is likely to be more deliberative by promoting thorough discussion of the case, and may also allow minority voices more equal time and respect in the discussion than a verdict-driven style.

Deliberation in Seattle

Returning to the present study, we can provide additional evidence that bears on the character of jury deliberation. Through the generosity of Seattle Municipal Court officials, we received even more extensive access than King County judges felt comfortable providing, and we were able to ask jurors on criminal trials more in-depth questions about their deliberations.

Looking exclusively at these municipal juries, we had a database of 267 Seattle jurors who served on sixty different criminal trials in Seattle Municipal Court, only three of which failed to return complete verdicts. Typical jury size in this court was six jurors, though there were cases with five or seven. Nearly a third (32.2 percent) of those participating in this study sat on juries hearing low-level assault charges, another 16.1 percent heard drunken-driving cases, and the rest heard a range of minor offenses (e.g., reckless driving). The median juror spent two days in the courtroom, with 91 percent spending three or fewer days there. The median juror deliberated for no more than one hour, with 84 percent deliberating for two hours or less.

The questions we asked these jurors in their post-service questionnaire were designed to capture some of the most essential components of jury deliberation, as described in Figure 5.4. Thus, we asked jurors if their analysis of the evidence and relevant law was thorough (i.e., careful weighing of evidence and the evaluative criteria given in the judge's instructions) and whether individual jurors treated each other with respect, listened to one another, and gave all jurors adequate opportunities to express their views.

Rather than looking at individual jurors, for this analysis it made more sense to look at the level of the jury, and Table 5.5 shows group-level means and minimums for the fifty-five juries that had three or more completed post-deliberation surveys.[35] Using the same five-point disagreement/agreement scales used earlier, this table shows that juries had scores skewed heavily toward the top-end of the scale (strong agreement) regarding weighing evidence thoroughly ($M = 4.51$), discussing judicial instructions ($M = 4.35$), listening to each other ($M = 4.41$), and having adequate chances to express their own views ($M = 4.50$). Referencing a survey item discussed earlier, the average juror also reported being treated well by his/her peers ($M = 4.40$), a treatment score falling between "very good" and "excellent."

By looking at the level of the jury—rather than the individual juror—this table shows even more striking evidence regarding deliberation. Table 5.5 shows the lowest (minimum) score within each group to give a sense for the experience of the juror who experienced the least high-quality deliberation. The average

Table 5.5. Jury-level descriptive statistics for deliberation measures in municipal criminal juries

Statement	Mean	SD	Average minimum score	Percent of groups with minimum response level		
				Agree/strongly agree	Neutral	Disagree/strongly disagree
"Jurors thoroughly discussed the relevant facts of the case."	4.52	.33	4.04	89%	9%	2%
"The jury thoroughly discussed the instructions the judge provided."	4.35	.42	3.73	67%	27%	5%
"All of the jurors listened respectfully to each other during deliberation."	4.41	.36	3.91	89%	7%	4%
"The other jurors gave me enough of a chance to express my opinions about the case."	4.50	.31	4.02	95%	4%	2%
				Minimum response level		
				Very good/excellent Good		Satisfactory/less than satisfactory
"How were you treated by fellow jurors?"	4.40	.46	3.68	71%	24%	7%

$N = 55$ juries for all rows. All variables are scored on scales ranging from 1 to 5.

minimum score across the fifty-five groups was closest to the fourth scale point in all cases, suggesting a "minimum experience" that was usually comparable to that of the rest of the jurors. Table 5.5 also shows the distribution of minimum experiences across the groups, and this analysis showed exactly how few juries included a member who gave their jury experience low marks. Only 5 percent of juries had a juror who reported a deliberation score below the scale midpoint (3) on the five-point scale, and only 7 percent of juries had a *single* member who felt the treatment they received from other jurors was no better than "satisfactory."

We also asked jurors to describe their own individual behavior in three respects. First, we asked them how often they spoke up to "explain evidence or facts," and the modal response (47 percent) was "three or more times." Only 11 percent of jurors reported never making this kind of contribution. Returning to the group level of analysis, we found that in two-thirds of the juries, every single member offered at least one comment relevant to the facts and evidence being discussed.

Second, we asked jurors how often they expressed their "own views" during the trial. Over two-thirds (68 percent) did so three or more times, with only one in twenty never sharing their own opinions on the case. At the jury level, it turned out that each of the eleven individual respondents who never spoke up sat on a different trial. In other words, though only 5 percent of individual jurors remained mum about their view, in the aggregate, this meant that exactly one-fifth of all juries had at least one member who remained silent in this respect.

Third, we wanted to know if jurors' personal experiences shaped their deliberations. Jurors generally understand that although their general life experience is valid—being part of what it means to be judged by a jury of one's peers—it is inappropriate to drag one's personal experience into the deliberation. A few jurors who were dismissed during *voir dire* even commented on this, such as a retired woman in the jury pool who wrote, "I did not expect to be seated on this particular jury due to my disclosure of a personal experience that might have tainted my objectivity." But one criminal juror said that although he and fellow jurors "were not permitted to know anything about the auto impact because no expert witness was asked to testify," he decided that "my personal experience is valid" in reflecting on the accident.

Was this a common sentiment? Forty-two percent of Seattle jurors reported that they *never* "spoke about [their] own experiences" during the jury deliberation, but slightly more (43 percent) did so once or twice, and 15 percent did so three times or more. At the jury level, only five juries (9 percent) had no member draw a personal connection to the case, and in 41 percent of the trials *every single juror spoke from personal experience at least three times*.

Were these personal reflections important to jurors in making their decisions, or were they more casual asides and comments? One way to know is to test the extent to which this behavior predicted jurors' overall satisfaction with their deliberation and the verdicts they reached. When compared alongside the other deliberation and participation measures we have just reviewed, how important are these personal expressions?

To find out, the Seattle jurors separately rated the "quality of the jury's deliberation" and "the jury's final verdict" on a four-point scale from "very unsatisfied" to "very satisfied." The median rating for the deliberation was 3.5 on the 1–4 scale (between "satisfied" and "very satisfied"), and the median verdict rating was 3.4. Only 7 percent of juries had an average rating below "satisfied," though 16 percent said they were at best "unsatisfied" with the verdict.

Table 5.6 then shows the correlations among the individual deliberation and participation measures with these two satisfaction ratings. (We look at these separately, owing to the high correlations among many of our predictors.) The clearest sets of results are the general correlation of deliberation measures with overall satisfaction and deliberation. All of the behaviors, except discussing the judge's instructions correlated substantially with jurors' satisfaction with their jury's deliberation. In addition, respectful listening and treatment were the keys to satisfying verdicts, a finding that emphasized the importance of the democratic relations among jurors above and beyond the rigor of their analytic process.

As to individual participation behaviors, these were not predictive of deliberation satisfaction, but they did foreshadow a satisfying verdict.

Table 5.6. Correlations of deliberation items with overall satisfaction with deliberation and verdict at the group level of analysis

Category and measure(s)	Satisfaction with deliberation	Satisfaction with verdict
Deliberation ("Jurors...		
thoroughly discussed the relevant facts...	.25**	−.03
thoroughly discussed the [judge's] instructions...	.13	−.10
listened respectfully to each other...	.31***	.29**
gave me enough of a chance to express my opinions...	.26**	.04
gave me excellent treatment")⁺	.22*	.28**
Participation ("How often did you...		
explain evidence or facts?	.05	−.19*
express your own views?	.10	−.26**
speak about your own experiences?")	.17	.06

Note: * $p < .10$, ** $p < .05$, *** $p < .01$. Minimum jury-level $N = 54$.
⁺ This phrasing adapts the maximum label ("excellent") from the response scale for the item, "How were you treated by fellow jurors?"

Returning to the question that sparked this analysis, it was speaking about evidence and views about the case that predicted verdict satisfaction. By contrast, talk about personal experiences related to the trial neither significantly contributed to nor detracted from jurors' overall assessments of the deliberation or their verdict. In other words, jurors acknowledged making personal comments during deliberation, but then did not end up seeing those as integral to high-quality deliberation and an appropriate verdict.

Returning to King County

Though the King County judges were not comfortable allowing us to look at their juries in detail, they did allow us to ask their jurors for the same two satisfaction ratings with which we ended the previous discussion. Thus, we step back into our larger dataset to examine simultaneously juror satisfaction in the Seattle Municipal, Kent, and downtown King County courthouses. This permits looking at 234 juries from both criminal and civil trials and ranging in size from five to twelve.

Staying at the jury level for our analysis, we found very high means for juror satisfaction with both deliberation and verdict. For deliberation, on the four-point satisfaction scale, the average for a jury was 3.38 ($SD = .45$), between "satisfied" (3) and "very satisfied" (4). Similarly, the mean score for verdict satisfaction was 3.24 ($SD = .59$). Looking at the distribution of these scores, only 13 percent of juries had an average deliberation rating below "satisfied," and 21 percent had a similarly low average verdict rating. There were differences of opinion among jurors, though, because 45 percent of juries had at least one member who was "unsatisfied" with the deliberation. Twenty-nine percent of juries had at least one member who was "very unsatisfied" with the jury's deliberation. The figures are similar but lower for verdict satisfaction, with 36 percent of juries having at least one unsatisfied juror and 21 percent having at least one very unsatisfied juror.

As one might have guessed, these average jury ratings for deliberation and verdict are correlated powerfully ($r = .65$). Less obviously, however, it is noteworthy that the *variation* in these measures also correlated ($r = .40$), which is to say that the more jurors differed in their assessments of deliberation, the more they diverged in their satisfaction with the verdict. This makes sense, in that a jury that does not see its deliberation in the same light may well exhibit equally mixed feelings about the verdict.

The correlation between deliberation and verdict ratings holds special importance for this study, given our core claim about the importance of jury deliberation in shaping jurors' civic behavior and attitudes. Given that interest, it is worth exploring in more detail this relationship and seeing if it holds up when other variables are taken into account.

We began by creating a pair of new variables measuring jury verdicts and considering their interrelationship. First, among those jurors who completed our post-deliberation survey, 249 served on trials reaching not guilty verdicts or findings for the defendant in civil trials. Six hundred sixty jurors found for the plaintiff in civil cases or found a charged defendant guilty on criminal charges. Another ninety-seven reached a mixed or ambiguous verdict. When the means of these three verdict outcomes were compared, there were no significant differences.[36]

A more powerful contrast occurred between these 1006 verdict-reaching jurors and the remaining 145 individuals who served on hung juries. As one might have guessed, the mean verdict satisfaction ratings varied significantly between those reaching full verdicts (M = 3.4, SD = .84) and those remaining hung on one or more charges (M = 2.3, SD = .98).[37] Expressed in correlational terms, the association was of moderate strength (r = −.33).

There was not room for both verdict and the hung jury variables in our subsequent analysis because of their particular relationship (i.e., hung jurors are all "missing data" when one compares different verdicts). Given the clear significance of hung juries relative to the direction of the verdict, we opted to include the former by itself. We placed the hung jury variable into a multilevel regression analysis, which makes it possible to look simultaneously at individual-level variables (e.g., juror perceptions) and jury-level variables (e.g., trial duration). Other variables included ones already familiar—the type of trial (civil vs. criminal), the seriousness of the charges, the days spent in the courtroom, the number of hours in deliberation, and, finally, jurors' sense of the trial's importance and their satisfaction with the deliberation.

The results of this analysis in Table 5.7 show that a juror's satisfaction with his or her jury's verdict bears no relation to the type of trial, level of charges, or days spent in the courtroom. The duration of the jury's deliberation has a marginal significance, but the more powerful effects come from whether the jury reached a verdict, the subjective importance of the trial to jurors, and jurors' assessment of the quality of their deliberation.

In sum, whether jurors are likely to reach a satisfying conclusion to their trial hinges not on the external features of the case or the trial so much as on the importance the jurors ascribe to it and, above all else, how they assess the quality of their deliberation. This finding is reassuring in that the legitimacy of the verdict *should* hinge on the quality of the deliberation, for that is the core of the jurors' job and the justification for their special role in the American system of justice. Were we to find only a weak connection between the jurors' deliberation and their verdict satisfaction, we would have been left to wonder on what basis jurors could judge their own verdict.

Revisiting the Voting Connection

Before concluding this chapter, we return one last time to the question of jury deliberation and voting. Perhaps a future study will permit direct inspection of the deliberative process in juries to see what *specific* aspects of this experience have the greatest civic impact. In the meantime, the best we can do is to

Table 5.7.   Individual-level and jury-level predictors of juror satisfaction with the verdict

	Estimate (γ)	SE
Fixed part		
Intercept	.61	.18
Hung jury [= 0]	.61***	.11
Trial type [= 1]	−.14	.09
Seriousness level of charges	−.02	.06
Total days spent in the courtroom	.01	.01
Total hours in jury deliberation	−.02*	.01
Perceived importance of jury in resolving case	.12***	.03
Satisfaction with the deliberative process	.51***	.04
Random part		
Intercept	.02	.02

Note: * $p < .10$, ** $p < .05$, *** $p < .01$. Minimum jury-level $N = 124$. Results are for a multilevel model with jurors grouped within their respective juries. Hung jury and trial type are dichotomous variables, and the effects shown are for all non-hung outcomes and criminal trials, respectively.

return to the relatively small sample at the Seattle Municipal Courthouse, where we at least have first-hand accounts of participants' experiences and their assessments of different elements of their juries' deliberations.

In linking these municipal jurors' survey responses back to official election records, we could make definite matches in the election archives for only 77 percent of those jurors, yielding an effective sample size of 170.[38] To conduct this test, we combined the two different sets of municipal deliberation items into separate scales—one assessing the perceived quality of the deliberation and a second measuring jurors' active engagement in the deliberation (see Appendix Section 5c).

When we regressed these variables, along with demographic control variables from the preservice survey, we found the pattern of results shown in Table 5.8: The key deliberation measure was the assessment of their jury's deliberation, not the relative frequency with which the individual jurors themselves participated. To get a sense of the size of this effect, consider that the overwhelming majority (91 percent) of municipal jurors had scores on our four-item deliberation measure between just two scale points—four and the maximum of five. The regression results suggest that the difference between that four and five is roughly a 7 percent increase in voting frequency (unstandardized regression coefficient, $B = .069$). By way of comparison, this is roughly analogous to the difference between deliberating and non-deliberating jurors in the National Jury Sample (chapter 3).[39]

Table 5.8.   Linear regression measuring the effect of jury deliberation quality and participation at the Seattle Municipal Courthouse

	Percentage of election voting in 2004	
Predictor	B *(SE)*	*b*
Percentage of elections voted in from 2003 general to 2004 primary	.513 (.06)	.581***
Age	.001 (.00)	.044
Education	.014 (.01)	.084
Respondent sex	−.017 (.03)	−.031
Self-identified as white	−.023 (.05)	−.032
Employed full time	.027 (.04)	.050
Self-identified as retired	−.042 (.07)	−.054
Frequency of speaking about one's experiences	.006 (.02)	.017
Deliberation quality	.069 (.03)	.129**
Deliberation engagement	.022 (.02)	.066
R^2	.38***	
N	179	

Note: * $p < .10$, ** $p < .05$, *** $p < .01$. On the measurement of deliberation quality and engagement, see Appendix section 5c. B denotes unstandardized regression coefficient, *SE* denotes standard error of estimate, and *b* denotes standardized coefficient.

A Final Word on Voting and Deliberation

Chapter 3 used a national archival dataset to show that jury deliberation, per se, has a causal link to future voting rates, and chapter 4 refined that finding by showing that in King County, jurors' overall subjective experience of service partially explained that effect. The Seattle Municipal jury analysis in this chapter pulls these findings together to suggest that the jurors' perceived experience of deliberation helps to tie the jury–voting connection together. For Seattle jurors, moreover, what mattered was not how much an individual participated, but rather the juror's sense of whether *the jury as a whole* weighed the evidence, followed instructions, listened, and let each other speak. The better the deliberation, the stronger the voting effect.

This chapter's aim, however, was broader than simply refining the jury–voting link. It began by giving a clearer sense of the kinds of trials on which jurors typically serve. Unlike those portrayed in films and in news accounts, the typical juror serves on an assault trial, an automotive injury jury, or a similarly unglamorous case. The median juror in our study was in court only five to six days, with the jury deliberating by itself for only part of a single day. For many sworn jurors, service was even briefer—lasting just two or three days. Even long trials did not produce overly long juror deliberation sessions because jurors were already weighing the evidence quietly in their heads as the trial progressed forward.

Though the juries in this study were not as diverse as the nation as a whole, they were generally fairly representative of the county or city population from which they were drawn, and over two-thirds of respondents perceived that their juries were made up of residents with diverse backgrounds. Though a minority of jurors expressed frustration with inefficient court officials and attorneys who used unduly technical terms and belabored their points, jurors from all backgrounds generally perceived that the court staff, attorneys, judges, and fellow jurors treated them with respect. Even those initially reluctant to serve and those seated on longer criminal or civil trials generally shared this positive assessment of juror treatment.

While these jurors' trials progressed, the jurors experienced strong and often mixed emotions. Those having strong positive feelings expressed a diffuse satisfaction but also a sense of civic pride in the process, themselves, and the performance of their jury. Those who simply felt badly most commonly vented frustration, mixed sometimes with warm sympathy and other times with a cool indifference. Generally, the jurors appeared to recognize and work through their emotions as they arose, or even set aside those feelings that might prejudice them, as in the case of the juror who felt "empathy for the defendant even though we fairly delivered a guilty verdict."

On a cognitive level, the overwhelming majority of jurors found their trials not only interesting but also *important*. Those two perceptions went hand-in-hand: If a trial was uninteresting to jurors, they almost always failed to see the importance of the case. Generally, they found criminal cases slightly more engaging than civil ones, but the key to capturing juror interest was the seriousness of the charges or claims, with few jurors doubting the importance of the higher-profile cases. Interest or importance aside, about a quarter of jurors admitted to finding their trials confusing at times. The sources of confusion jurors spontaneously mentioned ranged from legal definitions to language differences.

Past research has found considerable evidence demonstrating the generally high quality of jury deliberation. Moreover, jurors themselves have learned a meaning of deliberation that fits quite well with theoretical notions. In particular, they view their job as blending analytic rigor (in examining trial evidence and judicial instructions) with democratic fairness and respect (for fellow jurors).

In the Seattle Municipal Court, we got to see up-close the attention jurors gave to judges' instructions, the trial evidence, and each other's arguments, with most jurors, however, also interjecting their *personal* experiences into the deliberation. When it came to assessing their satisfaction of the jury deliberation, however, what mattered was the weighing of evidence—not whether jurors offered reflections on their own lives. Jurors' assessments of the verdict, moreover, were best predicted by respectful listening and how jurors treated each other, a finding that emphasized again how jurors balance the value of democratic social relations with the need for tough case analysis.

As in the Seattle Municipal court, the King County jurors overwhelmingly rated their deliberation favorably. Though we could not look into the deliberation room, the reports coming out of it showed that only one-in-ten juries emerged less than satisfied with its deliberation, though one-third of juries had at least one member who was dissatisfied with the verdict. Surveys also showed that jurors' overall satisfaction with the deliberation correlated strongly with their verdict satisfaction. Moreover, when a jury had divergence of opinion on the deliberation itself, it tended to yield sharper disagreement about the soundness of the verdict. A final analysis showed that whether jurors end up satisfied with their verdict depends not on external trial features—such as the seriousness of the charges or whether the case was in civil or criminal court. Instead, confidence in the verdict came most readily when jurors perceived their trial as important and believed they had deliberated well.

All of these subjective juror assessments—of their treatment by the court, their cognitive and emotional engagement, their deliberation—have importance in and of themselves. The data presented in this chapter offer considerable new insight into juror perceptions of the trial process. Nevertheless, the principal task of this book now repurposes these measures of the subjective juror experience to try to understand our central question—how and why jury service serves a civic educational purpose. We have already seen how subjective juror experience and perceptions of deliberation explain the jury–voting link. We now use these data to understand jury service's impact on a wider array of civic and political behaviors in chapter 6, followed by an investigation of attitudes toward public life in chapter 7. In doing so, the central tendencies of jury service—of an engaging and deliberative experience—become less important than the *differences* in jurors' experiences, as well as differences in the jurors themselves. As we shall see, these variations among jurors and service perceptions play important roles in understanding which individuals changed—and to what *degree* they changed—as a result of their brief visit to the courthouse.

Chapter 6

From Courthouse to Community

After serving five days on an assault/theft case at the Kent Regional Justice Center, one young male juror from Seattle found himself moved by the experience. When asked to reflect on his period of service, he wrote an answer that spilled out of the response-box and onto the margins of his survey questionaire:

> I truly felt that Jury Duty was the best civics lesson I've ever had. In no other way that I can think of are citizens so equally involved in the state's affairs. In daily life, our conversations and opinions rarely have serious consequences. For example, our sphere of concern may include communist China, but as joe citizen, we have zero influence. In the trial, our sphere of concern overlaps our sphere of influence and our involvement produces very real consequences. Thus, as Jurors and as citizens, we become more aware of the weight and responsibility of our decisions. Ultimately, this is a lesson in civics that a high school social studies class could never replicate.[1]

Of the thousands of jurors we interviewed, none made these connections quite so explicitly as this juror did. Had we coached our survey respondents to feed us responses like this, even then it would not have occurred to us to ask for "Jurors" and "Jury Duty" to receive capitalization (in the Old English tradition of emphasis through the use of capital letters). Juries and Jurors are even set off against the (intentionally?) lowercased "joe citizen," whose civic and political acts lack the "serious" or "real" consequences of jury deliberation. This juror, or should we say Juror, even becomes "more aware of the weight and responsibility" of his and other jurors' decisions simultaneously as "jurors *and as citizens*."

This survey response was, indeed, unique, but we began the King County study with every confidence that many others made this connection, consciously or otherwise. After all, the in-depth interviews in chapter 3 showed how jurors could spontaneously do the quick mental hopscotch from their period of jury service to voting in elections, which former jurors came to see as related civic responsibilities. Moreover, chapter 3 established the causal link from deliberating on a jury to becoming a more frequent voter—an effect replicated and extended in the final sections of chapters 4 and 5.

When we first presented preliminary findings to this effect in a 2002 article,[2] however, many readers wanted to know if the jury's civic educational impact extended beyond voting. On reflection, one could argue that jury duty and voting are, indeed, closely related, but together, they are *distinct* from the wider array of community, civic, and political activities that make up our public lives. In this view, both are formal citizen responsibilities—rendering official verdicts, filling out secret ballots—that stand closer to paying taxes and military service than to everyday voluntary opportunities for public engagement, like raising money for a school, writing a letter to the mayor, or reading the local section of the newspaper.

In this chapter, we address this question by continuing to explore the experience of jurors at the King County and Seattle courthouses. We narrow our sample slightly by looking only at those jurors who returned *all* of the surveys in our three-wave panel study. Previously, we looked at what jurors wrote on arrival at the courthouse, as well as their reflections on their service experience shortly thereafter. Now we can learn what happened in the months that followed their service, thanks to a final follow-up survey, which we collected after the 2004 presidential election. In the end, we arrived at a sample of 1,030 empanelled jurors who completed each of the three surveys, and this chapter focuses on how jury service influenced their lives as democratic citizens and engaged community members.

When the Connection Begins

When these thousand jurors were still doing their period of service, court administrators and their judges admonished each of them not to discuss the case. These jurors, like most, existed in a private limbo until they arrived in the deliberation room. Even if they had lunch and conversations with fellow jurors, they were not able to discuss the case or the contours of their jury experience in depth with anyone. Even the judge and attorneys' interactions with them were all focused on the case itself and the jurors' responsibility to reach a proper verdict.

At the trial's close, however, everything suddenly changed. Both the judge and jurors became free to reflect on the case and discuss it openly, and we believe that in this special juncture, there lies a unique opportunity to make good civic use of jurors' experience. Thus, we begin our exploration at the close of jurors' period of service to look at what judges say to jurors as they leave and, afterward, what jurors say to their own family, friends, and colleagues when reintegrating themselves into the lives they had put on hold while serving at the courthouse.

A Judge's Parting Words

After hearing the verdict and ending the trial, judges customarily dismiss the jury—or the judge might remain for a few minutes to talk with the jurors. Although they are free to disperse, the jury has become accustomed to listening attentively to the judge's words. During our period of study, most King County and Seattle municipal judges followed this tradition. When asked, 57 percent of the jurors in our study recalled their judge saying "something memorable" to them personally or to their "jury as a whole...at the conclusion of the trial." Ninety percent of those jurors who recalled the judge speaking to them wrote a brief note on the survey when we asked them to summarize their judge's words.

What did the judges say? To answer that question, we categorized the different recollections from the 198 juries on which one or more jurors recalled

Table 6.1. What judges said to jurors at the conclusion of a trial

Comment Category	Percent of trials in which one or more jurors heard the judge make the comment
Thank you and appreciation	68%
Affirmation of the important and difficult role jurors play	37%
Clarifications about evidence, proceedings	29%
Complimented jurors on their ability, actions, and/or decision	12%
Provided explanation to give closure	10%
Invited jurors to talk with the attorneys after the trial	5%
Asked jurors for any comments they wished to share	4%
Expressed surprise at the verdict	1%
Judge learned a lot from the experience	1%
Asked jurors to remind others of importance of serving	1%
Offered advise on how to deal with the case after the trial	1%

Note: N = 198 trials in which judges made one or more comments to jurors. These categories were not mutually exclusive, and the list shown excludes "other" and "unclear" categories, along with comments directed at exceptional categories of juries/jurors (e.g., alternates). Percentages show the proportion of juries on which one or more member(s) wrote summary recollections that two or more of our coders placed in the same category.

the judge giving a parting message. Table 6.1 shows the proportion of trials in which each of a series of messages was conveyed clearly to one or more jurors after the trial. More than two-thirds of the judges (68 percent) offered what amounted to a simple "thank you" and appreciation of the jurors' work. Similar sentiments included an affirmation of the jury's important role (37 percent) and compliments on the jurors' abilities and actions (12 percent).

For example, a young woman who served as a juror in a rape trial said that she did not "remember exactly" what the judge said but then did recall that "he thanked us for our time, continued to tell us how important our role was, and allowed for questions." She then added that she "learned a lot" in the post-trial debriefing "and appreciated the knowledge passed on by the judge and attorneys." This comment resembled many others in that jurors would begin by apologizing for not remembering precisely what was said but then proceed to recall clearly the appreciative and solemn sentiments of the judges, who routinely thanked jurors for their hard work and important role.

Some judges went even farther, and another juror serving on a civil trial recalled that her judge "thanked us for our service and invited us to visit with her in her chambers" or even "call later to talk about the experience." Though only 5 percent of trials ended with an explicit invitation to talk not only to the judge but also with the attorneys, juror comments suggest that this, too, was a common—if less memorable—invitation.

Even jurors sent away without deliberating were often given encouraging words and appreciation. A middle-aged man seated for a robbery trial at the Kent Regional Justice Center recalled the judge thanking him and his fellow jurors "despite the defense pleading guilty," thereby "eliminating the need for a trial." The judge said that "we had none the less done our civic duty and we should all feel proud."

Hung juries also got a pat on the back. For instance, a woman who took more than two weeks off from a full-time job served on a jury that remained hung after twelve hours of jury deliberation on a murder charge. As she recalled, the judge "thanked us for the time and effort we gave the case" and reminded us "that we gave our best." Another juror on a drug trial recalled that the judge offered consolation: "The judge explained that even though we had a hung jury, we did a good job." The judge added that "sometimes the jury is not provided enough information to make a decision."

The latter comment spills over into giving the jury some insight into the case. Though case-specific recollections were less frequent, many judges clarified evidence or other aspects of the trial (29 percent) or gave legal explanations to help provide jurors with closure (10 percent). One woman serving on a solicitation to murder trial for two weeks recalled at the end that the judge "told us to not anguish over the verdict—to leave it in the courtroom."

Judges often gave praise and reassurance about difficult jury verdicts. One juror wrote that her judge asked the jury "to remember that we did not reach the verdict alone, therefore we are not personally responsible for the outcome." Instead, the judge explained, "The verdict was reached through the collaborative and collective opinions of twelve, which is why the jury system works."[3]

Many judges gave jurors more than platitudes about public service, really *explaining* why serving on the jury mattered. One juror recalled that his judge said that "he understood how difficult it was for us to stand in judgment of a fellow citizen." Another juror from the same Kent courthouse recalled that her judge said "how important our time and consideration were to the defendants." A third wrote of her judge, "She convinced me of how important the jury system is, and the time I spent doing this was justified." A male juror from a felony assault case said that his judge made an even larger connection when "she emphasized our role in helping break the cycle of domestic violence."

Finally, a juror with a doctorate degree remembered that his judge impressed him by saying to the jurors, "You have served your duty as an American Citizen."[4] There, once again, is the capitalization in the jurors' own writing. Perhaps we read too much into it, yet we cannot help but see the elevation of the status of Citizen in quotes such as these—that the judges who give such remarks have successfully placed a civic frame around the jury experience. Whether that framing elicits civic engagement beyond voting, we shall see shortly.

Sharing the Experience

Our research suggests that jurors also do their part to reflect on and reinforce the significance of their jury experience. In developing this research project, we have conducted in-depth interviews with jurors weeks, months, and even years after jury service, and former jurors are usually happy to discuss their experience—most having done so many times already. When the first author of this book has spoken about this research at senior centers, nearly everyone in the room has had a jury story to share, and the details in these recollections are remarkably vivid. Jurors can remember which pieces of evidence were important, how the other jurors behaved, and, yes, even what the judge said to them.

One reason for this vivid recall is the gravity of the experience itself, which we have discussed, but another is that jurors frame and reinforce their memories of jury service *by talking about it.*[5] In our six-month follow-up survey, we asked jurors two questions. First, we asked, "After a trial is over, jurors sometimes discuss their experience with other people. Since the end of your most recent jury service, how many times did you talk about your jury experience with other people living in your household?" Ninety-six percent of jurors said that, yes, they had talked about their experience, and over two-thirds (72 percent) had done so at least "a few times." Twenty percent did so "many times." When we asked if jurors had discussed their jury experience with "friends, co-workers, or family members living outside your household," the results were nearly identical, with 96 percent of jurors having talked about jury service at least "once or twice." When these results are combined, it turns out that only 13 jurors (1.3 percent of the sample of over one thousand jurors) never talked about their experience.[6]

These conversations about jury service have importance in and of themselves, as a means of sharing experiences with others who may, too, get called on to serve. For the present study's purposes, though, the significance of this talk may lie in how it helps jurors think out loud about their service and connect it, directly or indirectly, with the other aspects of their lives. Direct study of the content of these conversations awaits future research. For now, we add these conversations to the aspects of jury experience that may spark future civic engagement beyond voting. For that purpose, we combined the two survey items into a single measure of talk about jury service ($\alpha = .79$), which we will employ later this chapter.

Civic Engagement beyond Voting

Judges' and jurors' discussions about the jury experience might have an influence on jurors' future civic and political actions, and to explore that possibility, we have to step back once more, this time to define more precisely these varied forms of public engagement. In chapter 2, we explained the importance of the jury's location at the nexus of political society, civil society, and the state, and we discussed the other actions democratic citizens can take to exercise their influence on their wider community and political world. Here, we introduce the specific survey items we used to measure those behaviors.

At the outset, we wish to make two points. First, it was as important to jurors as it was to us to distinguish among these different behaviors, rather than collapse them into a single gross index of civic/political engagement. As one Kent juror wrote spontaneously at the end of her survey, "From my perspective, involvement in politics is different from involvement in my community. For example, I am involved in my neighborhood and various community outreach programs. However, I am not involved in any political campaigns or movements to change current political-based issues." Though some researchers have argued that participation in voluntary civic associations cuts against one's effective involvement in politics,[7] we simply emphasize the importance of making these distinctions and expecting variation in how jury service connects differently to these diverse activities. The pattern of statistical results we will see below suggests that other jurors made equally fine distinctions when answering our questions.

Second, we acknowledge that we did not ask about *every* form of political or civic action that was important to the participants in our study. One respondent complained that "you have assumed that 'being a good citizen' is largely due to a person's political focus." He added that he does "very little politically" but remains "very involved in school and our neighborhood in a social way." To try to address such concerns, we *did* include questions about volunteering in neighborhood and educational groups, but another juror said that he felt "too shy" and not sufficiently "competent" to attend such group meetings. Instead, he noted that he financially supported "a large number of nonprofit organizations as well as many political candidates, though our survey did not "take that kind of commitment into account."

The range of actions we could have included in our survey might have been even wider, but we worked in a research environment far more constrained than those that have spawned broader investigations of public participation.[8] Our surveys had to pass muster with the King County and Seattle Municipal judges, who had legitimate concerns about what unintended purposes our surveys might end up serving.[9]

With those caveats in place, we were able to include in our survey a set of eighteen different measures of political and civic engagement. These provided robust measures of jurors' pre- and post-service levels of public affairs media use, campaign involvement and political action, local face-to-face talk about community and political affairs, and group-based participation in a variety of local civic and community associations. As explained in chapter 2, these different activities represent a variety of ways in which active democratic citizens can participate in civil and political society beyond the official act of voting (or jury service). (For details on the construction of these engagement scales, see Appendix Section 6a.)

The analysis of jurors' pre- and post-service civic and political engagement also required augmenting the set of control variables employed thus far.[10] Additional factors that we thought might influence political participation included whether a person rents or owns a home, their years living in their present city, and the degree to which their friends and family are politically engaged.[11] We also created a pair of items designed to separately capture a person's liberal-conservative self-identification and the strength of identification, if any, with a major political party. (See Appendix Section 6b for details on the political control variables.)

A Quick Test-Drive for Municipal Jurors

Delayed gratification has its merits, but before moving into an extended discussion of the complex ways jury service could stimulate change in civic and political behavior, we turn briefly to a familiar setting to conduct a quick test. In chapter 5, we saw a close-up view of deliberation in the Seattle Municipal Courthouse, whose judges had allowed asking detailed questions about what took place in the deliberation room. We created two scales—one measuring jurors' assessments of the overall deliberation and the other assessing jurors' own level of participation in the deliberation (see Appendix Section 5c). Would these measures of deliberation prove predictive of changes in jurors' subsequent behaviors?

To find out, we used partial correlations, a variant on methods we have already described. (See Appendix Section 6c for details on this method.) We calculated partial correlations between the two deliberation measures and changes over time in each of the political/civic engagement measures. We had the general hypothesis of positive relationships in each case because we expected that the more effective the perceived jury deliberation, the more inclined one becomes to participate in future public deliberation and related activities.[12]

As if to illustrate the limitations of our prescience, the result of these analyses was nonsignificant associations, with one important exception. Municipal jurors' assessments of the quality of the jury deliberation, which predicted voting change in the previous chapter, had a positive association with the level of participation in local community groups—a partial correlation (pr) = .10, but this did not reach statistical significance (one-tailed p = .14). The p-value (probability level) of .14 means, roughly, that there exists a 14 percent chance that the positive correlation we found in our sample was simply due to chance.[13]

Jurors' level of participation in the deliberation, by contrast, *did* yield a positive change in community group participation $(pr = .21)$ that surpassed the threshold of statistical significance $(p = .009)$. In other words, the odds of this correlation being a chance occurrence is less than one in a hundred; to be precise, the odds are nine in a thousand. The finding suggests that whereas high-quality deliberation is key to promoting the act of voting (see chapter 5), increasing one's participation in local groups may stem more from *personally* engaging in that deliberation. By speaking up in the jury and contributing to its analysis of evidence or movement toward a verdict, one gets first-hand evidence of one's potential efficacy in such situations.[14]

Regarding the *absolute* size of these effects, in the larger pool of social scientific effects, we would call them something between "small" $(pr = .10)$ and "medium" $(pr = .30)$.[15] One way of comparing the effects is to remember that the voting effects first reported in chapter 3 were roughly equivalent to correlations of $r = .07$, a decidedly small effect that, nonetheless, results in real increases in voter turnout in the range of 4–7 percent. (For more on relative effect sizes, see Appendix Section 6d.)

The foregoing analysis, though, was just a test drive, meant to introduce an analytic approach with a limited number of moving parts. This initial test used a very small sample, which limited the statistical power of our analyses (i.e., our ability to find significant effects in our sample that do, indeed, exist in the larger population). The full King County/Seattle sample will yield a much larger sample of sworn jurors, and that sample has sufficient size to also permit comparisons of the jury service–public engagement links between different subgroups of jurors, such as full-time workers versus retirees. The one remaining step is simplifying our analysis of the jury experience and further explaining the links to changing civic/political behavior.

Theoretical Links from Service to Engagement

We set out to investigate what aspects of jurors' experiences correspond to changes in their political and civic behavior over time. Chapters 3 and 4 showed that being part of an effectively deliberating jury could trigger an increase in voting, but those findings show a causal link that still lacks a sufficiently textured explanation. What *specific features* of the subjective jury experience link service to behavior change? To answer that question, we briefly revisit the different elements of jury service, then consider how those experiences might influence behavior for different subgroups of the larger population of jurors. Having done that, we will then be able to examine more closely the links between service and engagement.

The Many Facets of Jury Experience

At this point, we introduce no new feature of jury service but instead—as we did for political behavior—reduce the sheer number of different measures of jury experience to a manageable set of scales or distinctive items. When analyzed in this way, we found jury service assessments could be broken down into eight components: overall satisfaction, personal treatment, cognitive engagement, comprehension of the trial, emotional engagement, assessment of the deliberation and verdict, praise received from the judge, and whether jurors talked about their service experience with friends and family. (Appendix Section 6e describes the creation of jury experience scales.)

Each of these aspects of jury service has a straightforward reason for shaping post-service civic and political behavior. First, overall satisfaction with jury service positively reinforces one's civic/political behavioral habits. We tend to repeat those activities we find rewarding, just as when children typically are willing to play a game again if they won the first time they tried it.[16] In this particular context, people have their civic inclinations reinforced if they leave with an overall sense of satisfaction or even pleasant surprise at how enjoyable or rewarding the particular activity of jury service proved to be, in spite of the doubts many—if not most—jurors had when they first arrived at the courthouse.

The treatment one receives at the hand of court officials, judges, attorneys, and jurors could likewise be expected to increase future civic engagement by creating a cognitive association between public action (jury service) and receiving kindness, respect, or even esteem. This relies on an external incentive for engagement, in that one's future participation beyond the courthouse could become predicated on the anticipation of receiving the same kind of rewarding positive feedback—as opposed to the fruits of the participation per se (e.g., improving one's community). Receiving respect and other social/personal benefits constitute a kind of "soft incentive" to participate, and such inducements can be as effective at stimulating political participation as can anything else.[17]

The two-item cognitive engagement scale seeks to distinguish those jurors who found the trial interesting and important from those who doubted its significance and found it dull or even stultifying. Intuitively, one expects juries to make a more lasting impression when they captivate the attention of the jurors, and the theoretical reasons for that effect fit common sense. When one is interested in a subject, it engrosses one's attention and generates spontaneous cognitions (e.g., thoughts and questions about the case). Essentially, this activity leaves a wider cognitive footprint in one's memory, thereby facilitating the connections the activity might make with future activities.[18]

Jurors' comprehension (or confusion) during the trial also stands alone as a separate measure of juror cognition. This variable could spark both positive and negative effects, though for very different reasons. First, we anticipate that jurors who are able to understand a trial have a rewarding experience of mastery. That, in turn, should stimulate future engagement for most jurors.[19] At the same time, however, sometimes our personal failures can drive us to seek self-improvement.[20] In the jury context, this may mean that those able to follow a trial without difficulty remain smugly self-satisfied, whereas those who struggle might recommit to becoming better informed and engaged in public life to avoid such embarrassment or frustration in the future.

Emotional engagement has a similar intuitive appeal: It makes sense that an experience that triggers our emotions would have more impact than one that left us cold. Along these lines, the mechanism of emotion's influence may be reinforcement of the experience; when we experience something in emotional terms, it leaves a *deeper* imprint.[21] An emotional experience of jury service, however, might have countervailing effects, and if we had more precise measures of jurors' emotional responses, we could explore those in depth. As it is, we can further investigate jurors' positive versus negative emotional reactions, but an insufficient number of jurors gave open-ended descriptions of their emotions to permit detailed analysis of the paths from specific emotions (e.g., disgust versus delight) to future behavior. This is particularly important because we imagine that emotion can both stimulate engagement and prompt withdrawal from public life, depending on the nature of the emotion and how jurors process it. Again, such refined analysis is beyond the reach of our measurement tools, but we can at least foreground this challenge at the outset.

Juror assessment of the deliberation and verdict could stimulate future civic engagement, as discussed in the Municipal test-drive and earlier chapters. It bears mention, though, that when working with the larger King County sample, we *do not* have detailed juror recollections of their deliberation—only general assessments of overall deliberation, verdict, and the importance of the jury's role in the trial. Though abstract compared to the more detailed Seattle Municipal Court measures, the deliberation/verdict assessment scale should still distinguish between those jurors whose experience was too ordinary or unremarkable to spark or reinforce future public engagement versus those truly inspired by the quality and importance of their deliberation at the courthouse.

The final jury measures we consider are the judge's parting words and the post-jury service discussion of the trial with friends and family. As to the first of these, we created a simple contrast between those jurors who remembered the judge offering praise or affirmation versus those who recalled no closing comments from their judge.[22] This contrast excluded many jurors who recalled the variety of other responses shown in Table 6.1, but it set up a clear clash between the majority (54 percent) reporting no memorable feedback from the judge and the rest hearing "thank you" or being praised. This allowed testing the impact of the most common kind of judicial comment.[23] Consistent with the earlier discussion of positive reinforcement, we expect that jurors receiving praise from their judges will be more likely to seek out future public engagement in search of similarly "soft" rewards.

Finally, talking about jury service after the fact represents an effort to bridge the courthouse experience with the rest of one's life. Regardless of whether one's experience was triumphant or tragic, this conversational behavior could strengthen preexisting cognitive connections between being a juror and being a democratic citizen more generally. Rather than treating jury duty as an isolated, almost private responsibility performed exclusively while "on duty," these conversations increase the likelihood that jurors *remain jurors in spirit* after leaving the courthouse. Still wearing their jury duty badges after leaving the courthouse, these jurors become more likely than their peers to maintain a heightened sense of responsibility to continue their public service—in other ways—after being dismissed by the judge.

Different Effects for Different Groups

In each of the aforementioned ways, variations in the experience of being an empanelled juror could account for shifts in post-service civic and political participation, but these are all broad generalizations. Recall from chapter 3 that jury service affected voting only for one subgroup of the larger jury pool—those persons with a history of infrequent voting who served on criminal trials. Both prior voting history and the type of trial played a "moderating role"—that is, they influenced the effect of jury service on voting.

This chapter considers those same moderating variables, but thanks to the survey data at hand, we can also consider a range of other possible moderators. It turns out that the type of trial, jurors' past voting history, and many other variables moderate the impact of jury service. We will review each moderating variable later, when they are necessary to show the full complexity of specific findings.

Engagement Pathways Found (and Lost)

Table 6.2 reveals the general associations between the key facets of the jurors' service experience and changes in their civic and political behavior. Reading the overall set of effects, it is clear that (*a*) there are a preponderance of links between the jury service measures and (*b*) the effect sizes are all small (all *pr* < .10)—roughly equivalent to that of the voting effect in chapter 3.

Looking at the different political and civic behaviors, the most frequent links are to increased public talk—the informal conversations people have about community and political affairs. Every measured aspect of the jury experience (except whether jurors received praise from their judge and jurors' assessments of deliberation/verdict) contributes to increased public conversation post-service.

Deliberation/verdict assessments had *no* significant partial correlations overall. Though subsequent analyses showed deliberation satisfaction

Table 6.2. Partial correlations between subjective jury experience measures and changes in civic and political engagement measures, controlling for demographic and political variables

	Change in civic/political behavior					
Jury experience	TV news	Non-TV public affairs media	Public talk	Political action	Local community groups	Min. *df*
Overall satisfaction	.01	.06**	.08**	.05*	< .01	907
Personal treatment	.04*	.03	.09***	−.01	−.02	907
Cognitive engagement	.09***	.06**	.06**	−.01	.02	896
Comprehension of trial	−.06**	−.03	.09***	.03	.01	895
Felt emotion	.04	−.01	.07**	.06**	.06**	892
Assessment of delib./verdict	−.01	.01	.02	.01	−.02	898
Appreciation from judge	.05	.08**	−.04	.06*	−.01	570
Talk about service	.04	.01	.08***	−.01	.09***	907

Note: * *p* < .10, ** *p* < .05, *** *p* < .01. Behavior change reflects a partial correlation between jury experience measures and civic/political behavior measures in the long-term follow-up survey, after controlling for equivalent pre-service behavior measures. Partial correlations also control for ethnicity, sex, age, education, work status (retired, full-time, and other), years in residence, renting versus owning a home, political knowledge, political activity level of friends and family, strength of major party affiliation, and liberal-conservative self-identification.

effects for particular juror subgroups, this finding is particularly interesting, as it suggests that jury service can trigger civic/political behavior change regardless of how one assesses the particular deliberation/verdict in one's trial. This has to be reconciled with the chapter 5 finding from the Municipal court that increasing voting rates were related to deliberation quality. It may be that either the behavioral impact of deliberation quality requires the more precise measurement that was possible in the Seattle court, or it could be that deliberation quality links to voting but not other behaviors. We will revisit this issue in chapter 8, after reviewing the rest of the findings in this and the following chapter.

Finally, every significant correlation represents a *positive* association, as expected, with one exception. Those jurors who were *less* confident that they understood everything that was said during the trial registered an increase in their television news viewing relative to those jurors who followed the trial perfectly well. This corresponds to our earlier observation that a frustrating jury experience could trigger a self-improvement effect in precisely this way.

Next, we break down this general sample of sworn jurors to look at the more complex patterns that exist beneath these overall effects. To do so, we take the same split-sample approach first employed in chapter 3 to compare the jury-civic/political behavior link across a variety of different subgroups. We focus on the clearest patterns that emerge in relation to particular variable clusters, as well as interesting isolated findings that stand out from the rest. We begin with the same key splits from chapter 3—the type of trial and jurors' prior levels of electoral participation.

Juror Confusion during Civil versus Criminal Trials

The type of trial did not have a strong moderating effect on many of the jury-engagement relationships, but there was one notable exception. Those jurors who experienced confusion during their jury service had different outcomes depending on whether they participated in a civil versus a criminal trial. Recall that there was an overall negative relationship between trial comprehension and future TV news viewing, but it turns out this association was present only for criminal jurors ($pr = -.07$, $p = .03$), whereas the negative effect for civil jurors came for the general media use measure ($pr = -.14$, $p = .03$).

A simple comparison of mean before- and after-service average scores for TV viewing and general media use suggests that jurors who found criminal trials perplexing began watching more television news than before, surpassing the unchanging viewing rate of other jurors. Figure 6.1 shows this pattern, with those jurors experiencing confusion raising their media viewing rate (from 3.45 to 3.70 on a 1–5 scale), whereas those jurors who were less confused had only a modest gain (3.50 to 3.53), and those who understood the trial registered a trivial decrease in viewing rate (3.66 to 3.62). Following

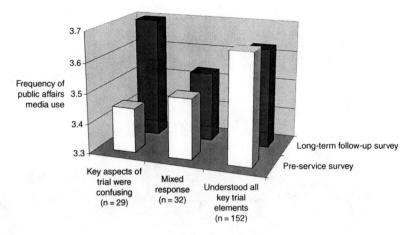

Figure 6.1 Changing frequency of public affairs media use among civil
jurors, broken down by jurors' comprehension of key trial elements

this same basic pattern, those jurors confused during *civil* trials similarly
raised their general interest in politics and radio/print public affairs con-
sumption relative to their peers.

This pattern of results helps to validate the choice to distinguish television news from other public affairs media in our measures of engagement.
Television has long been recognized as favoring coverage and investigation
of crime, especially violent crime,[24] and jurors may be changing their habits based on that fact. In both cases, we see the pattern of those jurors who
admit to a degree of confusion during the proceedings seeking out media to
address what they likely perceive as an important gap in their understanding of some aspect of criminal or civil law, enforcement, or justice. That the
type of trial signals the type of media they turn to suggests more about where
jurors choose to seek out information post-trial than any fundamental difference in the experience of these two types of trial.

Breaking the results down by trial type also revealed effects that the full-
sample analysis obscured. Relative to the criminal sample, the number of
civil jurors in our study was relatively small, and the overall patterns for
criminal jurors thereby drowned out behavioral impacts on civil jurors.
Specifically, there was a significant positive association between understanding civil trials and political action ($pr = .18$, $p = .008$) and community
group participation ($pr = .13$, $p = .049$). In both of these cases, however,
the pattern showed that juror confusion at civil trials *pushed down* public
engagement, as Figure 6.2 shows in the case of political action.

This constitutes the first (but not last) instance where it appears the jury
experience can dampen civic engagement. Though such effects are the
exception, once we have reviewed the full set of results, we will revisit them
to better understand them as a whole. At this point, it suffices to stress that

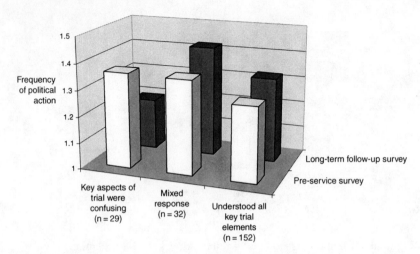

Figure 6.2 Changing frequency of political action, broken down by jurors' comprehension of key trial elements

the purpose of the present study was to develop a more complete description and explanation of the jury service-public engagement link. By looking at a wider range of behaviors than merely voting and by taking into account the many facets of jury service, we can discover details such as these, which underscore the sheer variety of experiences jurors have and how those variations lead to different civic outcomes.

Infrequent Voters and the Deliberative Challenge

To further compare these results with the original National Jury Sample in chapter 3, we also split these results by jurors' prior voting histories. Because the King County residents in our sample voted more frequently than the national average, the same split between those voting less than half the time and more frequent voters produced unbalanced subsamples, with roughly one-third (35 percent) being counted as relatively infrequent voters.[25] This split produced three related findings that underscore the importance of this distinction. First, only for frequent voters did public affairs media use rise in response to jurors' experience of trials that were cognitively engaging ($pr = .08$, $p = .03$) and satisfying overall ($pr = .10$, $p = .009$). For infrequent voters, the comparable effects were at or near zero. Second, political action rose *only for infrequent voters* in relation to cognitive engagement ($pr = .14$, $p = .02$) and jurors' assessment of deliberation/verdict ($pr = .13$, $p = .03$), with the frequent voters showing nonsignificant negative associations for these same variables. Third, infrequent voters *decreased* their involvement in community groups the more positive their assessment of the deliberation/verdict ($pr = -.14$, $p = .02$) and overall satisfaction ($pr = -.13$, $p = .03$).

Putting these pieces together, an engaging, rewarding jury experience appeared to spur frequent voters, who are already politically active,
to become more attentive to public affairs media, perhaps thereby further
advancing the political knowledge they can draw on when voting. At the
same time, infrequent voters appeared to be spurred by an intense and important deliberative experience to step into the political arena while decreas-
ing their involvement in non-political local groups. The latter result may
reflect a simple time-trade-off between the two activities, or it may represent a politicization of the previously disengaged jurors, who become drawn
into political action—voting, protesting, campaigning—and away from less
political public activities.

The presentation of two additional results clarifies this unexpected pattern of results. The jurors in our sample split into roughly three educational
groups—those who never graduated from college, those who have a college
degree, and those who have undertaken graduate study. Only the first of these
groups shows a decline in community group involvement in response to a
positive assessment of deliberation/verdict ($pr = -.15$, $p = .009$), with the other
educational groups having a near-zero partial correlation. By contrast, it was
those with the most formal education who started watching more public affairs
media if their deliberation/verdict was more satisfying ($pr = .16$, $p = .002$).

Looking across both the habitual voting and educational splits, one other
jury experience variable shows a strikingly similar pattern. For the less active
voters, hearing praise from the judge at the end of the trial was a harbinger of
community group *disengagement* ($pr = -.17$, $p = .03$), and the same association appeared for jurors without a college degree ($pr = -.14$, $p = .02$).

What could account for this pattern? Why would those most important
and satisfying deliberations and those that warrant heartfelt thanks from a
judge prompt a withdrawal from community group activity? Though we do
not have a direct measure thereof, one plausible explanation is that these
particular trials were among the most trying. It turns out that judges are more
likely to give thanks the longer the trial ($r = .19$), with praise typically coming after trials that extend over a week (6.4 days on average), versus only 4.4
days for those trials where jurors do not recall any such farewell. It might
well be that these trials leave less educated and engaged jurors with the
sense that working in groups is incredibly demanding. To these jurors, turning to private or mass political action might seem an attractive alternative.

This interpretation squares with an earlier study on the effects of participating in the National Issues Forums. Adult literacy students who participated in face-to-face discussions of national and international policy
issues through this program reported lower levels of group efficacy than did
nonparticipants ($r = -.18$).[26] In other words, forum deliberation made those
participants—all lacking even moderate formal English education—more
skeptical about the effectiveness of group-based political decision making
and action. When this result was discussed with adult literacy educators
using the Forums program, they offered this post-hoc explanation: For many

adult learners, these forums were the first experience of political group discussion, and group deliberation seems extremely difficult until one gets more practice with it. In the same way, less politically and educationally experienced jurors serving on particularly challenging trials may come away motivated to become engaged but disinclined to work in small and diverse community groups analogous to their jury.

The Mix of Jury Verdicts

If particularly demanding deliberations might have differentially influenced jurors, it is certainly likely that the nature of the jury verdict itself could have an impact on the jury's link to civic and political engagement. For this analysis, we split jurors who reached verdicts into three groups—29 percent who joined in a not guilty verdict (or found for the defendant in a civil case), 62 percent who reached a guilty verdict (or found for the plaintiff), and 9 percent who served on a jury that reached a *mixed* verdict—one with victories and defeats for both sides.[27]

There was only one respect in which jury verdict, per se, influenced civic engagement. Whether contrasting not guilty/defendant against guilty/plaintiff or making it a three-point scale with mixed verdicts in the middle, those juries finding guilt (or for the plaintiff) became more politically active relative to their acquitting peers ($pr = .09$, $p = .015$).[28] Inspection of the means showed that this was largely due to guilty verdicts spurring future action, along with not guilty verdicts presaging a slight decrease. More interestingly, Figure 6.3 shows that the largest increase in political activity after jury

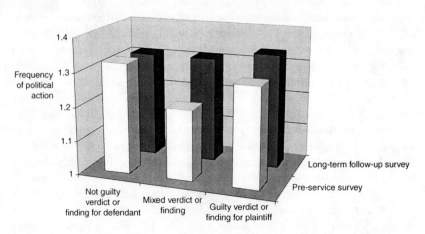

Figure 6.3 Changing frequency of political action, broken down by jurors' verdict

service came for those few jurors who reached mixed verdicts—a group too small to shape the overall guilty versus not guilty result.

Just as seemingly challenging deliberations generated complex civic/ political engagement effects, mixed-verdict juries also appear to have been in a special situation. Recall that in chapters 3 and 4, we found that the number of charges against a defendant increased the impact of jury service on voting. The best explanation that fit the data was simply that these extra charges complicated the deliberative task. The multiple charges did not amount to more *serious* charges, as we had initially suspected, but they did give jurors a more complex set of questions to resolve. Multiple charges also meant that jurors could negotiate compromises or arrive at morenuanced decisions through their deliberations.[29]

Advancing this argument further, the mixed verdict juries are precisely this kind of jury—one that has the opportunity to give a more complex lesson in deliberation. Though mixed-verdict jurors make up only a small segment of the total jury population, they could account for a significant portion of the overall effects initially shown in Table 6.2. Comparing the effects of the jury experience variables for this small subsample against the other verdict categories showed considerable differences, with the overall pattern being very clear: For those jurors reaching mixed verdicts, the quality of their experience was of tremendous importance.

As Table 6.3 shows, the size of the experience effects for mixed-verdict jurors is considerably larger as compared to the others discussed thus far. Inspecting these more closely, the general pattern was for jurors with less riveting and satisfying jury experiences to reduce their civic/political engagement slightly and for those with more engrossing and rewarding experiences to increase their engagement substantially. The clearest exception to that general pattern was the effect of discussing the jury experience after its conclusion: Those with the fewest trial-related conversations watched as much public affairs television as before, but those who discussed their jury service more frequently tended to tune out such media more often than they had in the past.

Looking at the many significant effects in this subsample, one pair that stands out is that mixed-verdict jurors appear to have become more engaged in local community life when they had emotional reactions and came away satisfied with their deliberation, verdict, and their important role as jurors. These jurors appear to have worked through both complex issues and, perhaps, their emotions. The emotional content from this subsample of jurors appears to resemble the general mix of emotions described in chapter 5, though there may be more emphasis on more powerful emotions and the arduousness of the deliberative task.

For instance, one juror who drove across the Lake Washington Bridge each day from Bellevue for a civil trial said that she "had empathy for both the defendant and the plaintiff and "had to consciously turn off this emotion when listening to evidence and deliberating." A young juror who served on

Table 6.3. Partial correlations between subjective jury experience measures and changes in civic and political engagement measures for mixed-verdict jurors, controlling for demographic and political variables

Jury experience	Change in civic/political behavior					
	TV news	Non-TV public affairs media	Public talk	Political action	Local community groups	Min. df
Overall satisfaction	−.03	.18	.09	−.01	.08	50
Personal treatment	−.01	.25**	.23*	−.09	.15	50
Cognitive engagement	−.12	.27**	.02	−.11	.16	50
Comprehension of trial	.15	.17	.17	−.12	.08	50
Felt emotion	−.08	.34***	.12	.14	.23*	50
Assessment of delib./ verdict	−.11	−.05	.33***	.06	.25**	50
Appreciation from judge	.26	.60***	−.14	−.09	.16	18
Talk about service	−.24**	−.18	.11	.03	.14	50

Note: * $p < .10$, ** $p < .05$, *** $p < .01$. Behavior change reflects a partial correlation between jury experience measures and civic/political behavior measures in the long-term follow-up survey, after controlling for equivalent pre-service behavior measures. Partial correlations also control for ethnicity, sex, age, education, work status (retired, full-time, and other), years in residence, renting versus owning a home, political knowledge, political activity level of friends and family, strength of major party affiliation, and liberal-conservative self-identification.

another civil case in the same courtroom wrote, "I felt that our responsibilities as jurors were significant, but I enjoyed hearing the discussion and different perspectives in the jury room. After the verdict was given, I considered the possibility that we could have been wrong, even though we tried our best."

Those mixed-verdict juries that had these kinds of engaging and rewarding experiences not only became more engaged in community groups but they also experienced similar boosts in their rate of public talk and public affairs media use. In sum, these data suggest that the distinctive task of challenging multi-issue deliberation on juries may have exceptional power as a stimulus of civic and political engagement.

Outside the Full-Time Workforce

As the foregoing example has shown, some of the most striking moderator effects become apparent when looking at smaller subsamples of jurors. After all, the largest groups of jurors already dominate the overall results, whereas the unique effects within these smaller groups can become obscured in the general figures. This is certainly the case in relation to the final moderator discussed herein—jurors' "work status." Two-thirds of jurors worked full time, and the general experience of that largest group shows up in Table 6.2. Three additional subgroups of jurors, however, had some noteworthy and distinctive results, and we consider their experience before closing this chapter.

After full-time employees, the second largest group of jurors was retirees, and they came to jury service with a different perspective. They arrived at the courthouse more eager to be sworn onto a jury, and though they had their own set of responsibilities and commitments, jury service did not take them away from a regular job. For retirees, the thank you and praise from the judge played a relatively critical role in spurring television news viewing ($pr = .25$, $p = .01$), public talk ($pr = .15$, $p = .085$), and political action ($pr = .30$, $p = .003$). In addition, post-trial conversations were a key for this group increasing its public talk ($pr = .23$, $p = .004$) and community group involvement ($pr = .24$, $p = .004$). Comparisons of means show that these all represent substantial increases in political/civic engagement for those jurors who received thanks and talked about their trial experience. The lone exception was the effect for television news: Those jurors who did *not* receive appreciation from their judge subsequently decreased their news viewing, whereas the viewing habits of those who got a pat on the back remained unchanged.[30]

Temporary and part-time workers made up the third largest bloc of jurors. Like the full-time workers, these jurors typically took time off from their regular jobs to serve on a jury. Demographically, they were quite similar in terms of ethnicity, age, education, and home ownership. Though a substantially larger percentage were women (71 percent versus 49 percent of full-time workers), jurors' sex did not prove an important moderator variable in its own right. Table 6.4 shows that for these jurors, the key to the jury service experience was whether it engaged their brains and their hearts. Not only are the partial correlations consistent across the full range of civic/political behaviors, but closer inspection of means shows a more subtle consistency. In each case, temporary/part-time workers who come to jury service will, by the end of the study period, *decrease their engagement unless they have a cognitively and emotionally riveting jury experience.* In other words, a stimulating jury experience does not promote engagement for these jurors; rather, it forestalls a decline.

The final subgroup considered here provides a stark contrast to the temporary/part-time workers. Ninety-seven percent of those who came to jury service in King County/Seattle while currently identifying themselves as homemakers were also female, though they differed only slightly on average from full-time workers in all other respects.[31] Whereas intellectual and emotional stimulation kept temp-workers from falling into civic decline, a satisfying deliberation and verdict spurred homemakers into action, at least in regard to watching television news ($pr = .50$, $p = .001$), general public affairs media ($pr = .29$, $p = .022$), and public talk ($pr = .39$, $p = .003$). As has been seen before, however, those same conditions actually promoted a *decline* in community group engagement ($pr = .28$, $p = .013$). Homemakers who had an

Table 6.4. Partial correlations between subjective jury experience measures and changes in civic and political engagement measures for temporary/part-time employees, controlling for demographic and political variables

Jury experience measure	TV news	Non-TV public affairs media	Public talk	Political action	Local community groups
Cog. engagement	.46***	.35***	.37***	.19*	.17*
Felt emotion	.07	.18*	.21**	.24**	.28**

Note: * $p < .10$, ** $p < .05$, *** $p < .01$. Minimum $df = 63$. Behavior change reflects a partial correlation between jury experience measures and civic/political behavior measures in the long-term follow-up survey, after controlling for equivalent pre-service behavior measures. Partial correlations also control for ethnicity, age, education, work status (retired, full-time, and other), years in residence, renting versus owning a home, political knowledge, political activity level of friends and family, strength of major party affiliation, and liberal-conservative self-identification.

especially satisfying and important deliberation became likely to withdraw from local group activities, but those with less remarkable deliberations remained unchanged in this regard.

Complex Changes in Civic Engagement

The significance of these varied findings becomes clearer when we pull back from the details to see the larger relationships between jury service and civic and political engagement. These results parallel those presented in previous chapters regarding voting in the general direction and size of the behavioral effect of jury service. Engaging and satisfying jury experiences tended to produce small positive changes in news media use, public conversation, strategic political action, and community group participation. The clearest link was from positive jury service experience to increased participation in informal conversations about community and political affairs. This may reflect the fact that conversations were the least taxing of the behaviors measured. Thus, the modest civic boost given by jury service most readily surfaces in the form of increased civic conversation frequency, the activity least constrained by the financial and temporal limitations of one's daily life.

With regard to jurors' detailed assessments of deliberation in the Seattle Municipal Court in particular, only post-service community group engagement had anything approaching a significant relationship with deliberation. This contrasted with chapter 5's finding of high-quality deliberation promoting voting. Instead, we found that increasing one's participation in local groups may stem more directly from *personally* engaging in that deliberation during jury service. This difference should not be overwrought, given the smaller sample in the municipal subsample, but it could mean that voting-in-deliberation translates to voting-in-elections, whereas *actively participating* in deliberation translates to *actively participating* in other groups. In retrospect, these close behavioral matches make perfect sense.

Behind these modest overall relationships lie stronger or more complex ones for different groups of jurors and different kinds of trials. Satisfaction with deliberation and verdict had a *large* positive effect on homemakers' attention to television news, and it also had a substantial impact on their use of general public affairs media and their political conversations.

For retired persons serving on juries, post-trial experiences were as important as anything else. Recall from the beginning of this chapter that the majority of jurors recalled their judge saying something memorable to them—usually a form of thanks or appreciation for their hard work, especially when enduring the most challenging trials. Within the subsample of retired jurors, praise from the judge played a positive role in promoting television news viewing, public conversation, and political action. Also, though 99 percent of jurors talked about their experience after the fact with friends, family, coworkers, and acquaintances, a subset did so more often than others. Post-trial conversations were the key for predicting which retirees became more conversational about community and political issues and more engaged in community group life.

A relatively rewarding and engaging jury service experience did not *always* yield a net positive change in behavior, however. Recalling the experience of temporary/part-time workers who served on juries, this group actually withdrew from public life *unless* they found their trial to be stimulating. In other words, an engaging jury experience forestalled a decline for these individuals. Similarly, those retired jurors who *did not* receive post-trial praise from their judge subsequently decreased their rate of television news viewing.

More rare but notable was the *negative* relationship between jury service and participation in community groups for two subsets of jurors— homemakers and infrequent voters. In both cases, the more important that jurors found their trial and the more satisfying their deliberation and verdict, the more likely they were to withdraw from local group activities. Interpreted in light of previous research with adult basic literacy students, this result may show that the most compelling deliberations can also make less engaged and politically connected citizens wary of exposing themselves to such difficult group processes in the future. Another negative result was more of a boomerang effect than a decline: Those jurors who were *less* confident that they understood their trial subsequently *increased* their television news viewing relative to those jurors who followed the trial perfectly well.

This discussion also returns us to the grouping variables first introduced in chapter 3—voter frequency and trial type. In general, the civil versus criminal contrast did not, in and of itself, explain considerable variation in jurors' experience or the educational impact of juries. One noteworthy exception was that juror confusion at civil trials sparked non-televised public affairs media use, whereas criminal jurors who struggled to follow their cases turned instead to television news, perhaps because of its relatively strong emphasis on violent crime.

Though every analysis controlled for jurors' pre-service behavior, it was revealing to further differentiate infrequent from frequent voters again. After all, voting frequency likely speaks to a kind of responsible civic habit distinct from the other kinds of engagement. This is analogous to political theorist Shelly Burtt's distinction between the "compulsion of duty" to vote and likewise fulfill civic obligations, versus the "education of the passions" and desires to take further action in public life.[32]

With this in mind, an engaging, rewarding jury experience tended to spur frequent voters, already *compelled* to act, to become even more attentive to public affairs media, perhaps augmenting their already considerable political experience. Infrequent voters, by contrast, responded to the quality of their deliberative experience; though it moved them away from community group participation, as mentioned earlier, it moved them toward political action—voting, protesting, campaigning, and even nonpartisan/political groups.

Finally, the experience of jurors with mixed verdicts sheds more light on the finding first reported in chapter 3, wherein the jury-voting effect became stronger the more charges the criminal defendant faced. Comparing the different verdict categories from the trials in our database, the largest increase in political activity after jury service came for those few jurors who reached mixed verdicts—split between plaintiff and defendant or guilt and innocence. Moreover, mixed verdict jurors increased their civic and political engagement after jury service most clearly when they had experienced strong emotional reactions and came away satisfied with their deliberation, verdict, and their important role as a jury. It appears that the challenge of weighing multiple questions or charges comes in the potential for more challenging deliberations, owing to the need to choose among many different verdicts or judgments before finishing the jury's work.

These findings validate and extend the civic educational model of jury service far beyond voting, though they add considerable complexity to the generally positive associations between the jury experience and civic and political engagement. Before we close the books on these data, however, we must augment these behavioral results with an investigation of how jury service influences how jurors view public life. After all, the model of democratic citizenship in chapter 2 stressed not merely behavior but also beliefs. Chapter 7 now applies the same jury experience variables introduced in this chapter to investigate the relationship between a juror's time at the courthouse and shifting civic and political perceptions. By the end of the next chapter, we should not only know whether jury service shapes both actions and attitudes, but also whether those attitudes shape the jury experience itself and the extent to which short-term attitude changes presage long-term changes in civic and political behavior.

Chapter 7

Civic Attitude Adjustment

Given the range of findings presented thus far, it is fair to wonder why no prior research had investigated the role jury service plays in shaping American civic and political life. In the course of our project, we discovered that at least one scholar had conducted precisely such a study. From 1989 to 1990, Paula Consolini, who was then a University of California-Berkeley doctoral student, visited San Francisco area courthouses with much the same purpose as ourselves. Our study to this point has focused on changing jurors' post-service behaviors, but Consolini focused on how service could change jurors' *attitudes*. She hoped to learn whether jurors change how they think about courts, democratic institutions, and themselves.[1]

Looking at twenty-six nonviolent criminal trials held principally in municipal and superior courts, Consolini conducted in-depth interviews and gathered pre- and post-service surveys from 126 sworn jurors and alternates, plus 159 prospective jurors who were not empanelled. She found that almost half (45 percent) of the jurors reported learning new factual information about the legal process. Consolini concluded that sworn jurors, "especially those serving for the first time, seemed to develop some greater depth of understanding and appreciation of the due process principles which they applied during their service." As one juror explained to her, the service experience showed "how the principles fit the logic of the process." With further interviews, Consolini found that most trial jurors and even some of those who did not become empanelled "reported greater depth of appreciation of general procedural rights like the right to an attorney and the presumption of innocence."[2]

It is encouraging that jurors gained more and deeper knowledge of the legal system as a result of their service. That particular benefit seems a straightforward matter of learning the very content and concepts that make up the trial and deliberative process itself. Consolini had tried to look farther—to see if jury service also increased jurors' appreciation of the jury system and the courts. In the end, she found that "trial jurors' evaluations of the jury system and court fairness improved significantly (by about twenty percentage points) as a result of their service."[3] Paralleling the findings presented in chapter 6, juror treatment by the court and the judge figured into these changes, as jurors who developed "respect" for their judge shifted their attitudes toward juries and the judicial system more than their counterparts did.

The most remote effect Consolini examined was whether jury service could bolster individuals' sense of political self-confidence.[4] It was at this point that the small sample size of the doctoral study limited its conclusions. Time and again, Consolini found patterns of results in the direction she expected, but they rarely reached statistical significance. When she inspected subsamples, statistical power dropped further still. For instance, the thirty-eight women serving on juries for the first time during Consolini's study increased their sense of political self-confidence considerably: 45 percent felt "efficacious" before serving, but 58 percent felt that way afterward. Similar results show that various jurors appeared to become more community-oriented and inclined toward public engagement.

All that was needed to establish the validity of these suggestive findings was a larger sample of empanelled jurors. Equipped with ten times the number of sworn jurors completing pre- and post-service attitude surveys, we now have such a survey. In this chapter, we explore the more challenging questions Consolini posed about the degree to which jury service changes not simply juror knowledge of the law and the legal process but also deeper attitudes toward juries, judges, public institutions, and themselves as community members and democratic citizens.

Measuring Attitudes

Looking for attitude changes, we make many of the same analytic choices as in chapter 6, but there are important differences in our approach. First, civic and political attitudes are, by definition, subject to sudden change in a way that behavioral habits are not. Our studies of electoral participation in earlier chapters required looking at voting rates over the course of years because differences in behavioral patterns can only be found with enough time points to see the patterns. Similarly, most of the behavioral survey questions in chapter 6 included the phrase, "In the past six months...." We compared responses between the pre-service and the long-term follow-up survey because only with that gap of time was it possible to see behavioral change.[5]

At least theoretically, attitudes can change quickly. Many models of public opinion emphasize the stability of general beliefs and predispositions, and over time, those underlying commitments can even create relatively fixed issue-specific attitudes.[6] Nonetheless, civic and political attitudes are matters of belief, and beliefs are subject to change through experience and persuasion.[7] Though past research leads us to expect considerable stability in such attitudes, there is evidence that attitudes such as political self-confidence can shift in response to changing circumstances and new experiences.[8] To capture the dynamic character of such beliefs, every wave of our jury survey—including the one conducted immediately after jury service—includes the same set of attitude measures.

The general survey sample for this research was the same as in chapters 4 through 6, with a few exceptions. For some of these analyses we, like Consolini, looked at both sworn jurors and those members of the jury pools who were not empanelled on a jury. In one analysis, we even look at prospective jurors' *pre*-service attitudes, which were inadvertently shaped by the erratic timing of jury orientation. For another section, we also followed Consolini in setting up a comparison group of King County voters who were *not* summoned for jury duty.

The particular civic and political attitudes we measured in this study are the very same ones introduced in chapter 2.[9] We used standard survey items from the National Election Study and General Social Survey to measure political self-confidence (a.k.a. political/internal efficacy) and political faith (a.k.a. external efficacy or perceived system responsiveness). To complement these political attitudes, we also measured jurors' civic faith (trust in fellow citizens to be responsible and engaged in public life) and civic pride (one's sense of personal civic responsibility). In addition, we looked at jurors' confidence in different public institutions, asking jurors to agree or disagree with statements that "the criminal jury system is the fairest way to determine guilt or innocence of a person" and "the civil jury system is a good way to settle many civil lawsuits." To see how far-reaching the attitudinal impact of juries might be, we also asked our survey respondents to rate "the average quality of the decisions" made by "the jury system," "state and local judges," the U.S. Supreme Court, and, for good measure, the U.S. Congress. (See Appendix Section 7 for details on these measures.)

Orienting (and Influencing) Jurors

An initial test of the malleability of these attitudes came to us unexpectedly during the course of our study.[10] As in other state and local jurisdictions, the jurors in our study all received a quick and basic orientation to jury service. During the period of our study, King County administrators treated the jurors-in-training to a videotape featuring Raymond Burr (of *Perry Mason* fame), who reminded jurors that "one of the most important services we perform in Washington state usually isn't followed by a standing ovation or a bouquet of roses." Thus, he welcomed them to jury duty—"an unappreciated, yet vitally important element of our democracy."[11]

Like their peers in other counties, the King County staff carried out the jury orientation routine exactly, day-in and day-out. Court administrators permitted us to distribute questionnaires to prospective jurors immediately after their orientation; however, there were many days when courtroom logistics made that impossible. Sometimes court officials would set aside a room of jurors, delay their orientation, and ask us to administer the questionnaire early. Other times, latecomers would miss the initial orientation, complete the survey, then get a makeup-orientation afterward.

In effect, an unintended natural experiment took place in which a random subset of prospective jurors took their initial survey *before* receiving their orientation. This enabled us to systematically compare the attitudes of prospective jurors who had just received an orientation versus those who had not. Limiting our analysis exclusively to those prospectives reporting to the King County Courthouse and the Kent Regional Justice Center, this yielded a sample size of 4,837 respondents.

It seemed unlikely that a mere orientation to jury service could change a person's sense of political self-confidence, but might it influence their attitudes toward *the jury itself*? We wanted to know if the mere orientation to serve could boost prospective jurors' trust in judges and the court system. Past research on workforce training would suggest that these effects are possible. It may seem a stretch to draw on such studies to understand *jury* orientation, but we believed new employee orientation is a more apt analogy than one might at first guess. After all, prospective jurors really *are* new employees of the court. Their new jobs are typically brief and poorly compensated, but they are jobs nonetheless.

The King County court's orientation has many of the hallmarks of a successful job orientation program. By celebrating the constitutional role and history of the jury, the court aims to build pride in an organization, and a sense of tradition can have considerable impact.[12] The King County orientation also addressed juror expectations, the court's function and purpose, and the responsibilities of both parties—features that are essential for establishing mutual trust between employer and employee.[13]

One interesting difference between jurors and most new employees, however, is that a substantial minority of the jurors who answer the court's summons are, in essence, being "re-hired." Some will be reporting to jury service for the second, third, or fourth time, and others may have even served on a jury during their last stint at the courthouse. Given this fact, we expected that the clearest effect of jury orientation would be on those prospective jurors who appeared at the court as a juror for the first time.[14]

Table 7.1 shows that jury orientation can, indeed, influence prospective jurors' attitudes toward the jury system and courts. Though, as we expected, a quick orientation does not shift one's broader civic and political attitudes,

Table 7.1.   Partial correlations of jury orientation with political and civic attitudes, broken down by prior service and controlling for demographic and political variables

Attitude	Never reported before	Reported but not served	Served before
Political self-confidence	.03	.02	< .01
Political faith	.02	.06	.05
Civic pride	.03	−.04	−.05
Civic faith	.01	−.03	−.02
Trust in jury system	.08**	.02	.05
Trust in courts/Congress	.02	−.01	.07*
Confidence in Congress	.01	< .01	.03
Confidence in U.S. Supreme Court	.03	< .01	.06*
Confidence in state/local judges	.01	−.03	.07**
Eagerness to serve on a jury	.05	−.02	.03
Willing to serve in the future+	.03	.03	−.02
Minimum *df*	767	447	537

Note: * $p < .10$, ** $p < .05$, *** $p < .01$.

+ This survey item read, "I would report to jury duty if asked to do so in the future."

Attitude change reflects a partial correlation between jury experience measures and civic/political attitude measures in the long-term follow-up survey, after controlling for equivalent pre-service attitude measures. Partial correlations also control for ethnicity, sex, age, education, work status (retired, full-time, and other), years in residence, renting versus owning a home, political knowledge, political activity level of friends and family, strength of major party affiliation, and liberal-conservative self-identification, as well as for the courthouse in which jurors served.

it does increase trust in the wisdom of the jury system, though only for new jurors. Those who have reported before—and, no doubt, been through a comparable orientation—experience no shift in their general assessments of juries. Veteran jurors, however, are the only group to gain a greater sense of trust in government after orientation. When this scale is broken down into its separate items, it is apparent that this boost is in their confidence in courts and judges.

One possible explanation for the latter result is the fact that those potential jurors who have previously served on juries have already established a general understanding—and positive view—of the jury service experience based on their past experiences. A quick comparison of means shows that those newcomers and veterans who filled out the survey before being oriented differed in precisely this way.[15] Watching the video for the second, third, or fourth time allows these individuals to focus more on the relationship between juries and judges within the legal system, a connection that may be more difficult to grasp for first-time jurors.

Subjective Service Experience and Attitude Change

This examination of jury orientation was really a warm-up for the real test—the impact of the *entire* jury service experience over a longer period of time. The orientation study, after all, looked at very short-term attitude changes—ones that may have faded over time. Moreover, given the range of juror experiences reported earlier, it is entirely plausible that the service experience produces more mixed results. These will likely vary depending on the juror's particular experience.

Before looking at the different elements of jury service, however, we begin with the same broad approach used by Consolini in her study of Bay Area courts. Thus, Table 7.2 compares the short- and long-term attitude changes

Table 7.2. Partial correlations contrasting unused jurors against dismissed and sworn jurors to assess short- and long-term political and civic attitude change, broken down by prior service and controlling for demographic and political variables

Jury experience	Jurors dismissed in *voir dire* (vs. unused prospective jurors)		Sworn jurors (vs. unused prospective jurors)	
	Short-term change	Long-term change	Short-term change	Long-term change
Political self-confidence	.13***	.06*	.03	< .01
Political faith	.02	.04	.04*	.05**
Civic pride	−.01	.03	.03	.01
Civic faith	−.05*	.03	−.06**	.02
Americans always do their part	−.05*	.03	−.03	.03
Americans consider voting a duty	.01	<.01	−.05*	−.01
Most Americans will make sacrifices	−.06**	.03	−.03	.02
Trust in jury system	.01	.04	.05**	.09***
Trust in courts/Congress	.04	−.07**	.04**	<.01
Confidence in Congress	.01	−.05*	−.03	−.02
Confidence in U.S. Supreme Court	.02	−.05*	.02	−.03
Confidence in state/local judges	.07**	−.06**	.10***	.04*
Minimum *df*	829		1,392	

Note: One-tailed * $p < .10$, ** $p < .05$, *** $p < .01$. Attitude change reflects a partial correlation between jury experience measures and civic/political attitude measures in the long-term follow-up survey, after controlling for equivalent pre-service attitude measures. Partial correlations also control for ethnicity, sex, age, education, work status (retired, full-time, and other), years in residence, renting versus owning a home, political knowledge, political activity level of friends and family, strength of major party affiliation, and liberal-conservative self-identification, as well as for the courthouse in which jurors served (owing to uneven distribution of orientation timing across the two county courthouses).

experienced by two contrasted pairs of jurors: those who were summoned but never used versus those who were dismissed during *voir dire*, and the unused jurors contrasted with sworn jurors.

The first of these comparisons shows that by the conclusion of their jury service, those who had been dismissed became more politically self-confident and more confident in the quality of decisions made by their state and local judges, but they also lost a measure of faith in their fellow citizens, wondering whether their peers would "always do their part" and be willing to "make sacrifices" (in a general sense). In the long term, the boost in political self-confidence remained, but these jurors had actually reversed course regarding public institutions—becoming more skeptical of not only judges but even the U.S. Supreme Court and Congress.

The second comparison contrasts sworn jurors with those who were never used in a courtroom, and the short-term changes included an increase in political faith, trust in the jury system, and trust in courts and Congress. Just as for dismissed jurors, the empanelled ones also experienced a short-term loss of civic faith—this time in their fellow Americans' understanding of voting as "a duty." As for the dismissed jurors, this civic skepticism faded over the long term, but the increases in political faith and trust in judges and juries remained—with the latter effect even increasing (albeit not significantly) in size. When these results were broken down by prior jury experience, as Consolini had done, there were minor and inconsistent differences among the subgroups.[16]

Having gone through these general results, we now return to the approach developed in chapter 6, whereby we examine the link between the variations in jurors' experiences and their changes after jury service. To begin this analysis, we looked at sworn jurors' short- and long-term attitude changes. Table 7.3 shows a clear general pattern of short-term attitude change: Each of the different metrics by which we assessed the jury experience shows a significant and positive relationship with changes in one or more juror attitudes. Moreover, Table 7.4 shows that most of these associations remained in place when we surveyed jurors several months later, though the size of effects had dampened somewhat by that point. Consistent with the general findings of Consolini's doctoral research, the strongest effects in both the short and long term are for confidence in juries and state and local judges.

There were two clear exceptions to these patterns. Though emotional experience was related to many behavioral changes in chapter 6, these tables show that it had little attitudinal impact (only registering one marginally significant correlation in Table 7.4). The other anomaly was that trial comprehension had the lone *negative* short-term partial correlation: Understanding trials was associated with a decline in both civic faith and confidence in the U.S. Congress, and the second of these negative effects persisted even through the long-term follow-up survey.

Table 7.3. Partial correlations between subjective jury experience measures and *short-term* changes in civic and political attitudes, controlling for demographic and political variables

Jury experience	Political self-confidence	Political faith	Civic pride	Civic faith	Confidence in jury system	Overall confidence in courts/Congress	Specific Confidence Item		
							U.S. Congress	U.S. Supreme Court	State/local judges
Overall satisfaction	.03	.10***	.06**	.06**	.29***	.14***	.09***	.07**	.17***
Personal treatment	.06**	.05*	.03	.06**	.23***	.16***	.08***	.14***	.19***
Cognitive engagement	.01	.08***	.04	.08***	.18***	.12***	.05*	.10***	.15***
Comprehension of trial	.10***	.05*	.06**	-.05**	.03	-.01	-.05*	.02	.01
Felt emotion	.03	-.01	.01	<.01	<.01	.02	.04	<.01	<.01
Assess. delib./verdict	.04*	.05*	.01	.10***	.25***	.11***	.10***	.05*	.11***
Appreciation from judge	.07**	.03	.06*	.03	.09**	.04	-.05	.04	.12***
Talk about service	.06**	<.01	.03	-.02	.04	.06**	.03	.04	.07**

Note: $* p < .10$, $** p < .05$, $*** p < .01$. Minimum $df = 577$ for Judge thank you, minimum $df = 905$ for all other analyses. Attitude change reflects a partial correlation between jury experience measures and civic/political attitude measures in the long-term follow-up survey, after controlling for equivalent pre-service attitude measures. Partial correlations also control for ethnicity, sex, age, education, work status (retired, full-time, and other), years in residence, renting versus owning a home, political knowledge, political activity level of friends and family, strength of major party affiliation, and liberal-conservative self-identification.

Table 7.4. Partial correlations between subjective jury experience measures and *long-term* changes in civic and political attitudes, controlling for demographic and political variables

Jury experience	Political self-confidence	Political faith	Civic pride	Civic faith	Confidence in jury system	Overall confidence in courts/Congress	Specific Confidence Item		
							U.S. Congress	U.S. Supreme Court	State/local judges
Overall satisfaction	.01	.12***	.09***	.04*	.22***	.08***	.04	.04	.12***
Personal treatment	.06**	.05*	<.01	.04	.18***	.07**	.04	.06**	.08***
Cognitive engagement	.02	.06**	.08**	.03	.13***	.05*	.07**	.03	.05*
Comprehension of trial	.13***	.03	.04*	.04	.06**	-.05*	-.05*	-.04	-.02
Felt emotion	<.01	.01	<.01	.01	.02	-.02	-.02	-.06**	.01
Assess. delib./verdict	-.01	.04	.03	.07**	.14***	.06**	.08**	.04	.04*
Appreciation from judge	-.02	.05	.01	.05	.08**	<.01	-.04	-.03	.09**
Talk about service	.02	.02	<.01	.01	.06**	.04	.04*	<.01	.03

Note: * $p < .10$, ** $p < .05$, *** $p < .01$. Minimum $df = 570$ for Judge thank you, minimum $df = 898$ for all other analyses. Attitude change reflects a partial correlation between jury experience measures and civic/political attitude measures in the long-term follow-t:p survey, after controlling for equivalent pre-service attitude measures. Partial correlations also control for ethnicity, sex, age, education, work status (retired, full-time, and other), years in residence, renting versus owning a home, political knowledge, political activity level of friends and family, strength of major party affiliation, and liberal-conservative self-identification.

Not only was jury service shaping post-service attitudes, but so were pre-service attitudes coloring how jurors experienced—or, at least, *subjectively* experienced—jury duty. Figure 7.1, for example, shows the relationship between jurors' overall satisfaction with their service and their degree of faith in the political system before and shortly after serving. This figure shows that those least satisfied with their service experienced a slight drop in such faith, those moderately satisfied rose slightly on this measure, and those jurors most satisfied with their time of service had a more substantial increase in political faith. More striking than the relationship between service satisfaction and faith, however, is the considerable relationship between jurors' *pre-service* political faith and their assessment of jury duty: Those with the greatest faith also reported the greatest satisfaction. Later in this chapter, we will return to this issue, for understanding the complex interplay of attitudes and service requires taking this into account more fully.

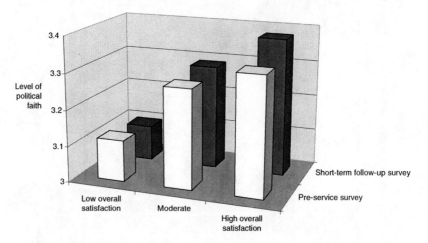

Figure 7.1 Short-term changes in political faith, broken down by jurors' comprehension of key trial elements

Trial Type and Political Profile

The key moderators of these relationships were similar to those featured in previous chapters, and we begin by considering the type of trial and voters' political profiles—their past voting history, their political knowledge, and their liberal-conservative self-identifications. Each of these trial and voter characteristics influenced the power and direction of effect that trial comprehension and satisfaction with deliberation/verdict had on jurors' various political and civic attitudes.

Starting with trial type and voter knowledge, the degree to which juror comprehension influenced long-term changes in attitudes depended on how politically sophisticated jurors were and which type of trial they attended. Those jurors who lacked basic political knowledge and became confused during trials experienced a drop in political self-confidence ($pr = .21$, $p < .001$)—an effect not found among more politically sophisticated jurors ($pr = .03$, $p = .268$). In addition, politically sophisticated jurors in civil trials gained political faith ($pr = .30$, $p = .002$) and civic pride ($pr = .22$, $p = .02$) to the extent that they understood the trial clearly. Politically knowledgeable jurors serving on civil trials also experienced stronger effects of deliberation and verdict satisfaction on civic pride ($pr = .23$, $p = .017$), trust in juries ($pr = .35$, $p = .001$), and general confidence in government ($pr = .21$, $p = .003$). In each contrasting case—with either low-sophistication voters and/or in criminal trials—the comparable effects were negligible or at least significantly lower.

Voter history by itself, and sometimes in conjunction with the type of trial, also influenced the effect of deliberation/verdict satisfaction on long-term juror attitude changes. First, infrequent voters serving on civil trials in which they favorably rated their deliberation/verdict experienced a net gain in political self-confidence ($pr = .29$, $p = .045$), whereas their frequent-voting counterparts experienced a nonsignificant effect in the opposite direction ($pr = -.12$, $p = .111$). For other attitudes, however, it was the *frequent* voters for whom deliberative satisfaction predicted modest gains in political faith ($pr = .12$, $p = .003$), civic faith ($pr = .12$, $p = .003$), trust in juries ($pr = .20$, $p < .001$), and general trust in government ($pr = .11$, $p = .004$). In each case, infrequent voters showed a near-zero or nonsignificant negative relationship between the same variables.

Political ideology also provided an interesting set of associations. For liberals and conservatives alike, satisfaction with deliberation/verdict bore no relationship to political faith and confidence in government. For political moderates, however, this aspect of the jury experience was a crucial predictor of change in political faith ($pr = .22$, $p = .001$) and confidence in the judgmental competence of government, especially state and local judges ($pr = .15$, $p = .022$). Moderates experiencing more deliberative satisfaction also had relatively large gains in their trust in juries ($pr = .25$, $p < .001$), though a similar effect was also present for liberal jurors ($pr = .15$, $p < .001$).

Taken together, these results suggest that the attitudinal effects of trial comprehension and deliberation were interlaced with jurors' political backgrounds. Civil trials were a particularly important setting for attitude development among the more politically sophisticated voters—but also for developing political confidence in less sophisticated voters. Meanwhile, frequent voters and moderates developed considerable faith in public institutions when they experienced a deliberation and verdict they found to be highly satisfying.

Work Status

As in chapter 6, the most striking differences among juror subgroups came from our crude measure of jurors' "work status." Once again, the preponderance of jurors were full-time employees, but those with different life circumstances had as distinct connections between jury experience and attitude change as they did with their shifting civic/political behaviors in chapter 6. Table 7.5 highlights the key experiential variables on which retirees, temporary/part-time employees, and homemakers differed markedly from full-time workers (and from each other, for that matter).

For retirees, the thank you from the judge and overall satisfaction were keys to shoring up these jurors' political faith and civic pride. Satisfying deliberation prevented what were otherwise declines in confidence in the jury system and government generally. For political self-confidence, deliberative assessment had one of the negative associations seen occasionally in chapter 6, such that a highly satisfying deliberation/verdict could actually shake a retiree's self-esteem ($pr = -.23$, $p = .004$).

For temporary/part-time employees, cognitive engagement and emotional experience were the keys to forestalling declines in various forms of civic/political engagement in chapter 6. These variables play the same role for attitude change, with the exception that a particularly engaging trial can actually yield a substantial *increase* in political self-confidence for this group of jurors, as shown in Figure 7.2. In addition, jurors from this group were more inclined to increase—or maintain—their previous levels of political faith, confidence in government, and civic pride if they *did not* understand the trial clearly. Perhaps, confused jurors who worked part-time were impressed by the performance of officials and peers in these trials, though it may be

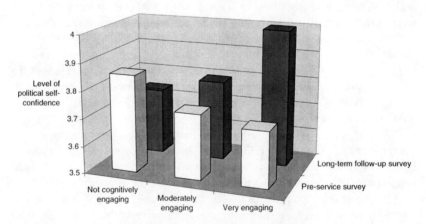

Figure 7.2 Long-term changes in temporary/part-time workers' political self-confidence, broken down by their cognitive engagement in the trial as jurors

Table 7.5. Selected partial correlations between long-term political attitude changes and subjective jury experience, broken down by work status and controlling for demographic and political variables

Work status / Jury experience	Political self-confidence	Political faith	Civic identity	Civic faith	Confidence in jury system	Overall confidence in courts/Congress
Retired						
Overall satisfaction	-.04	.21***	.24***	.18**	.14*	.15**
Assess. delib./verdict	-.23***	-.02	-.03	.07	.20**	.20***
Judge thank you (yes = 1)	.01	.23**	.26***	.07	.09	.13
Temp./Part-Time						
Cog. engagement	.57***	-.08	.19*	.02	.21**	.03
Comprehension of trial	-.07	-.21*	-.24**	-.02	-.11	-.17*
Felt emotion (yes = 1)	.24**	.30***	.26**	.23**	-.04	-.09
Homemaker						
Personal treatment	-.26**	-.11	.03	.37***	.32**	.34***
Assess. delib./verdict	.18	.11	.03	.23*	.41***	.31**

Note: * $p < .10$, ** $p < .05$, *** $p < .01$. Minimum $df = 82$ for retired, $df = 69$ for temporary/part-time, and $df = 47$ for homemakers. Attitude change reflects a partial correlation between jury experience measures and civic/political attitude measures in the long-term follow-up survey, after controlling for equivalent pre-service attitude measures. Partial correlations also control for ethnicity, age, education, work status (retired, full-time, and other), years in residence, renting versus owning a home, political knowledge, political activity level of friends and family, strength of major party affiliation, and liberal-conservative self-identification.

that those temp workers who found the trial very straightforward saw themselves rising to or above the level of officials and peers in that regard.

Finally, recall that in chapter 6, homemakers' civic/political behavior rose in response to particularly satisfying deliberations and verdicts. Here, we saw a similar pattern with three civic attitudes—civic faith (pr = .23, p = .05) and confidence in juries (pr = .41, p = .001) and government generally (pr = .31, p = .02). In addition, particularly respectful treatment by court staff, attorneys, and jurors yielded similarly large associations for the same three attitudes. Rather than stimulating positive attitude change, however, rewarding deliberation tended instead to limit a decline in civic attitudes. One last divergent finding for homemakers was found for no other subgroup of jurors: Those who felt mistreated by the courts actually *increased* in their political self-confidence (pr = −.26, p = .037)—perhaps gaining a better measure of themselves under what they considered adverse circumstances.

Linking Attitudes, Deliberative Experience, and Political Behavior

All of the relationships between jury experience and attitude shifts are interesting, in and of themselves, but the complexity of these links becomes clearer when we return to the issue raised earlier—namely, the effect that civic and political attitudes have on how jurors describe their jury experiences. Table 7.6 shows the full extent of these relationships, and when looking at these correlations in relation to one another, there is some evidence that these differences reflect *perceptual cognitive* impacts. The weakest effects civic attitudes have on trial ratings are for whether the judge thanked jurors—something surely done at the judge's discretion, not under the influence of the particular civic attitudes of the jurors. In addition, civic attitudes did not predict whether the trial sparked jurors' emotions, but it was associated with jurors' levels of *cognitive* engagement.

Theorizing the Reciprocal Attitude–Experience Link

Backing up from the particular context of this study, small group research has long recognized the role of attitudes and traits in shaping group life, and decades of studies show the influence such variables have on how people experience groups. The particular attitudes in our study, however, have not been connected to group discussion, though deliberation has been previously theorized to promote the very attitudes it tends to reinforce.[17]

Although political discussion is not synonymous with deliberation, two strands of research have demonstrated the potential for reciprocal relationships between citizens' political discussion and their civic attitudes and participation. The research of communication scholar Joseph Cappella and his colleagues' on the Electronic Dialogue Project demonstrates that

Table 7.6. Partial correlations between pre-service civic and political attitudes and subjective jury experience, controlling for demographic and political variables

							Specific Confidence Item		
Jury experience	Political self-confidence	Political faith	Civic identity	Civic faith	Confidence in jury system	Overall confidence in courts/ Congress	U.S. Congress	U.S. Supreme Court	State/local judges
Overall satisfaction	.05*	.12***	.10***	.08***	.14***	.11***	.04	.09***	.13***
Personal treatment	.02	.10***	.15***	.04*	.19***	.14***	.05*	.13***	.19***
Cog. engagement	.01	.12***	.08***	.06**	.16***	.12***	.08**	.11***	.10***
Comprehension of trial	.17***	.07**	.13***	.01	.08**	.02	<.01	<.01	.04*
Felt emotion (yes = 1)	−.03	.02	<.01	<.01	.03	−.03	−.03	−.01	−.01
Assess. delib./ verdict	−.03	.13***	.01	.08***	.07**	.05*	.05*	.04*	.02
Judge thank you (yes = 1)	−.01	.03	.05*	−.03	.02	.03	.01	.02	.05
Talk about service	−.02	.02	.08***	−.03	.03	.04	<.01	.06**	.03

Note: * $p < .10$, ** $p < .05$, *** $p < .01$. Minimum $df = 578$ for Judge thank you, minimum $df = 976$ for all other analyses. Attitude change reflects a partial correlation between jury experience measures and civic/political attitude measures in the long-term follow-up survey, after controlling for equivalent pre-service attitude measures. Partial correlations also control for ethnicity, sex, age, education, work status (retired, full-time, and other), years in residence, renting versus owning a home, political knowledge, political activity level of friends and family, strength of major party affiliation, and liberal-conservative self-identification.

participating in online deliberative discussion groups can increase people's argument repertoire, political engagement, and community participation. Cappella argues that there is a "spiral between deliberative discussion and [argument repertoire], with each being a causal force in the other's growth at a later time."[18]

Similarly, work by political communication researcher Dhavan Shah and colleagues provides evidence that citizen discussion "plays a critical role in the relationship between information seeking via mass media and participation in civic life."[19] This body of work supports the notion of reciprocal effects between deliberation and civic attitudes by showing how participating in online political discussions influences and is influenced by citizens' civic engagement.

Outside the particular domains of deliberation and discussion, it has been shown that the relationship between political self-confidence and participation in public life is a reciprocal one, with feelings of efficacy triggering behavior.[20] More generally, the civic attitudes we examine are more common among those persons who are the most politically active. These attitudes are often presumed necessary to support an active democratic public.[21] Thus, it is not altogether surprising that attitudes shape our experience of jury deliberation in much the same way that deliberation, in turn, reinforces civic identity, political self-confidence, and public trust.

In sum, we have reason to expect that political and civic attitudes are not merely influenced by one's jury experience but that the same attitudes shape the experience itself. Moreover, we can expect that the changes in juror attitudes that occur shortly after jury service might ultimately lead to long-term changes in political and community engagement. We will look more closely at each of these connections, and we begin by examining the interplay of attitudes and jury experience at the Seattle Municipal Courthouse.

Attitudes and Participation in Jury Deliberation

At this juncture, we return to the smaller subsample of municipal jurors because it permits us to look at jurors' more detailed descriptions of their jury participation. Specifically, this sample lets us see the extent to which pre-service attitudes shape individual jury participation in deliberation, as well as the extent to which that participation feeds back into those same attitudes.

To look at these connections, we conducted a *path analysis*. When done longitudinally, this approach literally draws paths between variables measured at different times to determine which of the hypothesized relationships among variables actually appear in the data. Using this approach, Figure 7.3 shows a simplified version of the path analysis to see the interplay of political self-confidence and participation in juries.[22] The result is that pre-service attitude shapes jury participation—with the more confident jurors speaking up more often. By contrast, the frequency with which jurors speak up does

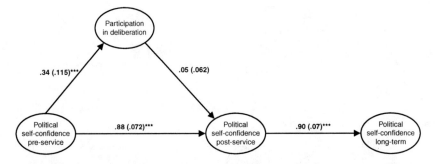

Note: *** p <.01. Numbers shown are standardized coefficients (and standard errors).

Figure 7.3 Interplay of political-self-confidence and participation in jury deliberation at the Seattle Municipal Courthouse

not, in turn, reinforce their post-service sense of political efficacy. (The high correlations along the bottom of the figure show the extent of political self-confidence's stability over time.)

The Interplay of Attitudes and Deliberation Perceptions

This result augments our earlier observations of how attitudes shape jurors' deliberative experience by showing that at least one attitude—political self-confidence—also shapes the extent to which jurors actively participate in deliberation. To go further, we set aside the municipal juries to look at the interplay of attitudes and deliberative experience for King County jurors who deliberated. We again deployed a path analysis, this time looking at the interplay of four variables: civic/political attitudes, perceived treatment by other jurors, whether the jurors reached a verdict, and overall satisfaction with deliberation/verdict.[23]

Figure 7.4 shows the most complex path model produced by this analysis. Using trust in juries as the focal attitude measure, the figure shows that pre-service trust in juries is associated with reporting more respectful treatment by fellow jurors. That, in turn, is associated with reaching a verdict—and with overall satisfaction with the deliberation/verdict. Finally, juror treatment and satisfaction *both* have significant effects on post-service trust in the jury system.

We ran the same analyses for each of the other civic/political attitude measures, and Figure 7.5 shows the results. Civic pride, political faith, and confidence in government all have positive associations with juror treatment, but only political faith has a direct effect on jurors' perceptions of their deliberation. Fellow juror treatment has a reciprocal relationship with two attitudes—civic faith and confidence in government,[24] whereas deliberation/verdict satisfaction has no significant direct paths back to attitudes.

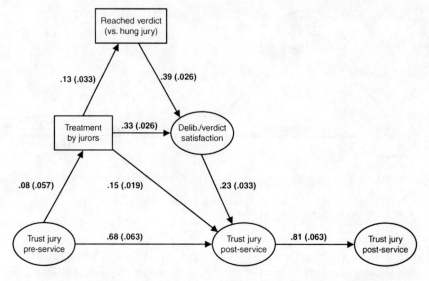

Note: All paths are statistically significant. Numbers shown are standardized coefficients (and standard errors).

Figure 7.4 Interplay of trust in the jury system, jury deliberation experience, and whether a jury reached verdict for deliberating jurors in King County

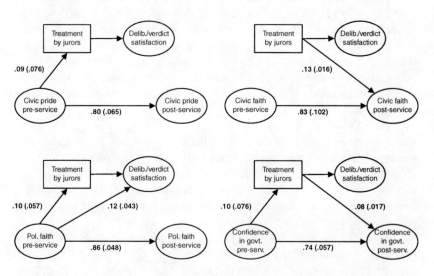

Note: All paths are statistically significant. Numbers shown are standardized coefficients (and standard errors).

Figure 7.5 Interplay of various civic/political attitudes and jury deliberation experience for deliberating jurors in King County

Underlying Reciprocal Connections between
Attitudes and Behavior

We now take one step farther down the causal path to consider the reciprocal relationships not between attitudes and jury participation but between
the attitudes and the civic and political behaviors discussed in chapter 6.
Previous research in psychology has shown ample evidence of attitudes
shaping behavior and vice versa.[25] In the political context, for example, citizens gather information and experiences—direct and vicarious—that help
them develop a set of beliefs about the political system and their place in it
(e.g., "I have important civic duties," or "Politics is a game I'm ill-equipped
to play"). These beliefs combine to generate civic and political intentions,
which in turn drive us toward (or turn us away from) various forms of public
engagement.[26]

At the same time, social psychologist Daryl Bem's self-perception theory
demonstrates that often the causal direction reverses itself, with attitudes
flowing from our behaviors. Bem's first postulate holds that "individuals
come to 'know' their own attitudes ... partially by inferring them from observations of their own overt behavior and/or the circumstances in which this
behavior occurs." Second, Bem points out that when our "internal cues,"
such as generalized civic/political attitudes, "are weak, ambiguous, or unin-
terpretable, the individual is functionally in the same position as an outside observer ... who must necessarily rely upon those same external cues
to infer the individual's inner states."[27] In the case of civic engagement, for
instance, citizens may ask themselves, "What must my attitude toward participation be if I am willing to participate in these ways, under these circumstances?" Thus, positive or negative experiences with jury deliberation or
other civic and political activities might translate into feelings of personal
political efficacy (or inefficacy), as well as trust in (or wariness toward) public institutions.

To investigate these links, we worked with political communication scholar
Mike Xenos to see the direction of relationship between the attitudes and
behaviors measured in our data. Briefly setting aside all aspects of jury service, just consider the initial and final survey waves we collected at the King
County and Seattle courthouses. These two surveys both measured the full
range of behaviors and attitudes described in this chapter and in chapter 6.
Taken together, these initial and final surveys provide a longitudinal dataset
capable of seeing which influences which—attitude or behavior? Using path
analysis, we can see which behaviors at Time 1 predict changes in attitudes by
Time 2, and vice versa.

Figure 7.6 shows the results of this analysis and our interpretation thereof.
(For simplicity's sake, we have set aside measures regarding confidence in
juries and government.) The broadest generalization one can draw is that,
indeed, attitudes and behaviors have a reciprocal relationship—with each
influencing the other in multiple respects. More precisely, beliefs about one's

competence in political and community arenas are important predictors of civic and political participation. Moreover, our public engagement experiences, including the most communicative aspects of public life (political conversation and media use), exert tangible force on the same attitudes that are also believed to predict their participation in the first place.

To interpret the mix of paths more precisely, Figure 7.6 groups behaviors (on the right-hand side of the diagram) into three theoretical categories—strategic politics, community engagement, and public affairs media use (sitting between the other two). On the left-hand side, attitudes pair up based on their internal versus external orientation. Internally-focused attitudes concern one's political self-confidence and civic pride—perceptions of *one's own* behavior and traits. By contrast, externally-oriented attitudes concern one's efficacy and civic pride; these constitute perceptions of *institutional and other people's* behavior. This grouping produces an elegant result: internal attitudes and community behaviors all generate positive

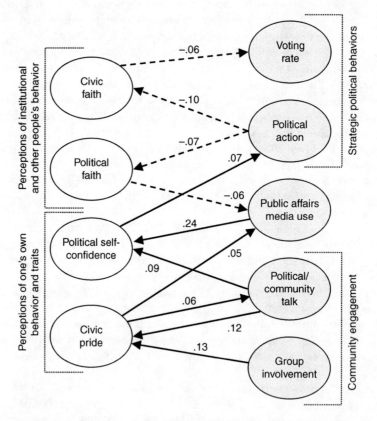

Note: All paths shown are statistically significant standardized coefficients.

Figure 7.6 Directional and reciprocal relationships between political and civic attitudes and behaviors

associations, but external and strategic political actions generate only negative associations.

The former paths fit with the general expectation of mutual reinforcement between civic/political behaviors and attitudes, but the other results
are more complicated. Strategic political engagement and media use appear
to depend on and reinforce a degree of *skepticism* about the public and its
institutions. Tracing the paths in Figure 7.6, the less faith one has in the
civic capacity of one's fellows, the more pressed one feels to get out and
vote; the less responsive (and responsible) one perceives institutions to be,
the more important one believes it is to stay informed about public affairs;
and the more one engages in politics, the more one comes to have doubts
about the responsibility and responsiveness of fellow citizens and institutions. The value of a modicum of public skepticism in democracy has been
noted by both political theorists and media scholars, and our findings suggest one way this relationship might manifest itself.[28]

Reshaping Attitudes through Jury Service to Change Behavior

The preceding discussion set aside the jury for a moment, but we can now
set it in the middle of at least a few of these causal pathways. Specifically,
because we have civic/political attitude measures taken shortly after jury
service, we can explore the possibility that the jury experience creates a
short-term attitude change that, in turn, generates longer-term changes in
civic behavior. We began our research with this premise in mind, and in this
final analysis, we test that initial assumption.

Given what we already know about jury service and civic/political attitudes and behavior, there were only a limited number of plausible complex
causal paths to investigate, and we have focused on a subset of variables
that have already demonstrated their interconnection. A three-wave path
analysis is complicated enough without the full complement of measures
included here. Moreover, only a few of the *potential* complex relationships
among attitudes, jury experience, and behavior actually occur when looked
at in this way. Were we to present each set of possible connections, we would
fill page after page with null results.

This is not to say that civic attitude change *never* mediated behavior
change in our data, and Figure 7.7 presents the most compelling of these
analyses. The figure focuses on King County/Seattle jurors' overall satisfaction with jury service and their ability to understand the full details of the
trial they witnessed. Key attitudes that shaped—or were shaped by—those
jury experiences included political self-confidence, political faith, and civic
pride. Finally, the behaviors linked to these attitudinal and experiential
variables were political action, public affairs media use, and public talk.[29]

The most straightforward results validate many of the earlier, partial findings, but the more novel result is that civic and political attitudes *do not*

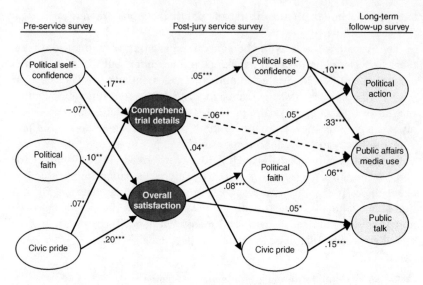

Note: * p < .10, ** p < .05, *** p < .01. Numbers shown are standardized coefficients.

Figure 7.7 Path analysis of the mediating role of attitudes in jury service's impact on political and civic behavior

completely mediate the relationship between jury experience and behavior. Trial comprehension influences each of the three behaviors through its effects on political self-confidence and civic pride, but it also has a direct *negative* effect on media use. Only political faith mediates the effects of overall trial satisfaction, which has direct impact on political action and political talk.

Assessing Changing Civic Beliefs in the National Context

This analysis of shifting civic attitudes ends in a place very different from where we expected to go. We have certainly validated the initial premise of Paula Consolini's doctoral dissertation, which began this chapter: When jurors had a satisfying, engaging service experience, many developed more positive attitudes toward not just juries and judges but also public institutions, fellow community members, and even themselves, as democratic citizens.

We did not anticipate, however, that jurors' short-term attitude changes would have only limited value as explanations for long-term behavior changes. A post-jury boost in one's political self-confidence, in particular, only goes so far in explaining the wide range of behavioral changes that result from jury service. Moreover, we found that one's civic and political faith have generally *negative* relationships with political behavior, such that a loss of faith might spur one to action and rising trust might nourish complacency. Thus, the mixed, limited, or even negative effects of jury service on these particular attitudes does not necessarily undermine the jury's power as a means of spurring civic engagement.

More fundamentally, the context of our study raised a question that we did not have adequate data to address, at least not to our satisfaction. As it happens, we conducted our study during a year in which the nation as a whole experienced substantial declines in some of the very same attitudes measured in our survey. For instance, the Gallup Poll found an 8 percent drop for public confidence in the criminal justice system and a 5 percent decline of confidence in the U.S. Supreme Court from May 2004 to May 2005. Confidence in Congress likewise dropped down 2 percent for independents (who already reviled it), 7 percent for Republicans, and 12 percent for Democrats, who make up a larger share of the King County—and especially Seattle—population.[30]

We had tried to prepare for this eventuality by collecting a comparison group consisting of a random sample of registered King County voters. We collected this mail survey in parallel with our jury sample, but we ended up with what we considered an unsatisfactory response rate of 20 percent and an undersized sample of respondents who completed both the initial and long-term follow-up surveys ($N = 205$).[31] In the end, we were not confident that this small sample was an apt comparison group; it skewed toward male, retired/unemployed, and highly educated—with almost half the sample having done graduate work. Even then, civic and political attitudes declined in this group over the course of the study.[32]

Their own methodological limitations not withstanding, previous studies on juror attitude change have consistently found that service improves attitudes toward jury service, the jury system generally, and/or the courts in which jurors serve.[33] Other research, including Consolini's dissertation, suggested positive attitude changes that reach farther—beyond the courthouse.[34] Thus, we have confidence that the positive effects we have found represent real net increases, for instance, in jurors' confidence in public institutions. What we remain uncertain about is whether jury service itself generated the declines in civic attitudes that we witnessed in this chapter and whether a rewarding experience limits such declines or represents a net civic boost, after taking into account the larger national trends, which we presume apply to some degree in King County.

One way of managing this challenge is to look again at the orientation effects and short-term attitude changes with this issue in mind. Given its narrow scope and brief duration, the juror orientation was only expected to affect attitudes toward juries and courts, and it did precisely that: For new jurors, it increased confidence in the jury system, and for returning jurors, it yielded a greater sense of trust in local/state judges and the U.S. Supreme Court. As expected, the direction of net change was positive in each case.

Even short-term attitude changes after jury service, however, were *not* all positive. The most relevant findings here were the comparisons of sworn jurors against those who showed up at the courthouse but never went through *voir dire*. Empanelled jurors, relative to their non-juror peers, experienced a short-term loss of faith in their fellow Americans' understanding of voting as "a duty." Their other significant attitude changes—confidence in institutions and civic faith—were all positive, and the lone negative correlation disappeared by the time of the long-term follow-up survey.

Now consider this long-term attitude decline: Relative to non-jurors, those jurors dismissed during *voir dire* had net drops in their confidence in public institutions by the time of the long-term survey—declines that *did not* appear in the short-term. Those declines could well reflect the national declines in public confidence that occurred during 2004, and their magnitude is relatively small even by comparison with the changes recorded in the Gallup Survey. While the population as a whole dropped 8 percent in its support for Congress, the dismissed jurors dropped just 4.3 percent.

We do not go so far as to suggest that this demonstrates a *net gain* in political faith, after correcting for the national change. After all, the Gallup survey does not synchronize perfectly with the time or sample frame of our own research, and it does not include the same measures. Nonetheless, this should caution one against interpreting net overall declines in civic attitudes in these data. The more robust findings, in our view, are those about the *relative* attitude changes among jurors depending on the juror's background and their trial experience, and we conclude this chapter by reviewing the main results from those analyses.

Revisiting the Variations in Juror Attitude Change

The civic attitude changes that occurred during and after leaving the King County courthouse clearly corresponded with jurors' subjective experience of jury duty. The general relationships for short- and long-term attitude changes (Tables 7.3 and 7.4) showed that *each and every* metric by which we assessed the jury experience had a significant and positive relationship with juror attitude change, and these changes faded only slightly over several months. The starkest difference from chapter 6 was that emotional experience played a relatively minor role in shaping jurors' attitudes, though it had been an important stimulus of behavior change.

The lone *negative* association paralleled the "boomerang" finding reported in chapter 6. In the short-term, better comprehension of the trial resulted in a *decline* in civic faith and confidence in the U.S. Congress, with the latter effect remaining significant in the long-term. Recall that confusion during trials could stimulate media use, perhaps out of a sense that one ought to learn more about the underlying causes of crime and the issues involved in civil disputes. Here, it is the jurors who find the trials at least somewhat challenging that may be, once again, humbled. This time, that humility could translate into the retention of faith in public officials and the complex problems they must manage, whereas the jurors who find the trials easy to follow doubt whether public officials merit even the modicum of deference they had previously offered them.

When the overall results were broken down by trial type and jurors' political backgrounds, civil trials were a particularly potent means of cultivating the civic beliefs of the more politically sophisticated, frequent voters—but also for developing the political self-confidence of less active and informed voters. Meanwhile, it was only frequent voters and moderates, as opposed to their respective counterparts, who developed considerable faith in public institutions when they had a satisfactory deliberation and jury verdict.

As was true for political behavior in chapter 6, work status proved the strongest background variable affecting civic attitude change. For retirees, the thanks from the judge and overall satisfaction were keys to limiting declines in political faith and civic pride, and a satisfying deliberative experience burnished confidence in the jury system and government generally. Paralleling the occasional association between deliberative satisfaction and *withdrawal* from community groups in chapter 6, a highly satisfying deliberation/verdict yielded a decline in retirees' political self-confidence. As before, we expect this effect involves the challenge that these trials present, and the decline in sense of personal efficacy may reflect the difficulty the jurors experienced working through the case, no matter how satisfactory the ultimate result may have been.

Temporary/part-time workers and homemakers also showed distinctive influence patterns. For temporary/part-time employees who served on juries, cognitive engagement and *emotional* experience were critical to forestalling declines in various civic attitudes, with the exception that an engrossing trial could *increase* these jurors' political self-confidence. Also, these jurors experienced the boomerang effect even more strongly: They often increased their level of political faith, confidence in government, and civic pride if they failed to entirely understand their trials. Finally, just as homemakers' civic engagement increased dramatically in response to satisfying jury deliberation and verdicts, the same strong, positive effect was present for civic faith, confidence in juries, and confidence in government generally.

These more narrow findings, along with the broader patterns of attitude change, go far beyond the straightforward civic boosterism of Tocqueville and others who have sung the praises of jury service. The overall pattern resonates with those positive portrayals of juries as a means of stimulating civic passions and convictions, but even the more refined results in this chapter have significance for how we think about the jury system, the jury service experience, and the administration of justice. We now turn to that subject in chapter 8, and we then draw out broader implications for democracy and deliberation in chapter 9.

Chapter 8

Securing the Jury

We began this book with an appreciation of a juror who was stranded on Boston's Southeast Expressway. Federal Judge William G. Young told that juror's story to a gathering of the Florida Bar Association in 2007 not to praise the jury but to forestall its burial. "The American jury system," he said, "is dying....It will never go entirely, but it is already marginalized....How is this possible, with our Constitution and every one of the 50 state constitutions guaranteeing the right to trial by jury? The general answer is that we do not care."[1]

The raw numbers support his view. Despite the popular perception of an ever-more litigious society, the total number of cases in federal and state courts has declined in recent decades. The proportion of cases that go to a jury trial, however, has declined even more rapidly. In federal courts, the percentage of criminal charges that end in jury verdicts dropped from 10.4 percent in 1988 to 4.3 percent in 2000, and the percentage of civil cases resolved by juries declined from 5.4 percent in 1962 to 1.5 percent in 2000.[2] In state courts, where the majority of juries become empanelled, the rate of decline is even steeper. In 1976, criminal juries resolved 3.4 percent of cases, but now they only account for 1.3 percent (35,664 cases). Over the same period, the rate at which civil juries accounted for case dispositions dropped from 1.8 percent to 0.6 percent (17,617 cases). Simply put, there are roughly one-third as many jury trials per year as there were in 1976.[3]

Judge Young's concern about the declining jury reflects anxiety about the independence of the judicial branch, the vitality of the constitution, and the rendering of justice for all citizens who might come before the court. Though there are signs of vitality in the jury,[4] many countries have scaled back or eliminated juries over the past century, and in the United States, recent legal reforms already have reduced the size and frequency of jury trials.[5] The plea-bargaining process has further reduced the deployment of criminal juries, and many critics suggest drastically reducing the use of civil juries or dispensing with them altogether.[6] The most radical reforms would greatly curtail the civil jury, in particular, because they fear that lay citizens cannot process complex evidence or reasonably assess punitive damages.[7]

In this chapter, we explore these arguments about the jury's role in the judicial branch—and in our larger political society. We consider a range of modern jury reforms and look at shifting public perceptions of the jury. Throughout, we offer a perspective informed by the preceding chapters, which have demonstrated the civic benefits of the jury. In this view, an ever-narrowing role for the jury—and diminished opportunities for jury service—may come at an unanticipated civic price.

Shifting the Debate on the American Jury

Few countries share the United States' commitment to trial by jury, and none relies on it to the same extent.[8] The American jury owes much of its good health to its establishment in the U.S. Constitution. The Sixth Amendment ensures that "in all criminal prosecutions, the accused shall enjoy the right to a speedy and public trial, by an impartial jury of the State and district where in the crime shall have been committed." The Seventh Amendment adds that "in Suits at common law, where the value in controversy shall exceed twenty dollars, the right of trial by jury shall be preserved, and no fact tried by a jury, shall be otherwise re-examined in any Court of the United States, than according to the rules of the common law."[9]

Even within the United States, where the Seventh Amendment enshrines the jury as a centerpiece of our legal system, a research note published in the *Harvard Law Review* observes that "concerns about jury competence preceded the founding of the United States and have troubled scholars and jurists throughout the history of the American judicial system."[10]

The jury—particularly the civil jury—has come under increasing scrutiny, as some critics suggest that the complexity of evidence and trials has increased over time, leaving lay juries ill-equipped to handle the challenging work assigned them. George Washington University law professor Dan Solove, for example, advocates abolishing lay juries and replacing them with professionals:

> We're in the 21st Century, and our legal system uses a method of adjudication that was invented in the Middle Ages. It's time for a more professional way of resolving legal disputes, one where the decision-makers are not a bunch of often-unwilling people plucked from the street, forced to upend their lives to resolve the disputes of others, and without the expertise to evaluate the facts and apply the law.[11]

Others critics have attacked specific roles that juries play in trials. Vanderbilt law professor W. Kip Viscusi, for instance, argues that "there is no evidence at all that juries can make punitive damage awards in a reliable and systematic manner." He has marshaled a wealth of mock-jury evidence to support such claims.[12]

The basic argument advanced by Viscusi, Solove, and others suggests that lay jurors are often incapable of serious and careful deliberation. In their view, a single expert judge (or small panel of judges) would be a more effective decision maker. This claim, however, overlooks the substantial literature, including the findings contained in our study, that underscore the seriousness of deliberation among groups of jurors. Notably, despite a real potential for faulty information processing and social pressure, lay juries generally engage in careful and elaborate deliberation.[13] As jury scholars Valerie Hans and Neil Vidmar observed in their classic work *Judging the Jury*, "The data from hundreds of studies of jury trials and jury simulations suggest that actual incompetence is a rare phenomenon."[14]

Indeed, this finding reflects a consistent theme related to research on the jury dating to a landmark study of jury trials held in Chicago in the 1950s. Five hundred judges completed questionnaires after 3,576 separate criminal trials, and in each case they reported how they would have ruled on the case had each been a bench trial. In 78 percent of the cases, the judge and jury would have reached the same verdict. For 19 percent of the cases, the judge would have found the acquitted defendant guilty, and in the remaining 3 percent, it was the reverse. In a comparable number of civil trials, the judges and jury again agreed on 78 percent of trials, and more recent research has produced comparable results.[15] Moreover, as one federal judge more recently admitted, "In the rare instances where I have thought the jury went astray, no celestial sign reveals that I was right and the jury was wrong."[16]

Critics point to examples of "runaway juries" that make awards based on irrational rage, rather than sober deliberation. But these cases—such as the famous lawsuit against McDonald's for making coffee too hot—are truly exceptional and often have sensible explanations beneath the surface.[17] Moreover, such sensational cases aside, the typical jury shows a commitment to real deliberation, listening to minority points of view, and taking their legal instructions seriously. As one participant in our study reflected, "I thought [the deliberative process] was really good. It was frustrating, because everyone had different ideas and felt very strongly about it. I think the process worked. I think everybody was very serious about it." When emotion came into play, it was sometimes simply a palpable feeling of obligation and responsibility *to deliberate carefully*, given the stakes for the defendant. As one team of jury researchers has concluded, an increasing body of "case studies and 'lab' or experimental studies, shows that rather than giving up when faced with voluminous evidence and conflicting expert opinions, juries take their fact-finding and decision-making responsibilities seriously."[18]

The democratic norms of jury service and deliberation, broadly understood by the general public and reinforced through jury orientation programs, provide jurors an opportunity to be heard even where the rules of a civil trial do not call for a unanimous verdict. In one civil trial we followed in chapter 3, for instance, a juror reported that the minority "did most of the talking." The juror recalled "a couple of times when it got heated and people were trying to talk over each other, but most of the time people raised their hands and the foreman said, 'So-and-so will be next.'" As this modest example illustrates, the jury presents ordinary citizens with the opportunity to exchange views and listen to one another, and in this way, the jury provides a critical safeguard against an overzealous prosecutor, an outmatched litigant, or a judge with strong preconceptions.

While the empirical debate on the vigilance and intelligence of juries continues, our own research adds another important dimension to the discussion. The jury must be recognized as more than one of many alternative means of rendering verdicts. Instead, it must also be recognized as a powerful means of civic education that reaches across all demographic and cultural divides. The jury teaches deliberation and inspires democratic engagement, and it has particularly powerful effects on the civic behaviors and attitudes of citizens who, short of jury service, might otherwise not be drawn into the public sphere. Thus, to replace juries with judges or to protect juries from challenging cases not only changes the rules of administering justice *but also limits the reach of the jury as a civic educational institution.* The net effect of our research in this regard is to move that claim from the status of conjecture to certainty.

The implications of our research, however, go much farther, and in this chapter, we explore in more detail what our findings mean for ongoing efforts to improve the performance of juries and the quality of the jury service experience. In so doing, we acknowledge the challenges facing juries and suggest appropriate responses to them, all of which fall well short of abolishing the jury altogether. We also discuss our research in relation to public perceptions and the popular reputation of the jury, as well as the relevance of our work for the adoption or expansion of juries outside the United States.

The Jury as Civic Outreach

Over the last thirty five years, U.S. courts and legislatures have made a concerted effort to ensure that all citizens have the opportunity to serve on a jury. The Supreme Court took a significant step in this direction in 1975 when it concluded in *Taylor v. Louisiana* (a case argued by Ruth Bader Ginsburg, who was later appointed to the Supreme Court) that a Louisiana law excluding women from jury service violated the Sixth Amendment commitment to a jury of a fair cross-section of the community. In its majority opinion, the Supreme Court explained that "community participation...is not only consistent with our democratic heritage but is also critical to public confidence in the fairness of the criminal justice system."[19] Over the succeeding twenty years, the Supreme Court addressed a series of other practices that limited participation in jury service—notably, the use of peremptory strikes on race or gender grounds—and consistently rejected such exclusionary tactics as unconstitutional.[20]

On the state level, a parallel effort has sought to end the practice of providing a wide ranging set of exemptions that permit professionals to avoid jury service. Such exemptions were often the product of political influence, whereby exemptions were traditionally "granted to every occupational group with sufficient legislative influence to obtain passage of an exemption statute."[21] In New York State, for example, *The New York Times* reported in 1996 that the list of exemptions had "grown absurdly, embracing not only surgeons, lawyers and police officers but optometrists, pharmacists, podiatrists, embalmers and people who fit artificial limbs."[22] In response, then-Chief Judge Judith S. Kaye led an effort to increase and improve public participation in jury service, ensuring that one million New Yorkers previously exempt from jury service would be involved in the system. Echoing Tocqueville and anticipating the findings of our study, *The New York Times* editorialized in favor of the change, suggesting that the commitment to wider participation in jury service "is good for the practice of democracy."[23]

Diversity and Deliberation

A traditional concern about juries, which the ending of professional exemptions has sought to address, is that they are largely composed of people with time on their hands and limited educational backgrounds. Given that some studies show many Americans lack basic knowledge about our legal system, one might presume that such widespread ignorance stands in the way of effective jury deliberation.[24] In addition to the already-cited research on jury deliberation generally, our data on jury deliberation in the Seattle Municipal Court show that jurors with low political knowledge or educational attainment can participate just as effectively in deliberation. Indeed, the quality of those jurors' deliberation did not hinge on those background characteristics. In other words, deliberation is an experience equally available to political novices and experts.[25]

An opposing concern is that juries, though diverse, end up disenfranchising the women and minorities who serve on them. In this view, juries cannot help but reproduce larger patterns of domination in society by privileging male voices and perspectives and discounting the perspectives of minority jurors. Numerous studies of mock juries over the years have found evidence of such effects, particularly a bias toward selecting white male forepersons (when not randomly assigned by the court). A more recent study suggests that crude sex bias may have given way to class-based status cues that give jurors a general impression of competence at deliberation.[26] This dovetails with a broader "difference critique," which emphasizes the danger of ostensibly objective and rational deliberation muting the voices of women and minorities.[27]

Comparing our results with the propositions drawn out of deliberative and difference theory, we find strong evidence to the contrary. Neither cultural nor status differentials appear to affect individuals' evaluations of their jury experience, as measured in terms of satisfaction with the deliberation, the verdict, treatment by other jurors, and overall service. Even when biological sex is compounded by other status differentials such as education, race, and work status, there was no clear pattern of difference in the subjective assessment of jury deliberation.[28]

Moreover, the civic educational benefits of jury service distributed themselves broadly. The behavioral and attitudinal changes jury service engendered did not vary noticeably between men and women, or along ethnic lines—though future research would do well to focus on a county with more ethnic diversity than King County, Washington. Moreover, it was homemakers—a mostly female group whose work status is often underappreciated—that showed some of the largest civic educational effects. Also, the jury service impact on voting that we began with in chapter 3 fell to those who were politically disengaged, which further suggests that ensuring a broad jury pool not only fulfills the Constitution's promise of equality but also helps the jury system spread civic impulses throughout the wider population.

Orienting Citizens to the Civic Purpose of Juries

Returning to Judge Kaye's crusade for jury reform, broadening the jury pool was, for her, only a first step in an ongoing effort to improve jury service. "I firmly believe," she has said, "that the work of jury reform is never finished. It requires ongoing attention not only to keep moving forward but also to guard against losing ground."[29]

Throughout her tenure as Chief Judge of New York's highest court, Kaye remained true to that credo and oversaw the preparation of a pamphlet for all potential jurors, underscoring the democratic benefits of jury service and highlighting the seriousness of the opportunity. This pamphlet prominently quotes Tocqueville at the beginning and is titled, appropriately enough, "Democracy in Action."[30] When the U.S. Postal Service released its Jury Duty stamp at the Manhattan State Supreme Court in 2007, Judge Kaye was on hand to celebrate "the important role of our citizenry in the delivery of justice. We rightly take pride in this uniquely American institution, which has been a great strength of our nation from its very beginnings" (Photo 8.1).

Such efforts to promote the civic value of jury service surely have some measurable impact, but the most important opportunity to frame the public's perception of jury duty comes when citizens arrive at a courthouse to begin their brief stint as jurors. Our analysis of jury orientation in chapter 7

Photo 8.1.   U.S. Postal Service stamp issued on September 12, 2007, to coincide with Juror Appreciation Day celebrations

suggests that the tremendous amount of work that many administrators put into organizing and carrying out jury orientation are not in vain. Moreover, we suggest that jury administrators approach the orientation period as more than an information-dissemination exercise. Orientation can be the best means available for *inspiring* jurors—not only to participate actively and take their job seriously but also to appreciate the unique civic educational opportunity that the jury provides.[31]

Many jury administration reforms have already done much to improve the typical juror's experience. Commenting on jury service in New York prior to putting her reform program into place, Judge Kaye recognized that "in the mind of the public, jury service was akin to tax audits and root canals—and they were right."[32] By contrast, courts now routinely invite jurors to serve on just one jury or for one or two days, whichever comes first, and this served to reduce jurors' uncertainty and anxiety about the process.

In recent years, jury administrators in many courthouses have made great strides to improve the jury service experience. For instance, they have streamlined procedures to assuage jurors' uncertainty and anxiety, and they now routinely schedule service deferments when necessary to fit within jurors' complex work and family schedules. Such accommodations may seem minor, but they serve to reinforce the idea that *jurors are public officials*, albeit poorly paid ones. Most courts now try to treat them with a level of respect befitting such an office, and this surely contributes to jurors' appreciation of the gravity of their role. Indirectly, these improvements in the jury experience probably have augmented its civic educational benefits.

Just as orientation can set the tone for jury service, so does the conclusion of jury service offer a special opportunity. Our research showed that for many jurors, the judge's parting words were very important. Most jurors remembered the praise and appreciation that judges offered, so judges should recognize that such gratitude does not come across as forgettable platitudes. Jurors serving on particularly difficult cases, or who were dismissed before getting to deliberate, also appreciated explanations from judges. More generally, court officials can remind jurors that it is normal—and probably healthy—to discuss the jury experience after leaving the court. Nearly all the King County jurors in our study talked about their service with family, friends, and others. Those who did so often got the greatest civic benefit from their period of service. Thus, it would serve the educational purposes of the jury for judges and jury administrators to not only thank jurors but also to encourage them to reflect on their experiences and talk about them with others.

Reforms that Improve and Empower the Jury

The most effective and appropriate jury reforms go even farther and aim to empower the jury as a deliberative body. Over much of the twentieth century, jurors were treated as potted plants during the trial itself, given little context or direction until after the trial ended, when they finally received their instructions. In the 1990s, however, a number of states began to experiment with strategies for empowering jurors. In Arizona, a nationally-renowned reform program implemented a number of changes, including allowing jurors to take notes, ask witnesses questions during the trial, and query the judge more directly during deliberations. Most controversially, the Arizona reform program included a rule that jurors be permitted to discuss issues arising in the trial before beginning their final deliberations (provided that they do not make any decisions about the case until all of the evidence is heard and the jury is given instructions on the law to apply). These innovations are encouraging to jury reformers. As one state judge put it, these new procedures help to overturn a system in which courts treated jurors "like

children" by way of "prohibiting note-taking, banning presubmission discussions, and barring questions to witnesses."[33]

Reform efforts like the ones undertaken in Arizona are still being evaluated and studied. The relevant scholarly literature, however, provides considerable support for expanding such initiatives. In the case of note-taking,
the evidence is clear that the reform makes sense. Jury researcher Valerie
Hans drew this conclusion from the juror note-taking studies:

> One can observe strong support for the reform among judges and jurors
> and no apparent negative effects. In some studies, note taking appears
> to enhance recall, evaluation, and more competent decision making,
> whereas other studies demonstrate no effects. There is some evidence
> that note taking may work best in conjunction with other jury aids, but
> that issue has not been extensively studied.[34]

As one judge who used the practice said, "I have been allowing juror note
taking for eight years and am a complete believer. I find it absurd that some
jurors are not allowed to take notes."[35] Studies of the practice echo that
impression, with one study finding a decided advantage in recalling information for those taking notes over those who did not.[36]

The case for allowing jurors to ask questions likewise is gaining broader
support. An early study that evaluated the practice in Wisconsin paved the
way for further experiments when it found that both judges and attorneys
believed that the jurors asked high quality questions and they did not dis-
turb the quality of the trial overall.[37] More recently, experiments with the
practice in New York State have underscored its considerable virtues. As
one judge, Erie County Supreme Court Justice Donna Siwek, explained:

> Permitting juror questions was an extremely positive experience for
> the court, the lawyers and the jurors. Despite their initial skepticism,
> the lawyers were pleasantly surprised at how smoothly the process
> worked and how insightful most of the questions were. The jurors
> universally appreciated the opportunity to ask a question that helped
> clarify or that was not covered on direct or cross. My initial concern
> that permitting questions would bog down the trial was completely
> allayed. Very often, when I read the submitted question with the attor-
> neys at side-bar, we all agreed, "Good question."[38]

Scholars have also come down on the side of this reform. Notably, Northwestern University law professor Shari Diamond's evaluation of the practice
in Arizona concluded that "Jurors not only use questions to clarify the testimony of witnesses and to fill in gaps, but also to assist in evaluating the
credibility of witnesses and the plausibility of accounts offered during trial
through a process of cross."[39]

Despite the support for allowing juror-initiated questions, some judges
and lawyers continue to be skeptical of the practice. The Minnesota Supreme
Court, for example, rejected the practice on the ground that it undermined
the role of jurors as neutral decision makers.[40] This decision, however, is

increasingly questionable in light of continuing scholarly research that demonstrates that jurors—like those in our study—take their charge very seriously and, rather than becoming advocates, "utilize questions to enhance their role as neutral fact finders."[41]

In the wake of an almost twenty-year effort to promote an active jury, there are important signs that it is beginning to shape a new consensus on how juries should function. Notably, in 2005, the American Bar Association endorsed a set of principles for jury trials, embracing a number of reforms designed to empower the jury.[42] In particular, that report recommended steps to promote increased juror understanding and active engagement during the trial, calling for permitting juror note taking, the use of "jury notebooks" (which could include relevant exhibits and other materials), juror-submitted questions, and an option to discuss issues in the trial before the case is formally submitted to the jury.

There is also increasing evidence that courts are adopting some of the reforms designed to promote an active jury. Reporting on a survey of a wide sample of judges, Valerie Hans found that the vast majority of jurors are permitted to engage in note taking. The use of juror-initiated questions, by contrast, is still relatively rare, as only around 15 percent of all trials studied allowed the practice.[43] In general, that practice is regulated by the presiding judge, although four states—Arizona, Colorado, Indiana, and Wyoming—specifically provide jurors with the opportunity to ask questions as a matter of law. Ten states specifically prohibit the practice.[44]

The most controversial innovation introduced in Arizona and the one that has yet to gain much traction is allowing jurors to discuss issues during the course of a trial. In addition to Arizona, both Colorado and Indiana permit this practice, but most states expressly forbid it. According to one survey, such discussions took place in only 2.2 percent of state civil jury cases and 1.3 percent of federal civil jury cases.[45]

As we noted in chapter 5, the jurors in our study generally did not wait until the close of evidence to begin the process of analyzing trial evidence and forming their opinions. Undoubtedly, early straw votes sometimes predicted the ultimate outcome, and some jurors were disappointed that they had no opportunity to discuss the issues with one another before that time. As one juror explained, he was "frustrated at not being able to discuss the process with other jurors." Another juror admitted to feeling "isolated" during the trial by the lack of discussion on the issues they were supposed to consider.

Although the practice of allowing pre-deliberation conversations remains rare, Arizona's support for the practice has enabled researchers to evaluate the practice in the case of actual Arizona civil jury trials. Their research concluded that both judges and juries viewed the practice very favorably, providing considerable support for this innovation.[46] Notably, eight in ten Arizona jurors studied appreciated the opportunity for pre-deliberation discussions; this sentiment was expressed by one juror who observed, "You have immediate questions all the time and it certainly answers them right now and you don't have to feel like you're alone."[47] Some jurors did voice concerns about such discussions encouraging prejudging, but that phenomenon is likely to happen in any case. Moreover, the studies did not find any evidence that the practice actually encouraged prejudgment, although about half of the lawyers and litigants unfamiliar with the practice were quite concerned with that possibility.[48]

Like the case of juror-initiated questions, courts are still uncomfortable with the practice of juror discussions before the close of evidence. Consider, for example, that a federal court of appeals overturned a verdict where jurors were allowed to discuss the issues among themselves before the close of trial. In so doing, it reinforced the prevailing sentiment that "we believe that the firmly-rooted prohibition against premature jury discussion is well-founded. An instruction that permits the jurors to discuss the evidence before conclusion of the case is erroneous."[49] By contrast, the judge who allowed the practice in that case anticipated the later research that would provide greater support for it:

> One of the jurors asked if they could discuss matters among themselves. This suggested to me that he was thinking, a trait that I believed should be encouraged. Had I said no, I would have been unable to explain why—because I could not then, nor can I now, think of any valid reason to preclude such discussion and a simple no would have left the jurors with the distinct feeling that the ways of the law are mysterious indeed....I firmly believe that jurors are more likely to do that which makes sense than to follow a command which is never explained because it is completely unexplainable.[50]

Another way of looking at this issue is to put it in the context of the generational shift that coincides with new communication technology. Younger jurors, accustomed to blogging, texting, and Twittering hourly, if not minute by minute, swim in a stream of near-constant social interaction—even in situations previously thought to be solitary, or at least quiet. Thus, we now have incidents of jurors texting from the jury box, conducting trial-related Internet research on their own, and blogging about their trial before it has concluded.[51] Courts will certainly strive to rein in such activity.[52] In our view, courts would be foolish to try to deny jurors' growing appetite for interaction. Instead, while stowing away jurors' mobile communication devices, courts should also gratify modern jurors' heightened social impulses by letting them ask questions during the trial, take notes while hearing evidence, and—at least during longer trials—engage in regularized face-to-face exchanges with fellow jurors before the attorneys' closing arguments.

Dealing with Legal Complexity

In embracing the virtues of an empowered jury, we remain mindful of the challenge juries face when confronted with especially complex criminal or, more often, civil trials. In addressing this issue, we must first emphasize that the majority of civil trials—particularly in state courts, where most jury trials take place—raise issues no more complex than the average criminal trial. Motor vehicle injury cases, for instance, have much in common with vehicular assault, just as a product liability suit might be no more complex than a criminal negligence case.

Complexity versus Technicality

We recognize that there are contexts where concerns about the jury's ability to process the relevant information, understand judges' instructions, and stay engaged during a long trial are legitimate. As jury scholar Neil Vidmar writes, "Over more than two decades, so many writings, both scholarly and journalistic, have been devoted to criticizing the institution of the civil jury that it becomes boring to recite the claims."[53] (We trust, of course, that such boredom does not impede the judgment of the jury's critics any more than courtroom tedium does for jurors themselves.)

With respect to particularly complex areas of the law, the U.S. Supreme Court has been sympathetic to this view. In the patent context, for example, the Court has ruled that, with respect to determining the basic question of what a patent claim means, the judge, and not the jury, should be the decision-maker.[54] In so doing, the Court concluded that judges are better suited to address such issues because their training better enables them to decide such issues correctly. Similarly, the Supreme Court has instructed judges to ensure a level of expertise on the part of any testifying experts so as to protect jurors from the challenge of sorting through "junk science."[55]

The most drastic response to the complexity of certain classes of civil cases is to remove juries altogether or substitute professionally trained ones for these specialized areas of law.[56] We are not categorically opposed to removing certain classes of issues from the purview of civil juries, particularly when cases are so obscure and rare that their removal denies only a handful of jurors of the civic benefits of jury service. The findings of our research suggest, however, that mundane technical complexity might dull engagement in some cases; deliberative complexity, by contrast, more often *enhances* jurors' experience.

Consider, for example, that in chapter 3, the hung jury was at least as likely to boost jurors post-service voting rates as were juries reaching verdicts. The transformative experience of jury service even on hung juries further underscores the importance of engaging citizens. The hung jury is not a case of successful citizen participation as a group; it may be the most personally frustrating and infuriating experience of failure in civic engagement. The struggle to avoid failure, however, lends intensity to the deliberative process and forces citizens to engage in a bitter conflict of individual opinions. Only a vigorous exercise of one's sense of civic duty would keep twelve strangers struggling for hours, often days, only to find consensus impossible.[57] Moreover, even when juries could reach agreement, cases with multiple charges and complex verdict forms brought about some of the strongest civic impacts seen in our research. Thus, deliberative complexity speaks directly to Tocqueville's conviction that the jury, in cases such as these, serves as the most effective school of democracy.

In many cases, the problem is not that jurors cannot handle some degree of complexity, but that the "hypertechnicality" of lawyers and judges leads to unnecessary confusion. In studying this subject, most researchers find that jurors can understand relevant concepts but falter when confronted with what Vidmar calls "the arcane concepts and abstruse syntax that characterize many instructions."[58] Thus, it is incumbent on judges to avoid becoming, as federal Judge William Dwyer put it, "obsessed with procedure at the expense of truth and common sense."[59]

Judicial Instructions

In short, we believe that the best approach to trial complexity is to make greater efforts to facilitate and enhance juror deliberation. Especially for complex civil trials, we believe that judges can empower juries by making a concerted effort to ensure that the relevant legal instructions are in plain English. They should also provide some guidance on how to deliberate. Particularly for cases involving complicated legal issues, the nature of the jury instructions can play a critically important role.

The Arizona reform program discussed earlier has gone farther by calling for the judge to offer jurors some guidance at the beginning of the trial to enable jurors to better understand the testimony on topics that, without some context, might be confusing. A challenge of providing such instructions is that, under current judicial practice, many judges do not decide on the exact jury instructions until the trial is actually completed. Nonetheless, judges can still offer jurors with an explanation of key concepts, even if they do not provide the formal jury instructions until the end of trial. As Erie County (New York) Supreme Court Justice John P. Lane reported:

> Jurors appreciate receiving preliminary instructions on the principles of substantive law. They find the evidence easier to understand when they know the underlying principles of the case. Things that we take for granted are new to jurors. For example, we may assume that jurors know what negligence is. The fact is that most do not. Similarly, early explanations of the burden of proof and the no-fault threshold are also effective. Of course, instructions are repeated in more detail at the end of the case.[60]

This type of approach is becoming more common, particularly in the criminal context. The American Bar Association Principles for Juries and Jury Trials recommends that preliminary instructions include the elements of the charges and claims so that the jury can better understand the nature of the evidence that will be presented.

In other cases, judges might make the lives of jurors easier by providing "special verdict" forms that provide questions on subsidiary issues that are necessary to decide in order to reach a final verdict. Our research suggests that this move might have a beneficial side effect: Creating the potential for mixed verdicts does make deliberation more challenging, but we found that it enhances the jury's civic educational effects for this very reason.

Models for Deliberation

More generally, judges should consider strategies for supporting and guiding jurors during their deliberation. In terms of models for deliberation, we found evidence that some jurors were concerned about the lack of guidance they received from the judge on how to deliberate effectively. As quoted earlier in chapter 5, one presiding juror in our study had this view:

> Though we were given instructions from the court on the law and on the claims made by both parties, we were not given suggestions on how best to handle jury deliberations. As presiding juror I felt a huge burden of responsibility to ensure a fair trial for all involved. It would have been helpful to have some suggested protocols or procedures to follow to ensure a fair and non-confrontational deliberation process.

Despite this concern about a lack of guidance, jurors in our study demonstrated an impressive ability to intuit critical strategies for effective deliberation. Most notably, juries tended to ensure that all members of the jury were provided with an opportunity to share their views. Indeed, in two-thirds of the juries we studied closely in Seattle, every single member of the jury seized their opportunities to provide their assessment of the relevant issues before their peers.

Another area where juries have often sought support and guidance during their deliberative process is how to proceed in the face of an impasse. The traditional response to this situation has been simply to declare a hung jury. As part of the jury reform movement in Arizona, however, judges were allowed to talk with the jury about the nature of the impasse and determine if answers to specific questions could be helpful. If the answer is yes, the judge is authorized to allow additional closing arguments by counsel, additional evidence, or some combinations of those measures to aid the jury's deliberations. More generally, we believe such a process affords the judge an opportunity to remind jurors of the principles of deliberation. Standard written instructions that a judge reads aloud could reemphasize both practical deliberative procedures, such as round robin discussions, and the principles of analytic rigor, equality, and respect inherent in the jury as a democratic body. For instance, the 9th U.S. Circuit Court of Appeals, in the Western United States, offers these words for judges speaking to deadlocked juries:

> As jurors, you have a duty to discuss the case with one another and to deliberate in an effort to reach a unanimous verdict if each of you

can do so without violating your individual judgment and conscience. Each of you must decide the case for yourself, but only after you consider the evidence impartially with your fellow jurors. During your deliberations, you should not hesitate to reexamine your own views and change your opinion if you become persuaded that it is wrong. However, you should not change an honest belief as to the weight or effect of the evidence solely because of the opinions of your fellow jurors or for the mere purpose of returning a verdict. All of you are equally honest and conscientious jurors who have heard the same evidence. All of you share an equal desire to arrive at a verdict. Each of you should ask yourself whether you should question the correctness of your present position.[61]

Such admonitions cannot help but promote continued deliberation. Though it will not always help a jury reach consensus, returning to the courtroom as a hung jury is, in fact, returning with a kind of verdict—one that also does little to diminish the civic lesson jurors will have learned from their labors.[62]

Pruning and Attacking the Jury

There is some evidence that the reform movement has helped to encourage both a more positive experience for jurors and a greater public willingness to report for jury service.[63] Making the jury service experience better should only augment the civic educational effects we have described. Increasing people's willingness to answer the summons and sit on juries will only help to spread the jury's benefits across an ever-wider swath of the population. These improvements, however, will only do so much good if the frequency of jury trials—and their size—diminishes further.

Stopping Short of a Jury Trial

Rather than trimming back the American jury, we are more inclined to restore it. Earlier, we noted that declining jury use has meant that fewer than one in five criminal charges and fewer than one in fifty civil cases end up before a jury.[64] If one can still hear the constitutional language of the Sixth and Seventh Amendments, those figures should sound surprisingly low. Though "in all criminal prosecutions, the accused shall enjoy the right to...an impartial jury," they are expected *not* to exercise that right. In civil suits, it is now uncommon to invoke "the right of trial by jury," no matter how well that institution has been "preserved."

Even in England, the modern jury's birthplace, signs of a declining jury abound. In March, 2010, the high court in London concluded the first criminal trial without a jury in over 400 years, sending four robbers to prison for ten years or more. An appeals court had earlier rejected the defendants' appeal for a jury trial by citing concerns about the "subversion of the process of trial by jury." In rejecting the appeal, the court cited the 2003 Criminal Justice Act 2003, which allows judges to identify cases in which a "real and present danger" of jury tampering exists.[65]

Many well-intentioned legal reforms have contributed to the declining size and frequency of jury trials. In particular, the plea-bargaining process has dramatically reduced the deployment of criminal juries. As New York University law professor Randolph Jonakait explains, "The prosecutor has the incentive to offer a plea that will result in a lesser sentence to remove the possibility that no punishment at all will be imposed, and the accused has the incentive to accept the lesser sentence" to remove the chance of serving many more years in prison.[66] These behind-the-scenes negotiations may benefit individual defendants and prosecutors, but their unintended consequence is to eliminate the public's role in the criminal justice system. Even when juries *indirectly* influence this plea-bargaining process (e.g., with both prosecution and defense pointing to past jury precedents when negotiating their deal), the civic educational benefit of jury service is lost for those prospective jurors who will, as a result of the plea-bargain, never be seated.[67]

We are more ambivalent about the role of alternative dispute resolution (ADR) and mediation because those practices at least involve more deliberative processes that may have some civic benefits for the litigants themselves. By some accounts, participants in such proceedings gain not only satisfactory resolutions to their cases but also a measure of appreciation for the value of dialogue, deliberation, and active engagement with public problems. It is no surprise, for instance, that advocates of these conflict-resolution methods are associated with the movement for deliberative democracy, which we discuss in chapter 9.[68] Still, it is fair to guess that depriving citizens of the important and unique civic educational opportunity of jury service has been an unintended consequence of the increased use of mediation and ADR.

These alternatives to jury trial, however, may well aid the civic educational purpose of the jury when they remove from the docket those cases that would otherwise strike jurors as frivolous, petty, personal, or simply trivial. In a minority of cases, we found some jurors shaking their heads in disbelief at the cases put before them, quietly signaling the same indignity that judges express when they throw out a case on similar grounds.

Disdain toward Juries

It is one thing to inadvertently roll back juries, but another altogether to run them down. This happens most subtly in popular cultural portrayals of juries and jury service, which all too often caricature them as bending to the will of all-powerful attorneys. To take one example, consider Robert Dugoni's 2003 legal thriller, *The Jury Master*. The novel opens with the jury's entrance: "They shuffled into the courtroom like twelve of San Francisco's homeless, shoulders hunched and head bowed as if searching the sidewalk for spare change." The jurors would soon bend to the will of David Sloane, the elite San Francisco lawyer representing Abbott Security in a wrongful death suit. Though the jury regarded him warily "like an unwelcome relative," his stirring closing statement brought all twelve around to his side. After completing his latest courtroom victory, the victim's mother berates him:

> Mr. Sloane…what you did to those jurors. I don't know how you did it, how you convinced them, they didn't want to believe you. I saw it when they came back. They had their minds made up.…My Emily is dead…that is something you can't change with your words.[69]

As overwrought as such examples sound, we worry that they have a corrosive force on public perceptions of the jury. If its moorings are weakened sufficiently, the jury system may be pried loose and sent out to sea by those who have a more active interest in its curtailment, if not its demise. Critics of the civil jury, in particular, have warned that America has become exceedingly litigious and that juries have become so reckless in their judgments that our legal system, our economy—perhaps even our society—will collapse without significant reform—specifically, tort reform. As the American Tort Reform Association warned in 2009:

> With the best alignment of political stars it's enjoyed in years, the powerful litigation industry has undertaken a coordinated and well-funded effort in state capitals across the country to roll back recent tort reforms, expand liability and gin up more personal injury lawyer-enriching lawsuits.[70]

Survey data suggest that these critiques have had some impact, as public attitudes toward civil lawsuits echo some of these concerns.[71]

Our research compels us to side with the view expressed by John Vail, the vice president and senior litigation counsel for the Center for Constitutional Litigation. In an essay about the unrecognized effects of tort reform, Vail writes:

> The debate about tort reform is largely cast in terms of corporations versus trial lawyers, so it fails to capture what is really at issue: Are citizens in a democracy entitled to make decisions, or must they defer to elites at every turn?…It is unusual today to talk about the right to sit on a jury as one of the fundamental rights Americans possess, at least as important as the right to vote, but the framers were wholly comfortable with the assertion.…From damages caps to health courts, tort reform seeks to take decisional authority away from the people. The debate about tort reform is a debate, ultimately, about whether ordinary people make the decisions that guide public life, or whether those decisions are made in corporate boardrooms.[72]

By analogy, how far would one get if one questioned the right to vote in elections? How easily can we roll back other constitutional protections, such as the freedom of speech in the First Amendment?[73] The jury has acquired a solid institutional status as a means of resolving legal disputes, but it may have lost some of its luster as a patriotic icon, as a bulwark of personal liberty against state and corporate power. Even more remote is any public knowledge of the Supreme Court's affirmation of the *juror*'s right to serve, as explained in chapter 1. The jury was not built to be an expensive legal luxury available only to wealthy civil litigants or brave criminal defendants, who stand up against the power of the prosecutor. Instead, its regular use is meant to be more comparable to that of elections. Its civic stature should compare more to that of judges, who are, in a sense, the jury's peer.

Far from a theoretical problem, we believe we can see the marks of these public attacks on the civil jury in our data. As we noted in chapter 3, some of the public criticisms of civil lawsuits have likely undermined the public's belief in the validity of such cases. The slightly lower stature of civil trials means a slightly reduced sense of duty for civil jurors, and this could even explain the reduced civic educational power of the civil jury. Thus, we found an increase in post-service voting only for criminal jurors, and this result faintly echoed through subsequent chapters.

Similarly, the declining national public confidence in the justice system we noted in chapter 7 had a parallel in our data with regard to juries, particularly civil juries. For those people who reported to jury service but never became empanelled, 76 percent expressed confidence in the civil jury at the outset, but that figure had dropped twelve points by the final round of surveys, after the close of the 2004 Presidential election. Over the same time period, this group experienced a similar but smaller drop in its confidence in criminal juries (down from 86 percent to 79 percent). Were that decline to continue, we can only expect it to further erode the jury's civic educational effects.[74]

Outside the United States

This last set of observations raises the possibility that the validity of Tocqueville's civic educational model of the jury depends on the time and place of one's investigation. It may well be that at the time he wrote *Democracy in America*, the jury was an even more potent educational force than we have found it to be in our own study. Just as we cannot assume that the effects we have found will prove constant over time, neither can we be certain that they be obtained across different national and cultural borders. Moreover, modern experiments using lay citizens to administer justice in South Korea, Kazakhstan, and other countries often create bodies that resemble the American jury only by degree—mixing jurors with judges, narrowly limiting the scope of the jury pool, and so on.[75]

Only future research will effectively test the geographic scope of Tocqueville's model, but it is already clear that at least some nations share a *faith* in his theory. As Australian legal scholars Kent Anderson and Mark Nolan have pointed out, the proponents of Japan's new "lay assessor" system marshaled two arguments in favor of greater public participation in the Japanese legal system—better legal outcomes (justice) and "the belief that it promotes a more democratic society."[76] In the words of the official Justice Reform Council, which outlined the proposed system:

> In Japanese society of the 21st century, it is incumbent on the people to break out of the excessive dependency of the state that accompanies the traditional consciousness of being governed objects, develop public consciousness within themselves, and become more actively involved in public affairs.[77]

The data from this study suggest that such statements are more than the optimistic words of government reformers. There is now real evidence that the jury system, in particular, can spark increased involvement in public life, and there is every reason to suspect that the participation hypothesis has validity, at least for people most in need of a civic boost. Thus, the jury system is not only a tonic that produces modestly satisfying results when regularly imbibed in the United States; rather, it might also be of value to nations, from South Africa to Iraq, that are working with relatively new, and potentially unstable, legal and political systems. If adapted effectively to local traditions and culture, the jury could serve to broaden public participation in such countries and smooth the transition to a democratic system of self-governance.

More direct civic educational programs have had success abroad, and the jury provides a powerful complement to such efforts, presuming that it can be institutionalized in a way that secures its deliberative and democratic character.[78] The jury might even have considerable civic educational potency for mass publics were a government to convene *national* juries, as has been suggested for high-profile class action lawsuits.[79] If used at the International Criminal Court, the jury system might even serve to teach global civics lessons.[80] Whether working in familiar or novel contexts such as these, our illustration of the civic power of jury service should hearten those who share a deliberative vision of democracy.

Chapter 9

Political Society and Deliberative Democracy

Lest our statistics drown out the voices of the individual jurors in our study, we begin this concluding chapter with the reflections of a King County juror. This particular person had served a previous time on a jury and had returned to the courthouse for another round:

> This is the second time in my life I've been called for jury duty, and I think now, as I did then, that our system is about the best anyone could have. I feel that most jurors take their responsibilities seriously and do their best to be fair and listen to all the evidence before making any judgments. In talking to the people around me, I was impressed with their attitudes about being called for duty. How fortunate we are to live in America!

The data presented in this book show that many fellow jurors have had equally inspiring experiences. In the broadest sense, then, Justice Kennedy was correct when he asserted, citing Tocqueville in *Powers v. Ohio*, that juries have a civic educational power. To pull together the findings shown in chapters 3–7, Table 9.1 summarizes the main results of our research on how jury service changes people's civic and political attitudes and behaviors. Referring back to the map of the state, political society, and civil society, the table shows that the jury has as wide a range of impacts as we initially expected. Those effects measure as small changes, with the only exception being that service at the courthouse has a relatively large positive impact on jurors' confidence in the quality of the jury system itself. From voting to community conversation, from group membership to public affairs media use, the different aspects of jury service had wide-ranging and intriguing connections to changes in jurors' post-service behavior. Important civic and political attitudes—such as confidence in oneself, one's fellow citizens, and public institutions—also changed in response to jury service.

As so often happens, though, careful inspection shows a more nuanced reality. We found that the impact of jury service varies considerably depending on a juror's background. Thanks to the legal advances cited at the beginning of chapter 1, the jury pool and the sworn juries themselves are now more diverse. Some groups, such as homemakers, that have received the jury's civic educational rewards would not have been found in the jury box in Tocqueville's era.

We discovered that each aspect of jury service has a different kind of impact on jurors, with the final jury deliberation not always providing the most important civic lesson. Moreover, the key aspects of jury service varied in certain respects for different subgroups of citizens. For instance, the full

Table 9.1. Summary of the civic and political impacts of jury service found in chapters 3 through 7

	Concept in chapter 2	Measurement in chapters 3 through 7	Size/ direction of effect	Key aspect of jury service experience
Government	Voting in elections	Voting in elections	+	• Deliberating (and quality of delib.) • Criminal trials (vs. civil), especially with multiple charges • Effects only for infrequent voters
	Confidence in the competence of public officials	Confidence in state/local judges	+	• Overall satisfaction/ treatment • Appreciation from judge
		Confidence in the U.S. Supreme Court	+/−	• Cognitive engagement in the trial • Satisfaction with deliberation/verdict • *Comprehension of trial had countervailing effect*
		Confidence in the U.S. Congress	+/−	• Treatment at the courthouse • *Emotional experience had countervailing effect*
	Confidence in jury system	Confidence in jury system	++	Nearly every aspect was important in contributing to this effect.

Table 9.1. (*continued*)

	Concept in chapter 2	Measurement in chapters 3 through 7	Size/direction of effect	Key aspect of jury service experience
Political Society	Campaign activity Political group involvement Directly contacting public officials	Political action	+	• Emotional engagement in the trial • Appreciation from the judge
	Confidence in one's political capabilities	Political self-confidence	+	• Comprehension of the trial • *Treatment at courthouse*
	Faith in the responsiveness of public institutions	Political faith	+	• Overall satisfaction/treatment • Cognitive engagement in the trial
Between Political and Civil Society	Discussion of local community Political conversation	Public talk	+	• Nearly every aspect was important in contributing to this effect.
	Following politics though news and public affairs media	TV news	+/−	• Cognitive engagement in the trial • *Comprehension of trial had countervailing effect*
		Non-TV public affairs media	+	• Overall satisfaction • Cognitive engagement in the trial • Appreciation from the judge
Civil Society	Civic/nonpartisan group involvement	Local community groups	+	• Emotional engagement in the trial • Talking with others about one's experience of jury service
	Civic pride in oneself	Civic pride	+	• Overall satisfaction • Cognitive engagement in the trial
	Civic faith in fellow citizens	Civic faith	+	• Satisfaction with deliberation/verdict

set of behavioral effects were much stronger for temporary and part-time workers serving as jurors when they found trial was cognitive and emotionally engaging. For juries reaching mixed outcomes (i.e., guilty on some counts, not guilty on others), the effects of the service experience on community group involvement and public conversations became much stronger if they were satisfied with their deliberation and verdict.

Our study found other complexities, as well. Jury service directly altered behavior, at least as often as it started a causal chain that leads from attitude changes, such as rising political self-confidence, to behavioral shifts. There were even some small countervailing effects. When jurors believed they had a firm grasp of their trials, for example, they subsequently turned away from television news and became less confident in the judgment of the U.S. Supreme Court.

This final chapter will touch on some of the details of our results, but we choose to reflect principally on the broader finding that the jury provides many citizens with a powerful deliberative experience and serves as an engine of civic renewal. With this as our launching point, we examine the jury system as a model of public deliberation beyond the confines of the courthouse. We also explore many meaningful opportunities for political engagement that draw on the principles of jury service, and we review the relevance of our research for the design of these deliberative public processes. We then conclude by considering the broadest implications of our research for the understanding and advancing the practice of democracy.

Comparing the Political Roles of Jurors and Voters

During the past century, Americans lost much of their faith in representatives. Populist movements rose up to protest what they saw as undue influence by business and a phenomenon of politicians associated with corrupt political machines, both of which were pushing private interests over the public interest. Enduring achievements of this Progressive Era of reform include the direct election of Senators and opportunities to vote on public issues through statewide initiatives or referenda.[1]

Over the last two decades, new political reform movements have again targeted the failings of political institutions and called for term limits, campaign finance reform, and opportunities to use the Internet to directly engage the public. In these ongoing discussions, commentators often fail to examine how the jury functions as a model political institution, uniquely situated at the crossroads of state, civil society, and political life.[2] Republican calls in early 2009 for "no taxation without deliberation," for instance, hailed the idea of sustained deliberation but did not make clear what role, if any, the average American might play in such a process.[3]

A civic reform necessarily involves some theory of the democratic citizen—some notion of who people are and what role they should play in politics and government. The Progressive Era's push for initiative and referenda stood on the premise that the good citizen was an *active voter*. Over the last twenty years, while the term limits movement arose as a populist response to the limits of our political institutions, many scholars and civic entrepreneurs have challenged the focus on voting per se, as the hallmark of democratic citizenship. Instead, critics have called for a commitment to *deliberative* public engagement, highlighting, in the words of political theorist Simone Chambers, the relative importance of "the communicative processes of opinion and will-formation that precede voting."[4] Briefly, we consider the problems faced by the voter model of civic engagement and contrast it with the deliberative model of jury decision making.

Initiative Elections and Deliberation

To appreciate the significance of political deliberation, and the limited value of voting as a standalone act, consider the nature of direct citizen voting on issues through the initiative process. A 2003 survey found that just days before a Washington State election, a majority of likely voters could not name a single measure on the ballot, even though their ballot included two statewide issues, one county amendment, and several local questions with fiscal impacts. Fewer than one in ten could give an argument pro or con on most of these issues. On the most prominent statewide measure, which proposed changing ergonomics regulations, the percentage who had the measure backwards (not realizing that voting "yes" repealed a law they favored) was greater than the margin of victory.[5] In such situations, citizen legislators are set up for disappointment, insofar as they may later recognize that they voted against what they actually wanted—either upon reflection, after receiving more information, or simply upon recognizing the broader context of the particular choice on the ballot.

The challenges of making an initiative system work is that citizens are often not sufficiently well-prepared, by their own admission, through a deliberative process to make a reflective judgment on what may well be critically important public issues. Particularly on ballot measure contests that have a strong advocate on only one side of the issue and those measures that do not garner significant public attention, citizens often do not receive sufficient information to weigh before deciding how to cast their vote.[6]

Contrasting the initiative system with the jury system highlights the degree to which this is the case. First off, public initiatives are often able to reach the ballot with minimal, if any, screening because well-funded groups (either motivated by ideological or monetary rewards) are often able to push for measures to be placed on the ballot without any requirement that they first be evaluated by an independent party.[7] Juries, by contrast, only hear cases once a judge or a prosecutor (sometimes with the aid of a grand jury) concludes that the issue is sufficiently contestable as to warrant resolution by a jury. Second, unlike the jury system (or even most candidate elections), a number of ballot propositions come to the public without the benefit of being tested through the process of adversary debate. In particular, where an issue concerns one interest group intensely and affects the public only diffusely, the public will often only hear one side of the story.[8]

Finally, even when citizens hear a two-sided debate on an issue of public significance, voting on ballot propositions asks citizens to make discrete choices out of context. As New York University law professor Clayton Gillette puts it, "Voters who face an opportunity to vote on one piece of the budget without simultaneously considering the effects of their vote on interconnected parts may skew the allocations that would be made if the entire budget were considered comprehensively."[9] This dynamic helps to explain what some have observed as a cycling effect where later initiative proposals are necessary to undo the effects of earlier ones, thereby inspiring later attempts to restore the impact of the earlier proposal.[10]

Participating in the initiative process can be an unsettling experience that emphasizes the significance of voting and provides little support in terms of facilitating the quality of deliberation that is necessary to make one's vote meaningful. By contrast, the process of participating in jury service is often a peak deliberative experience. Significantly, jury service provides citizens with an opportunity to participate in self-government based on a process of deliberation with fellow citizens and with the effect of rendering decisions that have real consequences for plaintiffs, defendants, and the state. Given that jury service represents a meaningful vote (i.e., one based on deliberation and a discernible impact), the Supreme Court may have understated matters when it explained that "with the exception of voting, for most citizens the honor and privilege of jury duty is their most significant opportunity to participate in the democratic process."[11]

The Jury Archetype for Group Judgment

There is another, more subtle way in which the jury stands as a counterpoint to voting. The voting model treats the citizen as a solitary decision maker. Democratic theorist Benjamin Barber calls voting closer to "a form of self-expression" than an act of civic engagement. More memorably, Barber describes the election day experience of most voters: "Our primary electoral act, voting, is rather like using a public toilet: We wait in line with a crowd in order to close ourselves up in a small compartment where we can relieve ourselves in solitude and in privacy of our burden, pull a lever, and then, yielding to the next in line, go silently home."[12]

The jury model of citizenship, by contrast, represents the citizen as part of a decision-making group. It is really more of a *jury* model than a *juror* model of citizenship. Whereas voting represents a private act in which one marks a secret ballot however one sees fit, the jury constitutes an archetype of collective deliberation.[13]

Juries have become a model for deliberation in the United States both because they exist in a highly institutionalized and ritualized context and because they directly involve the public. The essence of a jury trial is largely the same from one courthouse to the next. The details of the cases and arguments put forward differ, but federal and state laws ensure relatively consistent orientations, judicial instructions on deliberation, etc. Juries also draw a broad cross-section of the public. Through the official summons of randomly selected citizens (with current driver's licenses or voter registrations), juries form an officially constituted body that meets for the first time at the courthouse while awaiting assignment to a case. As we have seen, those who answer the summons do not constitute a perfectly representative sample of the public, but they are fairly representative, nonetheless. This helps to ensure that the norms and traditions of the jury percolate through the wider population, further reinforcing the archetype. Finally, juries yield public decisions and are, thereby, subject to public observation, albeit indirectly. Perhaps more importantly, as we saw in chapter 6, almost every juror *talks about their experience* with others, further strengthening the broader public conception of what it means to be a juror.

One of the hallmarks of serving on a jury is the aim to reach collective judgments without slipping into unreflective consensus-seeking, sometimes called "groupthink."[14] Judges often give poetic instructions to this effect, as in the case of Western District of Virginia, where the court offers these words to civil jurors: "It is your duty, as jurors, to discuss this case with one another in the jury room. You should try to reach agreement without violence to individual judgment, because a verdict must be unanimous."[15]

Because of the way the jury institution operates in the United States, it is likely that admonitions such as these are learned by jurors across the United States, and they likely yield the same sense of deliberative accomplishment and satisfaction we demonstrated in chapters 4 and 5. The jury draws private members of civil society into an institutionalized group decision-making body that, every working day, reproduces a broadly understood archetype of collective judgment that citizens can take back into their political and civil lives.

The Jury as a Model for Deliberative Reform

Many modern civic reformers believe our political system lacks sufficient opportunities to apply the deliberative lessons of the jury to public life. Deliberative democracy's advocates bemoan the limited quality of mainstream methods of public participation and seek to create a more deliberative civil and political society to facilitate better public decision making and dampen public conflicts.[16] More significantly, such civic opportunities also promise to *transform* how individuals think of themselves and act as citizens, in very much the same way Tocqueville envisioned juries promoting a concern for the common good and a sense of civic responsibility.[17]

Not surprisingly, advocates of deliberative democracy use the jury as an inspiration for their reform proposals. As University of California-Hastings law professor Ethan Leib writes:

> The strategy of making democratic institutions more deliberative often requires looking to institutions already in existence that can serve as points of departure for the institutional imagination. For this reason, deliberative democrats often look to the jury as a proximate example of a deliberative institution in our polity, where the voices of ordinary citizens speak about the laws that govern them.[18]

Citizens' Juries and Deliberative Polls

One of the earliest and most influential of these jury-inspired approaches to deliberative reform is the Citizens' Jury. This process grew out of the 1971 doctoral dissertation Ned Crosby wrote at the University of Minnesota. Crosby oversaw more than thirty Citizen Juries over the next thirty years, and they are now widely used in Australia, Britain, and elsewhere.[19] The Citizens' Jury process that evolved followed a set of design principles, such as producing a fair agenda, gathering a randomly-selected microcosm of the community (roughly twice the size of a criminal jury), providing high-quality information, minimizing staff bias, and allowing for intensive deliberation lasting four to five days. The Citizens' Jury seeks to learn whether a mix of information and in-depth deliberation can bring diverse individuals to a broad consensus on a narrow set of questions.

Consider these examples of Citizens' Jury tasks, which are typically called the "charge" a jury must meet. Should we pass a levy to improve our local schools? How should we manage the impact agriculture has on water quality in our state? How should we reconfigure the federal budget? How should we understand and address global climate change?[20] For each of these issues, reaching agreement on a set of detailed recommendations requires intensive learning and deliberation. In every instance, the citizen participants ended up feeling tremendously satisfied with their discussion process and their resulting judgments. Citizen jurors rarely thought they could have accomplished their task with *less* deliberation.[21]

The finer details of a Citizens' Jury have varied considerably from one jury to the next. The "jury" analogy is most vivid when the jurors hear testimony from advocates and their opponents, with the jury's task being to judge the quality of one side's viewpoint versus the other's. Also in the tradition of a jury, this procedural approach can involve cross-examination of one side by the other. Unlike the criminal or civil jury, however, the Citizens' Juries also get the chance to *directly* question both sides' witnesses, discuss the issues freely as the event unfolds, and even have a degree of control over the process itself.[22]

To appreciate the proximity of the Citizens' Jury to the archetypal jury, it is useful to contrast it with another popular and widely-used innovation, the

Deliberative Poll. Stanford University political communication professor James Fishkin invented this process "to approximate what the public *would think*, given a better opportunity to consider the questions at hand."[23] A typical Poll begins with a pre-deliberation survey (often conducted weeks or months in advance), followed by the distribution of a discussion guide to prospective participants. The citizens taking part in the Poll then meet and discuss the issue face-to-face in small groups and develop questions that, in a large plenary session, they pose to experts, advocates, and public officials. Afterward, they complete a post-deliberation questionnaire, and the featured result of this event is a comparison of how participants' views changed over the course of the Poll.

In essence, the Deliberative Poll tries to show us how individual citizens might "vote" if given a modest amount of time to talk through their thoughts on an issue and hear experts and partisans directly answer the questions citizens would like to put to them. Compared to a Citizens' Jury, the Deliberative Poll does not provide ample time for face-to-face deliberation to work through the nuances of issues and adequately hear and reflect on each other's views. After all, the Deliberative Poll does not *ask* participants to reason together to reach a collective judgment; instead, it asks them to sit together while refining their *private* judgments.

Perhaps owing to this difference in emphasis, the Deliberative Poll has also not sought to establish detailed protocols for structuring and moderating participants' small group discussions to ensure that they are fully deliberative, in the stronger sense of the term. When hearing expert testimony, it is ideal if experts and partisans, like litigants in a trial, can cross-examine one another and be subject to dogged questioning by the citizens themselves. This happens at times in Deliberative Polls, but the Citizens' Jury uses a design that makes certain this can occur. This helps ensure that when an expert makes a specious claim, it withers under their critics' cross-examination, and when a partisan gives a non-answer with vague platitudes or an unwelcome topic-shift, the unyielding follow-ups either reveal their inability to reply or force them to say what they truly believe, whatever the cost may be. In iterative processes with the luxury of more time, better use is made of outside opinions and information.

Finally, within the Deliberative Poll's discussion groups, there is also considerable variation in the style and quality of moderation. Simply having a moderator in the room with a written set of ground rules probably goes a long way toward removing the status inequalities that critics see in mock juries, but just as juries have judges (and, more aptly, forepersons) to navigate through the evidence and arrive at a verdict, so do Citizens' Juries employ professional moderators to help the jurors move through several days of testimony and discussion. This again reflects the different models— with the Deliberative Poll emphasizing the experience of the individual who needs limited assistance to reach a private judgment, and the Citizens' Jury providing an energetic, trained guide to help the jurors reach broad agreement on their final set of policy recommendations.

The Citizens' Initiative Review and Citizens' Assembly

Governments and civic associations have convened Citizens' Juries and Deliberative Polls to advise policymaking processes, to learn more about public sentiment, and for many other unofficial purposes. Such micro-deliberative processes can have measurable impacts on larger political and policymaking processes,[24] but the jury distinguishes itself by having a long-standing institutional foothold. Thus, many deliberative reformers have sought ways to similarly embed these new civic opportunities in civil society, politics, or even the state itself.[25]

Such institutionalization appears to have gotten underway for at least some deliberative designs, such as the Citizens' Initiative Review legislation, which the Oregon legislature passed with bi-partisan support in 2009.[26] This new law convenes a quasi-Citizens' Jury to review a pending ballot initiative by hearing and weighing testimony from proponents and opponents. The citizen panelists then draft a statement on the initiative, and this text appears prominently on its own page in the official Oregon voters' pamphlet published by the Secretary of State.

Oregon Senate Majority Leader Richard Devlin (D-Tualatin), chair of the Senate Rules Committee, offered this perspective on the Citizens' Initiative Review bill: "Oregon has long been an innovator in the area of direct democracy.... This bill represents another example of how our state continues to encourage and support citizen engagement in the process of governing."[27] It is true enough that this constitutes an innovation in direct democracy, but what makes the Citizens' Initiative Review unique is using jury-inspired small-scale deliberation to improve the quality of *large-scale* electoral participation, a process normally rooted exclusively in the voting model of citizenship. In essence, the Citizens' Initiative Review aims to promote more in-depth public deliberation on issues before voters reach their final, private judgments.[28]

When the Citizens' Initiative Review gets underway in 2010, it will come six years after another pioneering deliberative process, the British Columbia Citizens' Assembly. The assembled body was not modeled strictly on the jury, but it followed a number of its critical institutional features, including a random sample of citizens and a degree of formal legal authority.[29] Though both the Citizens' Assembly and Citizens' Initiative Review were designed to improve the direct democratic process, the most important difference was that the Assembly was empowered to *draft* a statewide measure, rather than merely comment on one. Whereas a typical Citizens' Jury gives policy recommendations, the Assembly actually wrote new election rules for British Columbia.[30]

In the end, the Assembly voted 146–7 in favor of adopting the Single Transferable Vote model, which lets voters rank candidates within multimember districts, in lieu of its traditional electoral system. The recommendation from the Citizens' Assembly was submitted to the British Columbia electorate as a referendum so that the general public could approve or reject it. The parliament had set a high bar for final passage by requiring 60 percent approval, and in a May 2005 election, 57 percent of the voting public supported the measure.[31]

Though the British Columbia Citizens' Assembly did not see its recommendations made into law, this process and its forerunners have certainly demonstrated that public microcosms can deliberate effectively. The Assembly, in particular, has helped settle the question of whether citizens can function at such a high level when playing a legislatively authorized role in an official policymaking process.[32] This important precedent has encouraged others to form official and unofficial Assemblies in Ontario, Canada, and the Netherlands.[33] The *San Francisco Chronicle* endorsed a legislative proposal to hold such an event in California.[34]

The failure of the Citizens' Assembly to bring about electoral reform, however, raises the possibility that there needs to be a significant departure from the jury model to advance these models of deliberation. Specifically, the Assembly's members engaged in a kind of rigorous deliberation appropriate for a decision-making body seeking to arrive at the correct verdict—the optimal solution to a policy problem when looked at by sober, thoughtful policy analysts. As one Assembly member wrote, in reflecting on how they ended up endorsing a unique form of the relatively obscure Single Transferable Vote system:

> The more we looked into it, the more overwhelmingly sensible it seemed. That is why we went with the more difficult to explain and lesser-known option....We wanted to give voters here the chance to choose a system that we had deductively reasoned to be the best, rather than a better known one that did not work for our region.[35]

Sensible as it sounds, in retrospect, this was a risky approach because the Assembly's deliberative judgment would ultimately be vetted by a direct democratic referendum, a process in which citizens act on impressions and signals, pulling together sound bites and weighing partisan endorsements.[36] The future success of such Assemblies might require working more closely with political parties and other influential electoral actors, and the Assembly members might do well to seek the most effective policy that can also pass muster with public sentiments.[37]

Popular Government

One response to this challenge is to take the deliberative model of public involvement a step farther. Rather than have a deliberative mini-public advise fellow citizens, this approach would form deliberative citizen bodies to *legislate*. Such efforts have historical precedents in ancient Greece and Switzerland, and California's established system of civil grand juries shows that modern citizens can play a useful—if imperfect—government oversight role.[38] More ambitious deliberative bodies like the 2009 Australian Citizens' Parliament, however, are legislatures in name only, since they lack a formal legal authority.[39] There has been no shortage of proposals to take the next step, however, and give citizens a kind of direct legislative power to complement their existing authority as jurors within the legal branch. We consider two of the most well-developed designs of citizen legislative bodies.[40]

Legal scholar Ethan Leib has drawn more direct inspiration from the jury than anyone since Ned Crosby developed the Citizens' Jury. Leib has put forward a bold, jury-inspired proposal in *Deliberative Democracy in America: A Proposal for a Popular Branch of Government*. Why tinker with improving direct democratic processes, Leib asks, when one can—theoretically—replace it altogether? Leib puts forward this alternative to the status quo model:

> The people need to have a more distinct voice in a [governmental] branch of their own. Let us call such a branch *popular* insofar as it aims to instantiate our ideas about popular sovereignty more concretely. As a practical matter, this branch would replace the initiative and the referendum; its institution would be established to address many of the shortcomings of those forms of direct democracy. Its functions could be brought about through national or state constitutional amendments, and its findings would enact laws...that could be repealed or vetoed by the relevant...executive or legislative branch (with a supermajority), or could be challenged in the judicial branch.[41]

Some of the distinctiveness of Leib's "popular branch" comes from his willingness to follow the jury as a "mandatory regime." As Leib argues, "There are very good reasons to compel citizens" to participate "from the perspective of civic responsibility and legitimacy, as well as representativeness and impartiality, all considerations militating toward mandatory jury duty and mandatory participation in deliberative assemblies."[42] To soften the blow for those reluctant to serve, his proposal would cover citizens' expenses for serving on these bodies, which Leib sometimes calls "policy juries." Citizens would also receive a fair stipend, comfortable amenities, and any necessary accommodations, such as translation services. Leib hopes that "service on policy juries could become constitutive of American citizenship in an age where there are few aspects of political culture that unify citizens."[43]

Along similar lines, in *Saving Democracy: A Plan for Real Representation in America*, democratic theorist Kevin O'Leary proposes establishing a third legislative branch, consisting of 43,500 citizens chosen by lot.[44] From there, he offers two variations. The first would convene a kind of state-sponsored Deliberative Poll: Each House district would have its own public assembly, whose one hundred members were chosen by lottery every two years. In exchange for nothing more than a per diem to cover expenses, these citizens would discuss issues in depth, and well-timed polls of this deliberating microcosm would be reported to public officials to influence pending legislation.

The second version of O'Leary's proposal is the People's House, a more powerful citizen body built on the same 435 district model. This House could introduce a few bills each session, pull dying bills out of committee for a floor vote, and reject legislation by majority vote (overridden by a three-fifths vote in the House or Senate). A citizen steering committee would set the agenda for the House, and each year, every district would nominate one of its members for the committee.[45] Among the most original details in O'Leary's blueprint is the grouping of Assembly districts into six geographic regions, then randomly matching each district up with one from every other region. This would create seventy-two quasi-national Assemblies with sister-city connections that could facilitate workable, wired national conversations.[46]

In tallying the benefits of Assemblies, O'Leary argues that they would give the public a space in which to exercise its voice, provide a system to promote public deliberation over special-interest politics, and break through legislative gridlock. Popular and sound ideas would reach floor votes in Congress, and elected officials might find passage of such bills irresistible, owing either to public pressure or the political cover provided by the Assembly.

Neither O'Leary nor Leib's proposals include detailed road maps to implementing a popular branch of government. Either proposal would cost tens of millions of dollars annually. Governments often are reluctant to cede any of their budget, let alone any degree of legislative authority. For instance, though the Oregon legislature authorized the Citizens' Initiative Review, it required private funding to foot the bill, and it established it as a one-time-only experiment. The Citizens' Assemblies established thus far have also been built to close after completing a single task. At the same time, many governments across the world have paid for Citizens' Juries, Deliberative Polls, and other deliberative processes. Over time, as such reform efforts are implemented and evaluated, policymakers and citizens may feel more comfortable expanding their reach. In that sense, the archetype of the jury can serve as a touchstone for the aspirations and strategies of those committed to promoting deliberative democracy.

Learning from the Jury

This review of deliberative proposals, experiments, and newly minted institutional practices should make plain that the deliberative democratic reform movement has considerable traction.[47] Though such reforms have already drawn some inspiration from the historical example of the jury, the jury system has more concrete lessons to teach those who seek to expand citizen opportunities for deliberation.

Prestige and Civic Impact

First of all, when assessing new deliberative processes in relation to the success of the jury, one must appreciate just how long it has taken the jury to mature into its present form. It seems that every major text on the American jury begins by reviewing its humble origins in England in various proto-juries, which bore little resemblance to the modern jury. It took centuries, for instance, for juries to establish their independence from the judge.[48] As we pointed out at the outset of chapter 1, even the right of *every* qualified citizen to serve on juries has been made secure only in recent decades. Though a process starting in the twenty-first century has advantages over those emergent at the dawn of the previous millennium, they, too, will require time to mature. They will likely endure challenges in court and revisions by legislatures, all of which will, hopefully, help new deliberative institutions to refine themselves over time.

It is likely that some of the power of the jury comes from its well-established prestige—the very reputation and public esteem that we have warned against tarnishing recklessly. The stature of the jury system—even the symbolically meaningful architecture of the courthouse and the jury box[49]—predisposes participants to be willing to answer the summons, and it likely increases their commitment to the rigors of the deliberative process, which, as we saw in chapter 5, can be emotionally taxing. New deliberative processes will have some novelty appeal, and Citizens' Juries and Deliberative Polls have partly succeeded because their organizers aim to capture some of the same drama of a trial or high-stakes public debate.[50] Nonetheless, we should be patient with new deliberative practices if they cannot, in spite of their virtues, secure wholesale public commitment in the near term.

One additional consequence may be the relatively thin civic educational benefit of new deliberative processes, at least initially. There has been little research to date on the long-term behavioral and attitudinal impact of participating in public deliberation.[51] At the same time, because these processes are *even more explicitly* connected to political society than the jury, their impacts on political behavior and attitudes should prove equal to—or greater than—that of the jury. Until participation in such programs becomes felt as the fulfillment of a civic duty—and until such activities have a meaningful, institutionalized role in the business of the state—they may not have the same consequences as serving on a jury.

When designing a deliberative process with civic impact in mind, it is also important to remember two ways in which "negatives" can become "positives." First, we saw in chapters 6 and 7 that jurors who became confused during trials did not necessarily become frustrated and withdraw from public life. In fact, there were times we saw a boomerang effect in which a discouraging sense of being lost during a trial spurred citizens to become more attentive to television news and other public affairs media. The practical lesson here is that one need not mollify those participants who recognize their need for greater civic knowledge; their newfound self-awareness could be the key to their reengagement with public life. Second, deliberative practitioners should not shield participants from any painful lessons about the responsiveness of public institutions—or other citizens—to their deliberative endeavors. Chapter 7 showed data linking voting and strategic political engagement to *lower* civic and political faith. Thus, if participants come to believe, as newly healthy civic skeptics, that their deliberation alone is not enough (i.e., that a meaningful policy impact requires further action on their part), that is a lesson well worth learning.

Drawing in the Wider Public

Who learns such lessons depends on who *participates*, and there again, the jury has much to offer. It is a well-established principle that deliberative events should ensure as diverse a group of participants as possible, and that often means making special efforts to include underrepresented populations.[52] Beyond the generic ethical imperative of inclusion that is essential to democracy, our data suggest that deliberative processes that successfully reach out to more politically marginal groups, such as those who vote infrequently, are potentially getting more bang for their civic buck. It is important, therefore, to recognize the particular needs of these groups and to make deliberative opportunities economically and socially viable for them.

We have already seen how many deliberative processes share the jury's commitment to random selection, though few go the additional step of making participation mandatory. When weighing this option, it is important to remember that mandatory service sometimes *lifts* a burden off participants, rather than placing one on them. Those who wish to serve but have professional or personal pressures holding them back can find relief in a legal mandate. As one of our King County jurors wrote:

> I was a foreperson on the jury and absolutely, thoroughly enjoyed the experience. Almost sorry I couldn't have been on a longer, more involved trial. It was interesting that after I got my summons, my employer automatically assumed that I would want to have them write a letter to try to have me excused. While it wasn't a hardship for me to serve, they considered it a hardship for them and the hospice patients we serve. Secretly I was glad that their letter didn't result in an excusal from duty. Good luck with your study!

Even the legally sanctioned processes in Canada and Oregon do not include that requirement, and it may be that compulsory participation has little future for new deliberative processes. In countries like Australia, however, where both voting and jury duty count as civic requirements, adding another may prove more palatable. Short of this, once more, the question of incentives arises, and until the service experience itself carries sufficient cachet to ensure a high response rate to randomly-distributed invitations, it is important to experiment with incentives that could yield more representative samples[53]

There is a less obvious way, though, in which juries involve the broader public, and this, too, merits consideration in other deliberative designs. The jury has partly achieved its archetypal status because the context in which it takes place—the courtroom trial—has been subject to careful public scrutiny. People watch trials on CourtTV and hear daily details from high-profile criminal and civil trials. Juries find their ways into television dramas, novels, and movies, and former jurors (and vicarious onlookers) blog about trials and juries constantly. Jurors themselves increasingly seek out a more interactive experience, and chapter 6 showed that nearly every juror talks about their period of service after the fact.

Deliberative programs like those we have reviewed earlier have had limited success garnering sustained public and media attention, but it is important to keep looking for ways to connect the larger public. If, as some critics claim, we now live in a world where both cable news and bloggers increasingly cater to those with the same predispositions, the opportunity for genuine reflection and reconsideration of one's views is likely to become more scarce.[54] Experiments in "teledemocracy" have strived to include large samples of the public in a simulated mass-deliberative process, and Deliberative Polls have often had their proceedings televised.[55] By providing exposure to balanced presentations through newspapers and other media, these efforts help deliberative processes reach far beyond the few who attend the signature events themselves. Drawing on the power of online and mobile communication technology, one obvious opportunity for innovation beyond the limits of the jury itself is for citizen deliberations to be videotaped and shared with the public. This approach promises to allow others to engage, at least on a vicarious basis, in the opportunity to engage in sustained deliberation.

The only caveat here parallels the concerns about televising Supreme Court oral arguments. The concern is that broadcasting such proceedings threatens to change their character, potentially leading participants to "play to the camera," to restrict their willingness to suggest controversial ideas, and potentially compromising privacy interests of individuals who do not want their views broadcast. If citizen participation in deliberative events became compulsory, this would become a concern, as opposed to when citizens freely choose to show up (and be viewed by the public). In short, just as juries have remained private in their deliberations, so are we mindful of the potential liabilities of videotaping and broadcasting such proceedings.

In every case, however, the materials prepared for a deliberative forum should be disseminated widely and citizens encouraged to participate in more informal, and ideally, more informed discussions on the same issues. Online forums could replicate and amplify the type of deliberation conducted at the focal public events. The 2009 Australian Citizens Parliament, for example, coupled itself with an Online Parliament, and the latter had the task of drafting proposals in online discussions that the Citizen Parliamentarians then considered in their face-to-face meetings.[56]

The opportunity to support online forums running in parallel with face-to-face events provides another new frontier for civic innovators. To date, such opportunities have emerged organically, as individuals use new technologies, ranging from blogs to Facebook and Twitter to videos posted on sites like YouTube, to engage in political discourse. The appeal of such technologies is that they promise to provide actual deliberative opportunities. Questions remain as to whether they can replicate the level of group cohesion, give and take, and effective discussion commonly found in juries and other face-to-face deliberative settings.[57]

Process Improvements

This brings us to consider the process of deliberation itself, as seen through the experience of the King County jurors described in chapter 5. From the many findings we have reported, we highlight four. First, it is not necessary to avoid complexity; jurors thrive when they have adequate time and resources to work through complex deliberative tasks, but they flag when weighed down by unnecessary technical detail. For the British Columbia Citizens' Assembly, for example, the challenge was to present to the citizens the full variety of voting systems without getting lost in the most arcane details about vote-counting systems. The citizens made choices on the scale at which their deliberation was most appropriate and stepped aside from debates that even mathematicians continue to wage.[58]

Second, male and female jurors alike experienced the trials in this study on an emotional level, and most had both positive and negative reactions to different elements of the trial. Emotion appears to figure into citizens' deliberations, even in a legal context that privileges rational and sober reflection. These results—and others we have reported elsewhere[59]—are good news for advocates of deliberation, because they suggest that women's communication style is not necessarily disadvantaged or ignored in deliberation. More generally, they emphasize the importance of *embracing* the emotional element of deliberation, as has long been the case for those civic reformers who give special importance to "dialogue," rather than exclusively the more analytic deliberative process.[60]

Third, a related concern is ensuring mutual respect among participants, a long-standing concern among deliberative democrats.[61] Here, we point to one particular finding in chapter 5: Whereas the deliberation measures predict juror satisfaction with deliberation (albeit modestly), the only measures that predict juror satisfaction with *the verdict* are jurors' sense of how they were treated by one another and how well jurors listened to one another. This finding foregrounds the importance of mutual respect in deliberative events, as these aspects of deliberation translated into jurors' satisfaction not only with the process but with their ultimate decision. To the extent that deliberative theory is still concerned with bolstering the legitimacy of public institutions, this result suggests that it may be the relational—rather than the rational—element of deliberation that most readily leads participants to view deliberative decisions as legitimate.

Though the overwhelming majority of jurors in King County felt respected by both their peers and court officials, we wish to stress the challenge that organizers of deliberative processes face as they try to give gracious, efficient service to a larger pool of jurors, many of whom have other responsibilities on their mind. When jurors end up feeling disrespected, mistreated, or taken for granted, the magic of jury deliberation disappears, sometimes resulting in something closer to a civic disenchantment. As one juror serving at the Kent Regional Justice Center wrote after such an experience:

> I felt the process was a waste of time. The court seems to function in it's own little world and goes about it's business without consideration of those called to participate in the process. While those that are asked to make the decisions must be content in doing their 'civic duty', the people who run the system enjoy salaries/benefits/social status in stark contrast to those who answer the call to serve.

We doubt this case was simply a problem of low juror compensation (though that small fact *does* make some jurors wonder how much the court appreciates their time, given their compensation of just a few dollars a day in most jurisdictions). Rather, we include this complaint to underscore the importance of ensuring that any deliberative process has on hand a staff or volunteers with enough good cheer, competence, and tact to make the citizen participants feel respected for their work.

A fourth procedural point returns us to the question of hung juries and the unanimous decision rule used in most criminal and many civil juries. Many comments from jurors, along with the hard statistical data, show that those who serve on hung juries often gain a great deal from the process, nonetheless. These situations call for judges to help jurors work through deadlocks or, if that fails, at least help jurors appreciate that it is their job to have worked through the evidence carefully together while respecting each juror's independent view. Neither judge nor jurors must force a unanimous judgment where none exists, and this principle would serve well those deliberative processes that some critics fear will succumb too easily to conformity pressure and a one-sided polarization of opinion.[62]

Moreover, some of the most critical safeguards for ensuring effective public deliberation—such as ensuring that group members are exposed to arguments to which they are not inclined—parallel some of the same features that have been built, over the course of centuries, into the American jury system.[63] Alluding to the research cited in chapter 1, on how culturally based cognitive biases inevitably influence the judgments of jurors and judges alike, deliberative public forums have more freedom to address such challenges directly than do courtrooms. One positive approach that designers can take is to address openly the different values—and perceptual biases—that we all bring to public issues, then to seek common solutions that accommodate the substantive and symbolic concerns of divergent cultural groups.[64]

Recentering the Jury in Democratic Theory

Viewing the jury through the lens of our political system and as an archetypal model of deliberative civic engagement, its virtues and key institutional features come into sharper focus. It foregrounds the limitations of the voting-centric conception of democratic citizens and reveals the need for direct democratic processes to provide more institutional support for citizen deliberation. In the jury context, deliberation is reinforced by the adversary system's commitment to providing jurors with balanced information, the leadership of the judge and foreperson to ensure all views are heard and considered, and the awareness that the deliberative process matters insofar as it will produce a binding legal decision. A political process designed along these lines would produce better results, avoid some of the trends in our society that spur increased polarization, and transform those who participate.

Meanwhile, the research we have presented shows that the jury already plays that transformative role for many—though not all—of those who answer their summons to serve at their local courthouse. Viewing our research in relation to the concern about declining social capital in the United States, the jury system may place limits on that decline.[65] Though the effects observed in this study are small, over time and across a large population they constitute a tremendous force that maintains a modest level of political and civic vitality across generations. Whatever forces imperil democratic public life, the jury system provides a counter force.

Tocqueville proved a useful starting point for mapping the educational effect of the jury, and his writings also proved useful in framing the jury not as an isolated legal exercise but as a vital part of political and civil society, even linking individual citizens to the state itself. In this sense, jury duty rises in stature from a custodial responsibility—one that gets a postage stamp and an Appreciation Day—to a more serious and fundamental duty. In its political aspect, the jury does have much in common with voting in elections. In its mandatory character, and the reluctance some feel toward it, answering the jury summons bears some resemblance to shuffling into the post office on Tax Day. In its communal qualities, the jury brings together strangers for face-to-face discussion of the fate of fellow citizens in a manner reminiscent of a neighborhood gathering or town meeting.

Connections such as these are far from mere metaphors. Many jurors leave the courthouse with a refreshed civic spirit and a greater willingness to engage with community and political life. In the end, though, we must not only recognize the jury's achievements in individual cases, important as those may be. We must also venerate the jury as an institution that links the state with both political and civil society and helps to make democratic society a reality. If permitted to endure in the United States and take deeper root in other countries as this new century progresses, the system of jury service will continue to bolster the legitimacy of democratic legal systems and shape the contours of deliberative reforms yet to come.

Further Reading

Though *The Jury and Democracy* presents an original argument, it builds on previous scholarship in law, civic engagement, political participation, and public deliberation. Two recent works that have celebrated the jury as a vital institution in American democracy include Jeffrey Abramson's *We, the Jury: The Jury System and the Ideal of Democracy* (Harvard, 2000) and William Dwyer's *In the Hands of the People: The Trial Jury's Origins, Triumphs, Troubles, and Future in American Democracy* (St. Martin's, 2002). Though we mainly suggest books here, we would be remiss not to recommend two pertinent law articles: Vikram D. Amar's 1995 essay, "Jury Service as Political Participation Akin to Voting," (*Cornell Law Review*, Vol. 80, pp. 203–59), and Barbara Underwood's 1992 piece, "Ending Race Discrimination in Jury Selection: Whose Right Is It, Anyway?" (*Columbia Law Review*, Vol. 92, pp. 725–74).

The only work to consider at length the lasting impact of jury service on the jurors themselves is Paula Consolini's 1992 U.C.-Berkeley doctoral dissertation, *Learning by Doing Justice: Private Jury Service and Political Attitudes*. Funded by the National Science Foundation, this landmark study helped to close the gaps between jury research, political participation research, and studies of the relationship between legal institutions and political attitudes, and it is available online at our project website, www.jurydemocracy.org.

Books that have looked more closely at the mechanics and pitfalls of the jury system include Neil Vidmar and Valerie Hans' *American Juries: The Verdict* (Prometheus, 2007), Randolph Jonakait's *The American Jury System* (Yale, 2003), Valerie Hans and Neil Vidmar's *Judging the Jury* (Perseus, 1986), and Neil Vidmar's edited *World Jury Systems* (Oxford, 2000). Other titles have looked more closely at how jurors make decisions, as in Norman Finkel's *Commonsense Justice: Jurors' Notions of the Law* (Harvard, 1998), or the recent wave of work on civil juries, prominently including Valerie Hans' *Business on Trial: The Civil Jury and Corporate Responsibility* (Yale, 2000) and Cass Sunstein et al.'s *Punitive Damages: How Juries Decide* (Chicago, 2002). A useful general resource is the Center for Jury Studies at the National Center for State Courts (www.ncsc.org).

Among the best works that focus squarely on political participation and civic life include Sidney Verba, Kay Schlozman, and Henry Brady's *Voice and Equality: Civic Voluntarism in American Politics* (Harvard, 1995), Mark Warren's *Democracy and Association* (Princeton, 2000), and Cliff Zukin et al.'s *A New Engagement? Political Participation, Civic Life, and the Changing American Citizen* (Oxford, 2006). Then there is always Alexis de Tocqueville's classic, *Democracy in America* (Penguin, 2003), which could be read alongside a compelling recent biography, *Alexis de Tocqueville: A Life* (Yale, 2007), by Hugh Brogan.

Also, Jackman and Miller's book, along with Theda Skocpol and Morris Fiorina's edited volume, *Civic Engagement in American Democracy* (Brookings Institution, 1999), bring renewed attention to the important role that institutions play in shaping democratic society. On the debate between the relative importance of cultural norms versus institutions in shaping public life, contrast Robert Putnam's *Bowling Alone: The Collapse and Revival of American Community* (Simon & Schuster, 2000), which documents a decline in civic engagement and social capital, with Robert Jackman and Ross Miller's *Before Norms: Institutions and Civic Culture* (Michigan, 2004), which disputed Putnam's claims.

Works that come closest to making our argument may be those that celebrate the importance of deliberation in public life and argue that the experience of deliberating can transform a person's self-concept, attitudes, and public behaviors. Recent works on this theme include James Fishkin's *When the People Speak: Deliberative Democracy and Public Consultation* (Oxford, 2009), Amy Gutmann and Dennis Thompson's *Why Deliberative Democracy?* (Princeton, 2004), Diana Mutz's *Hearing the Other Side: Deliberative versus Participatory Democracy* (Cambridge, 2006), and Mark Warren and Hilary Pearse's edited volume on the British Columbia Citizens' Assembly, *Designing Deliberative Democracy* (Cambridge, 2008). Chapter 6 of John Gastil's *Political Communication and Deliberation* (Sage, 2008) links this literature explicitly to the jury.

Methodological Appendix

This Appendix provides additional information on the data and statistical analyses presented in *The Jury and Democracy*. Complete survey instruments are available at the Jury and Democracy Project (www.jurydemocracy.org).

Additional Information for Chapter 3

Section 3a: Matching Protocol for National Study

The matching software compared alpha-sorted juror and voter datasets to look for unique name matches. Ideal pairings found one unique match of first, middle, and last name, but there were many other acceptable name matches (e.g., matching first and last names, with a juror having a middle initial matching only one corresponding middle name in the voter dataset). When a juror's name matched multiple names in the voter database, additional tiebreakers were employed depending on available data (e.g., matching suffixes, such as "Jr." or "III", or matching street numbers). Finally, 6 percent of the matched records were manually identified; for these cases, the matching software identified "candidate voter matches" that were visually compared to the juror in question to look for a unique match (e.g., voter "Rebecca Ann Janowitz" matching juror "Becky Ann Janowitz").

Section 3b: Characteristics of the National Jury Sample

Table A3.1 provides more information about the jurors in the National Jury Sample, including the type of trial they served on, their role as a juror, the trial's outcome, and the rate at which they could be positively matched with voting records. Table A3.2 provides National Jury Sample data by county/parish, the election and jury record coverage periods, as well as the average pre-jury service voting rates.

Additional Information for Chapter 4

Section 4a: Recruitment Letter

Below is the text of the introductory letter received by King County jurors. At the King County and Seattle Municipal courthouses, prospective study participants heard an introduction to the study from one of the survey administrators then received the invitation letter shown in this table, in addition to a consent form and copy of the survey.

University of Washington
National Survey on Community Life

Dear King County juror,

You have the opportunity to participate in important research being conducted by the University of Washington with a grant from the National Science Foundation. This project explores how King County residents participate in community life and public affairs.

This is the first of three parts to this study. If you volunteer to take part, you will complete a brief survey today, then receive a second survey 1–2 weeks after you have completed your jury service. You also will be re-contacted near the end of this year to check in one last time. At each point in the study, your participation will involve filling out a short survey that takes just 10–15 minutes to complete. When the study is done, you will receive a complimentary copy of the study's main results.

Your participation is voluntary, and we will be grateful if you are able to take part. This research project requires the involvement of a broad cross-section of the public. We want to make sure that your voice gets heard.

Please read and complete the attached consent form before proceeding with the survey. The consent form will provide detailed information about the study, and at your request, we will provide you with a copy to keep for your records. If you have any additional questions, a University of Washington research assistant is present in the jury assembly room to assist you.

Sincerely,

John Gastil, Project Director
National Survey on Community Life
Department of Communication

Table A3.1. Juror counts, trial characteristics, and voter matching rates by county/parish in the National Voting Sample

County/Parish	Total Jurors	Trial Type		Juror Role or Trial Outcome					Voter Matching	
		Civil	Criminal	Alternate	Guilty Plea	Canceled Trial[1]	Hung Jury[2]	Complete Verdict	Matched Voters	Match Rate
Boulder	573	366	207	4	25	14	31	499	327	57%
Cumberland	2,251	534	1,717	130	8	47	0	2,065	1,189	53%
Douglas	1,815	1,249	566	60	46	160	94	1,450	1,289	71%
El Paso	2,208	786	1,422	50	116	290	35	1,707	1,303	59%
Orleans[3]	2,131	355	1,776	87	574	161	263	1,004	1,436	67%
Summitt	2,429	1,024	1,405	222	71	98	50	1,980	1,841	76%
Swain	435	55	380	23	10	0	0	402	251	58%
Thurston	1,395	295	1,100	0	54	48	81	1,193	978	70%
Total	13,237	4,664	8,573	576	904	818	554	10,300	8,614	65%

[1]Includes mistrials, dismissals, withdrawn cases, settling out of court, or waiving the right to a jury (after the trial began).

[2]Includes any jury that hung on one or more of the charges.

[3]Thirty-five percent of the Orleans Parish jurors are from an oversample of non-jury verdict outcomes.

Table A3.2. Official election and jury record coverage periods and average pre-jury service voting rates by county/parish in the National Voting Sample

| County/Parish | Election Data Collected | | Jury Start and End Dates | | | Avg. Pre-Jury Voting Rate |
	Earliest	Latest	Earliest Start	Latest End	Median Start	
Boulder	1994 General	2004 General	8/19/1996	6/20/2002	7/19/1999	63.3%
Cumberland	1992 Primary	2004 General	3/21/1995	2/7/2000	4/6/1998	37.2%
Douglas	1987 Primary	2004 General	2/10/1997	8/4/2000	3/22/1999	44.0%
El Paso[1]	1992 Primary	2004 General	8/1/1995	9/30/2004	5/3/2002	43.4%
Orleans	1994 Primary	2004 General	12/1/1997	11/9/1999	12/7/1998	59.3%
Summitt	1994 Primary	2004 Primary	7/2/1996	3/10/2000	3/8/1999	55.7%
Swain	1992 Primary	2004 General	4/26/1995	8/31/1999	4/4/1997	33.7%
Thurston	1994 Primary	2003 General	5/29/1994	11/9/1996	10/31/1995	71.1%

[1]The El Paso jury data was available through an online service, iDocket, which at the time of the study, had data from 2000–2004, but one trial originating in 1995 was accessible as well.

Section 4b: Path Analytic Test of Jury–Voting Connection

Into this analysis, we also introduced the demographic measures we collected in the King County survey, plus a straightforward measure of political party membership. The political party item came from the long-term follow-up survey completed online and by mail months after service. King County judges had been concerned about asking questions on political ideology or party too close to the trial dates, lest attorneys become concerned about our survey influencing trials or should they file a request for our survey data to explore the potential for a mistrial. (Complete questionnaires were returned by 1,088 of those empanelled jurors invited to take this final survey.) The third survey included the National Election Study measure of party membership, "Generally speaking, do you think of yourself as..." Responses to this question were dichotomized with 1 indicating membership in the Democratic or Republican Party (79% of all jurors), with the rest identifying with no party or a third party. (The third survey is discussed in depth in chapters 6 and 7.)

To probe jurors' subjective assessments, we combined the earlier measures of engagement (interest in the trial) and experience relative to expectations. Responses to these two items were averaged together to create a single Experience index, with higher scores indicating a more positive and engaging jury service experience (on a scale from 1–5, $M = 3.86$, $SD = .71$).

Amos 5 path analytic software was employed to test the hypotheses, which explicitly distinguish among direct and indirect effects (Byrne 2001). As path analysis goes, the default path model employed was straightforward, even if the many paths in Figure A4.1 might look like a spider web to those whose eyes have not yet adjusted to such diagrams. First, all predictor variables were assumed to covary with one another. To ensure a model solution, however, all covariant paths to Deliberated were removed, except for the possible covariance of trial type and Deliberated, in the event that civil or criminal trials in the sample were more likely to end prematurely. (Alternative models testing for these covariate paths produced no significant relationships. This is not surprising in that juror characteristics (age, etc.) are unlikely to affect whether a trial goes to deliberation.) Second, all predictors were given direct paths to both Experience and post-jury service voting rate. We predicted significant paths to post-jury service voting rate from only Experience, Deliberated, and the trial type dummy variable, along with the taken-for-granted effect of pre-service voting rate. All other control variables were assigned paths to post-jury service voting rate as a means of accounting for any direct influence they had on post-service voting.

Before examining the significance and size of effects (a.k.a., "individual parameter estimates") of the path analysis in Figure A4.1, it was necessary to confirm the overall fit of the model. "Fit statistics" assess whether the set of paths we have specified have an acceptable overall correspondence to the reality of the data we hope to model, and the fit in this case was strong enough to permit proceeding to the main results.

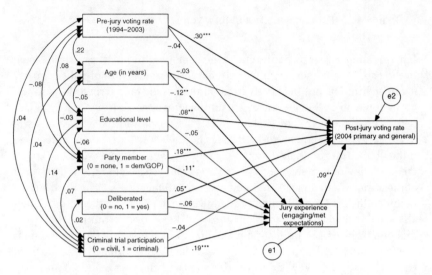

Note: * $p < .10$, ** $p < .05$, *** $p < .01$.

Figure A4.1   Standardized coefficients from path analysis of hypothesized predictors of post-jury service voting in King County for pre-service infrequent voters

This particular model produced a nonsignificant $X^2 = 4.33$ (*df* = 8, *p* = .826) a result suggesting exceptional model fit, since the chi-square test routinely detects unaccounted variance in large samples (Bentler and Bonett, 1980, p. 591). Even though the model passed the chi-square test, we turned to better fit indicators, such as the Bentler-Bonett normed fit index (NFI), which compares the minimum discrepancy of the tested model against a baseline. The obtained NFI value of .987 suggests a very good fit, as Bentler and Bonnet (1980, p. 600) found that only "models with overall fit indices of less than .90 can usually be improved substantially." An alternative fit measure is RMSEA, a population discrepancy measure that compensates for model complexity. The RMSEA value for this model was .045, which is safely below the .05 limit indicating a close fit (Browne and Cudeck 1993).

Table A4.1 provides a summary of the directional paths in the separate models we created for both infrequent and frequent voters. The group of jurors with a previous history of frequent voting demonstrated no relationship between jury service and post-service voting rate, a finding consistent with Study 2. In addition, the model yielded most of the hypothesized relationships for infrequent voters. For infrequent voters, Criminal Trial had a direct positive effect only to Experience (B = .345, *b* = .195), as did the control variables Party Member (B = .181, *b* = .108) and Age (B = −.008, *b* = −.116). Variables with significant direct paths to post-service voting rate included Deliberated (B = .044, *b* = .055) and Experience (B = .038, *b* = .092), along with Party Member (B = .128, *b* = .184), Education (B = .016, *b* = .078), and, of course, pre-service voting rate (B = .731, *b* = .301).

Table A4.1. Path analytic direct effects on jury experience and post-jury service voting for King County jurors, broken down by pre-jury service voting frequency

| | Infrequent Pre-Jury Service Voters (N = 843) | | | | Frequent Pre-Jury Service Voters (N = 937) | | | |
| | Direct Effect on Jury Experience | | Direct Effect on Post-Jury Voting Rate | | Direct Effect on Meeting Expectations | | Direct Effect on Post-Jury Voting Rate | |
Predictor	B (SE)	beta	B (SE)	beta	B (SE)	beta	B (SE)	beta
Vote Avg. Pre	-.209 (.31)	-.035	.731 (.09)	.301***	-.238 (.23)	-.046	.427 (.06)	.248***
Deliberated	-.114 (.10)	-.058	.044 (.03)	.055*	-.047 (.09)	-.024	-.013 (.02)	-.019
Criminal Trial	.345 (.09)	.195***	-.030 (.03)	-.041	.029 (.07)	.017	.003 (.02)	.006
Age	-.008 (.00)	-.116**	-.001 (.00)	-.032	<.001 (.00)	-.008	<.001 (.00)	.014
Education	-.026 (.03)	-.054	.016 (.01)	.078**	-.017 (.02)	-.039	.005 (.01)	.031
Party Member	.181 (.11)	.108*	.128 (.04)	.184***	.219 (.09)	.123**	.079 (.03)	.132***
Jury Exper.	—	—	.038 (.02)	.092**	—	—	.007 (.01)	.021

Note: * p < .10, ** p < .05, *** p < .01. Standard errors reported as .00 are less than .005. Fit Statistics (default model): X2 = 4.33 (df = 8, p = .826); NFI = .987; RMSEA = .045.

Additional Information for Chapter 5

Section 5a: Juror Treatment Perceptions

Table A5.1 shows that correlations among the four juror treatment items (juror perceptions of the treatment they received from judges, staff, attorneys, and fellow jurors) ranged from .44 to .61, all relatively large positive associations. When similar survey items correlate at this level, it is often prudent to integrate them into a single, overarching scale. Methodologists call this "data reduction" because it exchanges the complexity of separate items, such as these four, for the simplicity of an integrated scale—in this case, an overall measure of juror treatment . Doing so also has the important advantage of reducing the risk of multicollinearity in regression and similar analyses, a problem that arises when different independent variables are so correlated with one another that they cancel each other out when trying to predict variation in a dependent variable (see Cohen et al. 2003).

Table A5.1.   Intercorrelations among empanelled juror perceptions of treatment by judges, staff, attorneys, and fellow jurors

	Treatment by Judges	Treatment by Staff	Treatment by Attorneys
Treatment by Staff	.58***		
Treatment by Attorneys	.61***	.51***	
Treatment by Fellow Jurors	.44***	.50***	.42***

Note: * $p < .10$, ** $p < .05$, *** $p < .01$. Minimum $N = 1406$. Coefficient alpha (α) = .80.

Section 5b: Coding the Seriousness of Charges and Claims

There is no uniform standard for a criminal trial's gravity, but all could agree that murder is more serious than petty theft. To code the seriousness of criminal charges in King County, we had one coder use the State of Washington criminal code, which ranks charges by severity, while the other coder used common sense judgment about the seriousness of different charges. These two approaches were highly correlated ($r = .80$), and we combined them into an index of criminal charge seriousness. (This correlation was calculated at the jury level of analysis [$N = 223$] between the records-based ten-point seriousness scale and the commonsense four-point scale.) Crosstabulation was used to inspect the scales and set their recodings into a three-point scale (low = 0–.5, mid = 1, high = 1.5–2). By this metric, 52 percent of criminal jurors served on trials with lower ratings, 27 percent served on trials rated at the index midpoint, and the remaining 19 percent served on the most serious trials. (The National Jury Sample in chapter 3 simply used the lay judgments as the basis for its codings.)

Civil trials were more difficult to code. We might agree that compensation for a dented fender is trivial compared with medical malpractice, but motor vehicle accidents—a category representing 40 percent of civil trials in King County—vary widely in their seriousness. When we had a civil legal scholar code these data and compare them against commonsense rankings, the correlation was not even statistically significant. We then checked both ratings against the actual size of civil awards sought, and the layperson seriousness scale correlated powerfully ($r = .71$) with the awards sought. For its more intuitive appeal, we opted to use the layperson scale as our index of civil charge seriousness, which simply distinguished between less serious cases (61 percent) and more serious cases (39 percent). The reason for the dichotomy was that scale points 1 and 4 together accounted for only 5 percent of the data. Essentially, the distribution was already binary, and we collapsed scale points 1 and 2 to create the "low" level (0) and collapsed 3 and 4 to create the "high" level (2).

Section 5c: Measuring Perceived Deliberation Quality and Engagement

First, jurors' perceptions of the overall deliberation in terms of weighing evidence, following instructions, listening, and providing speaking opportunities were largely and somewhat uniformly correlated, so we treated them as a four-item scale. When making a scale in this way, it is necessary to assess its coherence or *reliability*, and there is a formal statistic to make this assessment. The more individual items in a scale and the higher and more uniform their inter-correlations, the higher that scale's overall reliability will become. What constitutes adequate reliability is a matter of debate, but the lowest conventional standard we have seen for a small survey scale is .60, with all methodologists preferring reliabilities (a.k.a. Coefficient alpha, or simply the Greek symbol "α") of .70 or higher whenever possible. In the case of jurors' deliberation perceptions, the scale had sufficient reliability (Cronbach's $\alpha = .83$).

The three items concerning jurors' own behavior were also all intercorrelated, but the rate at which jurors interjected their own personal views was more weakly associated with the measures of expressing opinions and explaining evidence. Thus, we combined only the latter two items into a modestly reliable two-item scale ($\alpha = .61$) and left the other survey question as a single-item measure of relating one's personal experiences.

Additional Information for Chapter 6

Section 6a: Civic Engagement Measures

Though we had a theory about how the eighteen survey items could be assembled into composite measures of four aforementioned types of engagement, it was necessary to turn again to statistics to validate that transformation. We used a *confirmatory factor analysis* on the pre-jury service engagement measures to check our theoretical model against the actual relationships among the eighteen measures.

We used a principal components analysis with varimax rotation and Kaiser normalization. The four factors explained 49 percent of the total variance. By comparison, an exploratory analysis found six factors, explaining 60 percent of the variance; the only notable differences were that this solution split the community groups into two factors and tossed TV news and educational groups into a sixth, hodgepodge factor.

The factor analysis tried to identify common factors underlying our large set of survey items, and in the confirmatory approach, we asked for the best-fitting solution with the number of underlying factors fixed to four—the same four engagement factors we had intended to build into our survey. The right-hand columns in Table A6.1 show the "factor loadings" of each of the eighteen items on the four underlying factors identified by the factor analysis. The higher the loading, the better the item fits on the factor, and to simplify the table, we removed any loadings below .30.

Overall, the factor analysis fits our theoretical expectations quite well, though we had not anticipated nonpartisan civic group participation falling into the political action factor, and we were not sure whether persuasion-oriented political conversation would fall under the broader category of political action or public talk. What the factor analysis tells us is that the frequency with which one tries to persuade in political conversation can be better predicted by the rate at which they engage in other forms of public talk than by their propensity for taking political action. In addition, Table A6.1 shows that these factors appear quite distinct—with only a handful of low cross-factor loadings, such as in the case of politically persuasive talk, which does have a weak loading on the political action factor. (To validate this factor analysis, we even took the additional step of factor analyzing jurors' follow-up surveys in the same way. This analysis produced identical factors, with similar factor loadings and still no cross-factor loadings above .37.)

Before creating our final engagement scales, however, we conducted a reliability analysis similar to the one described in section 5c to see if each of these factors produced reliable measurements. The scales measuring political action and public talk produced straightforward, reliable scales, but the other two scales required closer inspection. The reliability analysis for the public affairs media uses items suggested that reliability would increase (from $\alpha. = 52$ to $\alpha. = 61$) if we detached TV news viewing from the other survey items. We opted to do so, partly because past research on public engagement has found television news viewing to be a distinct kind of media use, sometimes even having negative relationships with other forms of civic engagement—contrary to the effects flowing from other media (McLeod et al. 1996; Moy and Gastil 2006).

Table A6.1. Item means, standard deviations, and factor loadings for political and civic engagement measures

				Loadings for four-factor solution*			
Combined scales and individual survey item	Response Scale	Mean	SD	Media Use	Political Action	Public Talk	Local Groups
Public affairs media use (α = .61)							
[How often] would you say you follow what's going on in government and public affairs…?	1–4	3.39	.74	.71		.36	
How often did you learn about politics and public affairs reading news in magazines, in newspapers, or on Internet websites?	1–5	3.89	1.05	.71			
How often did you learn about politics and public affairs watching television news programs? (Dropped from scale)	1–5	3.42	1.20	.60			
How often did you learn about politics and public affairs listening to the news on the radio?	1–5	3.56	1.18	.47			
Political action (α = .80)							
How often did you attend political meetings, rallies, speeches, or dinners?	1–4	1.36	.70		.81		
How often did you do an hour or more of volunteer work for a political cause, a political party, a candidate, or an initiative campaign?	1–5	1.24	.63		.81		
How active have you been in political groups?	1–4	1.48	.73		.75		
How active are you in nonpartisan or civic organizations?	1–4	1.11	.41		.62		
Have you contacted a public official, agency, or board?	1–2	1.32	.47		.45	.33	

Table A6.1. *(continued)*

				Loadings for four-factor solution*				
Combined scales and individual survey item	Response Scale	Mean	SD	Media Use	Political Action	Public Talk	Local Groups
Public talk (α = .73)							
How often have you discussed local community affairs with other members of your community?	1–5	2.72	1.13			.79	
How interested are you in local community politics and local community affairs?	1–3	2.22	.55			.64	
How often have you talked to people to learn more about a political issue, a candidate, or a ballot initiative?	1–5	3.02	1.16			.64	
How often have you talked to someone to change their mind about a political issue, a candidate, or a ballot initiative?	1–5	2.22	1.16		.37	.57	
Community group participation (α = .50)							
How active are you in charitable or service organizations?	1–4	1.79	1.01				.72
How active are you in religious congregations?	1–4	1.90	1.09				.65
How active are you in educational institutions?	1–4	1.76	.94				.52
How active are you in cultural organizations?	1–4	1.52	.83				.47
How active are you in neighborhood groups and associations?	1–4	1.60	.85				.37

Note: Behavioral frequency questions began with the phrasing, "During the past six months…." Complete item wording is in the Methodological Appendix.
*Factor loadings below .30 are not shown.

The community group participation items presented a different problem: They did not combine to form an adequately reliable scale, and removing any one item did not increase scale reliability. After all, recall that reliability depends on both the average inter-item correlation *and the number of items in a scale*, and though, for instance, religious group involvement has only weak associations to neighborhood and cultural group participation, its removal still causes reliability to drop. We opted to keep these items together, nonetheless, because no single pair of them was so strong as to merit separate analysis. When the time came to analyze this aspect of civic engagement, however, we took special care to consider these items individually, as needed.

Section 6b: Measuring Control Variables

We asked in the pre-service survey, "These days, how active are your adult friends in politics or community affairs?" Twenty-six percent of the jurors in this sample said their friends were "not at all" active, 64 percent said their social network was "somewhat" active, and 11 percent said their friends were "very" politically active. A second item asked the same question regarding "adult family members and relatives," yielding comparable percentages (40 percent inactive, 50 percent somewhat active, 10 percent very active). To control for differences in the political activity levels of survey participants' friends and family, we combined these two items into a single two-item scale ($\alpha = .57$).

This study, by design, overlapped the 2004 election period, which gave jurors the opportunity to act on any newfound civic impulse their jury service might have given them. Such action, however, might well have been further conditioned by a juror's leaning toward liberalism or conservativism or, more likely, by the degree to which they viewed themselves as part of a viable political party with a clear stake in the election.

For the political partisanship measure, we combined two items—one's party identification (Democratic, Republican, or other party affiliation, if any) and, for those with a party, the *strength* of that identification. By combining these items, we created a four-point scale measuring the strength of major party affiliation. Twenty-two percent of the sworn jurors in the present sample viewed themselves as independent (or favoring a third party), and they were coded as 0 on this scale. Twenty-seven percent only "slightly" supported one or the other major party (coded as a 1), 35 percent "strongly" supported a party (coded as a 2), with the remaining 16 percent offering "very strong" support to their preferred major party. (Only 2 percent of the sample preferred a third party, including three who wrote-in, on the space provided, "Green" and two who wrote "Socialist Workers Party." No other party name received more than one mention.)

The left-right self-identification measure we used was the same referenced in chapter 4, with one exception. Of the 203 people in this sample who had "missing data" on the liberal-conservative measure, 174 *did* choose to tell us what party they belonged to and the strength of their affiliation, as discussed above. These were very strongly correlated ($r = .78$), such that if one self-identified as a very strong Republican, one was either "conservative" (36 percent) or "extremely conservative" (64 percent). Therefore, for Democrats, Republicans, and independents with missing values on left-right ideology, we substituted the average liberal-conservative score from the other respondents who shared their same party affiliation strength.

Mean substitution is one of the cruder ways of handling missing data, but in an extreme and isolated case like this, it works reasonably well without unnecessarily complicating the analysis. This revised ideology measure and the major party strength of affiliation measure were only marginally correlated, with strong liberals being more partisan than strong conservatives ($r = -.06$, $p = .08$).

Section 6c: Partial Correlations from Deliberation to Engagement

Like a regression equation, the partial correlation method of analysis can control for any number of other variables before measuring the degree of association between two focal variables. The advantage it presents is that when multiple predictors share considerable overlapping variance—and the control variables are of little analytic interest in and of themselves—the partial correlation shows the full size of association between predictor and dependent variables.

For these data, we ran partial correlations between each of the two municipal deliberation measures and the set of civic engagement measures. Like the longitudinal voting analyses shown in previous chapters, these analyses provide evidence suggesting *causation*, rather than mere association. The partial correlation tries to predict behavior measured in the long-term follow-up survey based on jurors' descriptions of their service experience recorded months earlier. Equally important, the partial correlation controls for the baseline behavior measured in the initial pre-jury service survey. In other words, the partial correlation seeks to explain the *change* in behavior that occurred between the beginning and end of our study. To further boost our confidence in the validity of any observed association between jury experience and behavior change, the partial correlations also control for the influence of the aforementioned set of demographic and attitudinal variables, including ethnicity, sex, age, education, work status (retired, full-time, and other), years in residence, renting versus owning a home, political knowledge, political activity level of friends and family, strength of major party affiliation, and liberal-conservative self-identification.

Section 6d: Comparing Effect Sizes

An alternative approach to getting a sense of absolute size is to compare these effects with the wider range of associations discovered in past social psychological studies. In particular, a team of researchers recently integrated more than 25,000 studies involving over 8 million human participants to determine the general nature of effects in social scientific research (Richard, Bond, and Stokes-Zoota 2003). Consider, for instance, the effect sizes of these social behavior effects, all of which should be recognizable to readers but none of which previously had a clear "effect size" in one's mind:

$r = .11$ represents the relative ease with which one can influence a person with low self-esteem relative to one with self-high regard.
$r = .18$ represents the influence-advantage people with high social status have over their less prominent peers.
$r = .23$ represents the greater satisfaction people generally feel working for a democratic leader versus an autocratic one.
$r = .34$ represents the greater probability that people will disclose personal information to people they like versus those they dislike.

The range of effects in chapter 6 fall roughly in this range, with the larger correlations representing a stronger behavioral impact.

Section 6e: Creating Jury Experience Scales

We expected that the experience assessment items would reduce to just four factors (overall satisfaction, treatment, cognitive/emotional engagement, and satisfaction with deliberation/verdict) to which we would add the post-service variables introduced at the start of the chapter—hearing from the judge and discussing the jury experience with friends and family.

The results of the factor analysis of these survey questions, however, did not support a straightforward set of four factors. First, as Table A6.2 shows, the three overall satisfaction measures loaded weakly and diffusely across the first three factors. These three items were kept together as a single scale ($\alpha = .72$), but the factor analysis emphasizes that overall satisfaction is less a distinct factor than an overarching assessment of one's jury experience, which relates to the more discrete elements measured more precisely by other items. Given the present purpose of focusing on the particular aspects of jury service that trigger behavior change, this satisfaction scale will receive relatively less attention in subsequent analyses.

Next, the personal treatment factor showed strong loadings on the four related survey items, which yielded a reliable personal treatment scale ($\alpha = .80$). Even here, though, the relationships among items were slightly uneven, with perceptions of treatment by fellow jurors standing apart from the other three items slightly. The other three treatment variables had an average inter-item correlation of $r = .57$, whereas the jury treatment variable had an average correlation with those three items of $r = .45$—a strong but modestly weaker association. In the interest of parsimony, the items stayed grouped together.

The cognitive/emotional engagement factor proved to be a measure of cognitive interest and perceived importance, but not emotion, per se. This

Table A6.2. Item means, standard deviations, and factor loadings for jury experience measures

				Loadings for four-factor solution*			
Combined scales and individual survey item	Response Scale	Mean	SD	Satisfied/ Treated	Delib./ Verdict	Cog Engagement	Misc.
Overall satisfaction with service (α = .72)							
Rate your [overalll] experience at jury duty	1–5	3.67	1.08	.46	.45	.40	
Rate your experience as a juror in relation to your initial expectations	1–5	3.79	.87	.36	.41	.36	
I felt that my time was well-used by the court	1–5	3.57	.97	.32		.50	
Personal treatment (α = .80)							
How were you treated by the judges?	1–5	4.47	.80	.82			
…the court staff?	1–5	4.39	.80	.79			
…the attorneys?	1–5	4.02	.95	.79			
…fellow jurors?	1–5	4.24	.86	.66	.37		
Assessment of deliberation/verdict (α = .73)							
Rate your satisfaction with the verdict	1–4	3.23	.92		.82		
Rate the quality of the jury's deliberations	1–4	3.37	.82		.81		
The jury played a very important role in resolving this case	1–5	3.94	1.05		.48		
Cognitive engagement (α = .50)							
The trial was very interesting to think about	1–5	3.93	.85			.75	
The case… was important enough to take up the time of a full jury	1–5	3.50	1.20			.76	
Single-Item Measures							
Did juror feel emotion during trial [yes = 1]	0–1	.79	.41				.72
Some important aspects of the trial were difficult for me to understand. (Reversed)	1–5	3.93	.95				-.57

Note: Behavioral frequency questions began with the phrasing, "During the past six months.…" Complete item wording is in the Methodological Appendix.
*Factor loadings below .30 are not shown.

pair of items yielded a fair reliability for a two-item scale (α = .58). The two items that did not cohere to this factor were left as separate measures. Though the emotion and comprehension measures stood in the fourth factor together, they did so only as the detritus of the forced four-factor solution; in reality, they were not the least bit correlated with each other (r = .01).

Section 7:   Civic and Political Attitude Measurement

A confirmatory factor analysis with the same design as in chapter 6 yielded results consistent with this set of six attitudinal factors—the core set of four civic/political attitudes, plus trust in the jury and trust in other institutions (see Table A7.1). When these items combined into scales, their reliability tended to be low but adequate (α = .65 to .69), with more reliability for the venerable measure of political self-confidence (α = .86) and wholly inadequate coherence for civic faith (α = .44). (This scale pretested well with real jurors before the formal study began, but once in the field, scale reliability proved elusive.) In addition, the lowest loading item on the jury system trust scale was set aside to increase that scale's conceptual clarity and reliability.

Table A7.1. Item means, standard deviations, and factor loadings for political and civic attitude measures

| | | | | Loadings for six-factor solution* | | | | | |
Combined scales and individual survey item	Response Scale	Mean	SD	Political Self-Confidence	Political Faith	Civic Pride	Civic Faith	Trust in Jury System	Trust in Courts/ Congress
Political self-confidence (α = .86)									
I think I am better informed about politics and government than most people	1–5	3.41	.97	.87					
I have a pretty good understanding of the important issues facing this country	1–5	3.91	.79	.86					
I consider myself well-qualified to participate in politics and community affairs	1–5	3.62	.92	.86					
Political faith (α = .66)									
There are many legal ways for citizens to successfully influence what government does	1–5	3.62	.82		.80				
Under our form of government, the people have the final say about how the country is run, no matter who is in office	1–5	2.55	1.04		.65		.33		
People like me don't have any say about what the government does (Reversed)	1–5	2.39	.94		.74				

Table A7.1. (*continued*)

Combined scales and individual survey item	Response Scale	Mean	SD	Loadings for six-factor solution*					
				Political Self-Confidence	Political Faith	Civic Pride	Civic Faith	Trust in Jury System	Trust in Courts/ Congress
Civic pride (α = .65)									
People like me play an important role in the life of my community	1–5	3.82	.76			.73			
I take seriously my responsibilities as a citizen	1–5	4.13	.65			.69			
I often fail to do my part to make my local community a good place to live (Reversed)	1–5	2.47	.91			.81			
Civic faith (α = .44)									
Americans always do their part to try to make their local community a better place to live	1–5	2.60	.90				.76		
When asked to do their part, most American citizens will make sacrifices on behalf of the nation	1–5	3.43	.86				.72		

Notes

Chapter 1

1. Chapter 8 revisits Judge Young's remarks. The full text of this speech is available online at http://www.floridabar.org/DIVCOM/JN/jnnews01.nsf /8c9f13012b96736985256aa900624829/5d3d1e61610d7e5c8525731500519 20d.

2. Posted online December 14, 2005, at the blog "Sanguinary Blue" (http://sanguinaryblue.blogspot.com/2005/12/civic-responsibility.html).

3. The absence of comprehensive, national jury service reporting require-ments makes more precise figures impossible. The first figure comes from the 2006 Annenberg Public Policy Center Survey on the Judiciary (http:// www.annenbergpublicpolicycenter.org/Downloads/Releases/Release_ Courts20060928/Courts_Release_20060928.pdf). The second comes from a survey by the National Center for State Courts (Mize, Hannaford-Agor, and Waters 2007, p. 10). These numbers are slightly higher than the 2008 national Harris Poll on the jury (http://www.harrisinteractive.com/harris_ poll/index.asp?PID=861), which found that 24 percent of respondents had sat on a jury.

4. More favorable recent portrayals exist, such as the Russian film *12* (directed by Nikita Mikhalkov) and the BBC mini-series *The Jury* shown on Masterpiece Theater (http://www.pbs.org/wgbh/masterpiece/jury).

5 The juror stories that do get told often represent exceptional cases, such as the juror who sat on a child murder trial, then afterward painted a portrait of the child "in happier times" as a gift to the child's grieving grandparents (Welborn 2009). Many other tales appear in the "Deliberations" blog that was maintained by trial lawyer Anne Reed (http://jurylaw.typepad.com/ deliberations).

6. de Tocqueville (1835/1961, pp. 334–37). John Stuart Mill expressed similar views on the educational benefits of political engagement (Pedersen 1982), as did Rousseau (1761/1950).

7. Strauder v. West Virginia (1880).

8. Abramson (1994, pp. 105, 108–12).

9. Vidmar and Hans (2007, pp. 73–74).

10. Smith v. Texas (1940).

11. Batson v. Kentucky (1986, pp. 92–93).

12. For example, in civil trials in the state of Washington, each side may make only three peremptory strikes.

13. Batson v. Kentucky (1986, p. 121), ellipses from original opinion omitted.

14. Abramson (1994).

15. Smith v. Texas (1940).

16. Swain v. Alabama (1965).

17. As criminal defendants were not in a position to track jury selection practices years before they were charged with crimes, this was a largely useless tool (Batson 1986, pp. 92–93). Abramson (1994, p. 134) reported that for the next twenty years "not a single federal court found use of peremptory challenges to violate *Swain* standards."

18. Appendix to Amicus Curiae Brief for Elizabeth Holtzman, District Attorney, Kings County, New York. The brief supported the position of James Batson in Batson v. Kentucky (1986). Capitalization, spelling, and punctuation edited for style.

19. Batson v. Kentucky (1986).

20. Holland v. Illinois (1990, pp. 488–89).

21. Holland v. Illinois (1990, p. 489).

22. Franken (1986a–d, 1987a–b) provided contemporary coverage in the *Columbus Dispatch*.

23. Interview with Robert Lane, Chief Appellate Counsel, Ohio Public Defender Commission, conducted by Cindy Simmons on June 29, 2009.

24. This rationale for jury integration had been invoked by Justice Thurgood Marshall in the opinion in Peters v. Kiff (1972), which stated, "When any large and identifiable segment of the community is excluded from jury service, the effect is to remove from the jury room qualities of human nature and varieties of human experience the range of which is unknown, and perhaps unknowable. It is not necessary to assume that the excluded group will consistently vote as a class in order to conclude, as we do, that its exclusion deprives the jury of a perspective on human events that may have unsuspected importance in any case that may be presented." Justices William O. Douglas and Potter Stewart joined the opinion.

25. Brief for Petitioner in Powers v. Ohio (1991, p. ii).

26. Transcript of petitioner's oral argument in Powers v. Ohio (1991).

27. Powers v. Ohio (1991, p. 407); see also Amar (1997).

28. Powers v. Ohio (1991, p. 406), quoting Balzac v. Porto Rico (1922).

29. Powers v. Ohio (1991, p. 407), ellipses and bracketed words as in original.

30. In his dissent, Justice Antonin Scalia complained that Powers might be freed if he was granted a new trial. (Charlotte Golden, the only eyewitness to the murders, died in 1990.) "The Court," Scalia wrote, "uses

its key to the jailhouse door...to threaten release upon the society of the unquestionably guilty... since a denial of equal protection to other people occurred at the defendant's trial, though it did not affect the fairness of that trial" (Powers v. Ohio 1991, p. 430). The jailhouse door, however, never swung open for Powers. When the case went back to the trial court, the judge determined that the prosecutor had peremptorily struck each of the seven African Americans on the belief that they would have trouble imposing the death penalty, not because of racial stereotypes (interview with Robert Lane, see note 16)

31. The U.S. Supreme Court decisions recognizing that citizens of all races have a right to serve on a jury have not created uniformly race-blind jury selection in the United States. In the Equal Justice Initiative's (2010) report "Illegal Racial Discrimination in Jury Selection: A Continuing Legacy," the non-profit law organization reported that racial discrimination in jury selection remains "widespread, apparent and seemingly tolerated...especially in serious criminal and capital cases." It reported that in Houston County, Ala., cases from 2005 to 2009 in which the death penalty was imposed, prosecutors used peremptory strikes to remove 80 percent of the African Americans qualified for jury service. As a result, in half of the six capital cases, the juries were all-white. In the remaining three, there was only one African American on each jury. The population of Houston County, the group reported, is 27 percent African American. The group also found that after the Batson decision, prosecutors in states including Pennsylvania and Texas had been trained on how to exclude people on the basis of race.

Chapter 2

1. Janara (2002), pp. 64–65.
2. Janara (2002), p. 78.
3. Tocqueville (1835/2002, Book I, Chapter 5, and Book II, Chapter 7).
4. Tocqueville (1835/2002, Book I, Chapter 5).
5. For modern political theory on this subject, see Cooke (2000, pp. 948–49), Pateman (1970) and Warren (1992).
6. Delli Carpini, Cook, and Jacobs (2004); Chambers (2003); Gastil (2008); Thompson (2008); and Ryfe (2002).
7. Warren (1996, p. 121).
8. Abramson (1994, p. 9).
9. Matthews, Hancock, and Briggs (2004).
10. Dahl (1989, pp. 220–22). For Dahl's critique of the American constitution in these respects, see Dahl (2002).
11. There is no simple metric for measuring polyarchies or democracies, but their number is certainly on the rise. See Halperin, Siegle, and Weinstein (2005, p. 11), who use the Polity IV coding scheme (http://www.cidcm.umd.edu/inscr/polity/report.htm). For an alternative assessment of political freedom across the globe, see the Freedom House inventory of political freedom (http://www.freedomhouse.org/template.cfm?page=15).
12. Tocqueville (1835/2002, Book II, Chapters 5 and 7).
13. See Elstub (2008) and Hendriks (2006a).

14. Putnam (1995a, 1995b). These themes were developed further in Putnam (2000).

15. On the debate over declining social capital, see Bennett (1998) and Koniordos (2005). For extensions of Tocqueville's views on civil society, see Edwards, Foley, and Diany (2001).

16. On initiatives, see Smith (2002). On campaign mobilization, see Holbrook and McClurg (2005) and Popkin (1994). For a very readable introduction to American elections and voting generally, see Maisel (2007).

17. Evans and Boyte (1992); Hershey (1993).

18. Weintraub (1997, p. 15).

19. Warren (2000, pp. 32–33). Warren also argues that Tocqueville is guilty of making such sharp distinctions, but we do not share that view. Nor do Weintraub and Kumar (1997), who share Warren's concern about dichotomizing these spheres.

20. Cohen and Rogers (1995). For the "demarchy" variant of this approach, which might be characterized as bringing such groups more fully into the state itself, see Burnheim (1985).

21. On the interplay of institutions, civil society, and civic engagement, see Skocpol and Fiorina (1999).

22. Weintraub (1992, p. 57).

23. Putnam (2000, p. 67).

24. Amar (1995, pp. 205–6).

25. Kahan and Braman (2008); Kahan, Hoffman, and Braman (2009). Similar findings have been produced for decades. In 1965, for instance, political scientist Theodore Becker and colleagues demonstrated how a group of mock jurors, led to believe they were giving meaningful input on a real case, applied their political–cultural values in showing leniency toward a son who granted his father's wish to be euthanized. As Becker concluded, "We have decision makers who are in a judicial-decisional context confronted by clear law," but who ultimately judge based on "the decision maker's own personal view of propriety, justice, etc." (Becker et al. 1965).

26. Posner (2008, p. 116).

27. On the interconnection of politics and courts in the U.S., see Ferejohn (2002). On the politics of Supreme Court nominations, see Moraski and Shipan (1999).

28. Abramson (1994, p. 67); see chapter 2 in that volume for history and commentary on this practice. In 2002, South Dakotans even voted on—but rejected—an amendment to the state constitution sponsored by a coalition ranging from anti-abortion to pro-marijuana groups that would have made explicit the jury's right to "judge laws." For contemporary coverage of the debate in South Dakota, see Liptak (2002b).

29. See Mara (2001). For a wider overview of the subject that considers the tensions between the virtues of trust and skepticism toward citizens and institutions in democracy, see Warren (1999).

30. See Habermas (1996, p. 110).

31. Matthews et al. (2004, pp. 31–33). For studies showing U.S. juror attitude change toward juries and courts, see Allen (1977), Cutler and Hughes (2001), and Hans (2002, p. 226).

32. See the "Ramblin' with Roger" blog at http://rogerowengreen.blog-spot.com/2007/02/jury-duty.html.

33. Deneen (2005, p. 15).

34. For a classic film famously portraying the potential to sway juries through slick lawyering, see *The Mouthpiece*, loosely based on the notorious career of New York attorney William Fallon. For other historical and contemporary examples, see the reference book *Reel Justice* (Bergman and Asimow 2006).

35. See Consolini (1992), Cutler and Hughes (2001), and Matthews et al. (2004, p. 56).

36. Matthews et al. (2004, p. 66).

37. On the sense of civic duty, pride, or identity, see Finkel, Miller, and Opp (1989) and Youniss, McClelland, and Yates (1997).

38. Burkhalter, Gastil, and Kelshaw (2002, p. 411–18). On the varying meaning of deliberation across these diverse contexts, see Gastil (2008).

39. We use the term "civic pride" in parallel with a phrasing ("civic identity") we used in a previous publication from this research project (Gastil et al. 2008a).

40. On deliberative conversation, see Gastil (2008), Moy and Gastil (2006), and Mutz (2006).

41. See Bandura (1986) on self-efficacy; on political efficacy, see Craig, Niemi, and Silver (1990) and Niemi, Craig, and Mattei (1991).

42. See, for example, Finkel (1985) and Freie (1997).

43. See Evans and Boyte (1992), Leighley (1995), Putnam (2000), and Verba et al. (1995).

44. Bandura (1986) integrates the best of behaviorism into his work, having studied in that tradition. For a very readable critique, see Schwartz (1986).

45. The deliberative literature is deep and wide. For a broad overview, tying it to an even larger literature on political communication, see Gastil (2008). Chambers (2003) provides an overview of deliberative theory, and key theoretical works include Cohen (1997), Fishkin (1991), and Gutmann and Thompson (1996). Reviews of the research are also provided by Delli Carpini, Cook, and Jacobs (2004), Mendelberg (2002), Ryfe (2002), and Thompson (2008). Descriptions of different deliberative processes include Button and Mattson (1999), Gastil and Levine (2005), and Pearce and Littlejohn (1997). For representative examples of individual studies of deliberation—or something like it—see Cappella, Price, and Nir (2002), Cook, Barabas, and Jacobs (1999), Denver, Hands, and Jones (1995), Fishkin and Luskin (1999), Gastil and Dillard (1999), Luskin, Fishkin, and Jowell (2002), and Niemeyer (2004). For cautionary notes, see Karpowitz and Mansbridge (2005), Mendelberg and Oleske (2000), and Sanders (1997).

46. Mathews (1994, p. 195). Some may recognize this language resembling a theme in the 2008 Obama presidential campaign, which asked voters to "be the change you want to see in the world." That quote goes back at least as far as the writings of Gandhi (see, for example, http://en.wikiquote.org/wiki/Mohandas_Karamchand_Gandhi).

47. Gastil (1999).

48. Anderson and Nolan (2004, p. 943).
49. See, for example, Pope (1986).

Chapter 3

1. Amar (1995, pp. 205–6). Portions of this chapter are adapted from Deess and Gastil (2009) and Gastil, Deess, Weiser, and Meade (2008).
2. Pateman (1970).
3. Pateman (1989). Mansbridge (1999) explains how difficult it would be to design a randomized treatment with a sufficient sample size. These are precisely the problems we solve in this chapter.
4. Interviews were conducted by research assistant Jordan Meade. Each interviewee volunteered to answer questions after being invited to take part in this study by the bailiff at the end of each trial. Forty percent of those invited to participate agreed to do so, and a sub-sample of those were interviewed. For additional details on these interviews, see the first study reported in Gastil, Deess, Weiser, and Meade (2008).
5. The theme of juror bonding is common in the literature on juries, including Knox's account (2005) of juries in Australia. See also Matthews, Hancock, and Briggs (2004, p. 66–67).
6. Teddlie and Tashakkori (1998).
7. The exact question sequence is as follows: Q1. Does serving on a jury remind you of any other activities you have done in your life? Q2. Talk a bit about what serving on a jury means to you. Do you think it is an important activity? Q3. Do you think of jury service as a responsibility? What other kinds of responsibilities do you have that you might think of as related? Q4. What does it mean to perform a "civic duty"? What would you say are the civic duties that a citizen has? Q5. Now that you have served on a jury, do you think differently about any of these duties or responsibilities? Why?
8. In each case in this section, italics are added for emphasis. They do not necessarily mark the interviewees' changes in tone while speaking.
9. Mathews (1994).
10. Fishkin and Luskin (1999); Crosby and Nethercutt (2005).
11. In addition, given public distrust of government, people might report more positive experiences in deliberative forums sponsored by nongovernmental organizations than governmental ones.
12. Green and Gerber (2004).
13. For additional detail on the Olympia Project and criminal juries, see Gastil, Deess, and Weiser (2002).
14. Data available at http://www.census.gov.
15. Before analyzing the link between jury deliberation and voting history, it was necessary to match registered voter names with the names extracted from jury lists. Matches were made following a series of logical rules, which were used to create a database comparison program (written in C++ for the Olympia Project, then in Access for future research). This program began by removing all sets of identical names on the voter registration lists. When a name appeared multiple times on the jury list, the program deleted all but the most recent trial experience for that name (eight instances). Next, the

program merged the jury and voting data for any juror whose name perfectly matched a registered voter's name (first, middle, and last name). This produced 1,115 study participants (80 percent of the original sample). Finally, the program merged juror and voter records when there were adequate and unique matches, which included the following: records that matched on first and last name, as well as middle initial, when only one of the two names had a full middle name ($n = 84$); records that matched first and last name with one middle name missing ($n = 161$); and records with identical middle and last names with the first three letters of a related first name matching, such as Debbie Sue Thompson and Deborah Sue Thompson ($n = 35$). These matching guidelines resulted in the rejection of only 1.6 percent of the names in the original juror database we had compiled.

16. In the parlance of social scientific research, investigators seek to design a study that has sufficient "statistical power" to detect differences. That power depends on two factors, only one of which is under the researcher's control. The first is the size of the difference or effect. In our case, we anticipated a relatively small effect. Using Cohen's tables (1988), the criminal juror sample had adequate statistical power to detect an effect size (r) of roughly .08 or greater, and the civil juror sample had sufficient power to detect an effect of .18 or greater.

17. Green and Shachar (2000). The results presented in this section (Tables 3.1–3.4) all use linear regression models, the same method employed in the earlier publications on which this chapter draws (Gastil, Deess, and Weiser, 2002; Gastil, Deess, Weiser, and Meade, 2008). Comparison analyses done with multilevel regression models yielded similar results, with the same patterns of significance but slightly reduced coefficient sizes. For more on multilevel modeling, see Chapter 5 in this volume, which discusses this approach and interprets the statistical results of such analyses in Table 5.7.

18. Kerr et al. (1976) found that jurors tend to express dissatisfaction when voting in the minority.

19. Whether a juror has a conclusive experience or not depends largely on random assignment. One has no control over whether one becomes an alternate or a seated juror, and individual jurors have no bearing on the likelihood of a trial ending prematurely. Individual jurors may lead their juries to hung verdicts, but there is no strong evidence of a relationship between the social/psychological characteristics of individual jurors and the likelihood of hung verdicts. More importantly, there is no evidence whatsoever of a connection between a person's past political behavior and the likelihood of their contribution to a hung jury. Though it is certainly the case that the jury pool differs from the larger population (see Knack, 1993) and empanelled jurors differ from excused jurors (see Wigley, 1995), it is highly unlikely that once empanelled, juror characteristics determine whether one has positive or neutral/negative deliberative experiences, as defined herein. In any case, past voting frequency can be controlled statistically, and our analyses employ this control.

20. Green and Gerber (2004).

21. Bessette (1994, p. 217).

22. Hans (1993). See Wheeler (2001) for a comic deconstruction of this popular perspective, or read Hans (2002, p. 50) for a more straightforward account.

23. Imwinkelried (2001).

24. Hans (2000) and Vidmar and Diamond (2001) challenge the perception that civil juries typically struggle to manage the information given to them.

25. See Thompson, Mannix, and Bazerman (1988), Gastil (1993), and Nemeth (1977).

26. Tjosvold and Field (1983).

27. Petty and Cacioppo (1986, 1990).

28. For additional detail on the National Jury Sample, see Gastil, Deess, Weiser, and Meade (2008).

29. Hans et al. (2003).

30. Such a view is contrary to the spirit of most deliberative theory, which yields ideas like Deliberation Day that aim to stimulate discussion *without the guarantee of resolution*. See Ackerman and Fishkin (2004).

31. Warren (1992); Crosby and Nethercutt (2005).

32. Freie (1997, p. 134).

33. We chose this approach among the many alternative means of testing this interaction for the straightforward reason that the high–low voter participation split provides a readily interpretable result highlighting a key contrast between two populations (Abelson, 1995).

34. Tocqueville (1835/2002, Book I, chapter 16).

35. The exclusion of counties in the Northeast was not accidental. The potential counties contacted in that region refused to release jury participation records citing post 9/11 security changes.

36. The remaining 85 jurors had relatively idiosyncratic experiences that fell outside these categories.

37. With a sample of 794, the Olympia Project found that deliberation had a significant effect on voting ($b = .077$). To reliably detect (i.e., power = .80) an effect of this size in a sub-sample required a sample of at least 761 jurors, with a one-tailed alpha set at .10. Striking such a balance still guards against false positives (10 percent chance) more than false negatives (20 percent chance), but the fact that this study is partly a replication justifies the directional tests and the relative balance of Type I and II errors. In the end, the smallest subsample our dataset yielded was 999, which had a power of .88. On statistical power generally, see Cohen (1988).

38. Ninety percent of the jury trials selected for study began after January 1, 1996, and ended by December 21, 2002, with the bulk of trials from 1997 to 2000. For those jurors who registered to vote after the beginning date of the voter history file, only elections after their registration date were examined. To create a normal distribution of voting rates and reduce the impact of floor and ceiling effects, records with no history of voting or a history of voting in every single election were removed.

39. A small fraction (4 percent) of jurors served on more than one jury during the study period, and they were removed from analysis to permit clear contrasts between different jury experiences.

40. These variables all came from the Trial Outcomes family, that is to say the different types of trial results jurors could experience. For criminal jurors, the categories were alternate, guilty plea, hung (on one or more charge), jury verdict, and other (mistrial, case dismissed by judge, withdrawn

charges, or defendant waived right to jury trial). For civil jurors, the categories were alternate, hung (on one or more question/claim), jury verdict, and other (mistrial, case dismissed by judge, withdrawn claim, or out-of-court settlement). For both criminal and civil jurors, the omitted category was "cancelled trial." Jurors with "cancelled trial" outcomes were empanelled but only participated in trials that resulted in neither jury deliberation nor a courtroom verdict (from either a jury verdict or guilty plea). Thus, it provides the most appropriate comparison for each of the other forms of jury experience. To the extent that this study constitutes a "natural" or "quasi-experiment" (Cook and Campbell, 1979), the cancelled trial condition can be conceptualized as a control group. In regression terms, this group served as the "reference group" against which the other conditions were contrasted (Cohen et al. 2003, p. 313). In addition, seven dummy variables were created for the county/parish categorical variable, and a dummy variable was created to distinguish randomly entered Orleans Parish cases from the over-sample of trials that did not result in jury verdicts; these served as control variables in regression analysis.

41. This variable was truncated at six or more charges to reduce its skew (from 3.8 to 2.3).

42. The fact that increased voting shows persistence over time is not surprising because previous voting behavior is the best predictor of future behavior, but it is important to note that the effect does not degrade at an unexpected rate. Instead, it shows a persistent impact on civic engagement that can be measured even five years later; in some counties that is long enough for the person to serve on a jury again.

43. Average duration in hours was 9.03 (SD = 5.06) for hung juries, versus 3.57 hours (SD = 3.33) for verdict-reaching juries. t = 14.04, two-tailed $p < .001$.

44. Goodin (2003).

45. Reuben and McFarland (2006).

46. Jacobs, Delli Carpini, and Cook (2004).

Chapter 4

1. See http://nikolasschiller.com/images/jury_duty.jpg. The summons contains stern language, and every year, there are examples of judges who do, indeed, send out warrants for arrest and levy fines against summoned jurors who fail to answer their summons. Typically, this is done to raise public awareness more than to punish specific scofflaws. When the D.C. Superior Court did this in 2008, for instance, Chief Judge Rufus G. King III said, "The point of this whole thing is to get people to serve on juries. It's not to lock them up" (Alexander, 2008).

2. The interview was conducted by research assistant Sarah Perez on February 26, 2009.

3. All interviewees presented in this study are anonymous.

4. The county jurors served in either the King County Superior or District Court.

5. King County upgraded its juror facilities after our study concluded. Jurors now report to an elegant, spacious room on the main floor of the courthouse. The building still shows its edge, however, as at least one bathroom stall thus far has had a block of concrete fall into it, harming none but destroying the toilet (and some of the staff's confidence in the safety of the restrooms).

6. When delivering our juror surveys for these courthouses, we were so struck by the difference in aesthetics across the courthouses that we added into our questionnaire an item asking jurors to describe "the seating, facilities, and other accommodations provided in the jury assembly room." A narrow majority of downtown King County jurors kindly rated their facility as "neither pleasant nor unpleasant," with roughly one-quarter falling on either side of the scale midpoint. In Kent, a plurality (42 percent) said their assembly room was simply "pleasant," with another 38 percent giving the neutral rating. The Seattle Municipal Court, by contrast, earned high marks, with more than two-thirds giving their headquarters the highest rating possible and only 6 percent saying it was anything less than pleasant.

7. Owing to logistical difficulties at the King County Courthouse, some jurors (selected at random) actually completed our pre-jury service survey *before* their orientation. This created a natural experiment on the efficacy of the orientation materials, which we describe briefly in chapter 6. See also Gall and Gastil (2006).

8. See Dillman (1999). Appendix Section 4a shows the text of the recruitment letter we used.

9. We tested to see whether the mode of survey (face-to-face, mail, online) had an effect, and we found none of any consequence.

10. Our response rates were similar to others for surveys conducted at the courthouse under similar circumstances (e.g., Losh, Wasserman, and Wasserman, 2000). That study also addresses jurors' reluctance to serve; among other factors, those who fail to appear or excuse themselves from jury duty tend to view it as a less important civic duty, and as many as one third doubt they will learn from the experience. For the most part, however, those excusing themselves from duty cite personal hardship as their principal reason (Richert, 1977).

11. Wilber (2008). Even worse than the case of Liz Lemon, this juror skipped out *during* the trial and had to be replaced with an alternate.

12. These and all other differences reported herein are statistically significant, in this case with a chi-square difference test.

13. On the history, contemporary practice, and controversies regarding *voir dire*, see Vidmar and Hans (2007), chapter 4. For a critique of the practice from the perspective of a former federal judge, see Dwyer (2002, pp. 164–167).

14. $X^2 = 10.6$, $df = 2$, two-tailed $p = .031$.

15. On the juror selection techniques used by attorneys and their limited effectiveness, see Lieberman and Sales (2006).

16. The overall model was not significant, but a three-level education variable approached significance, $B = .541$ ($SE = .238$), $Exp(B) = 1.552$, $p = .09$; a willingness-to-serve trichotomy (reluctant, neutral, eager) was significant, $B = .541$ ($SE = .238$), $Exp(B) = 1.718$, $p = .02$.

17. Toobin (1994), p. 42.

18. Powers v. Ohio (1991). On the history and practice of discrimination in jury selection and related issues, see Part II in Hans and Vidmar (1986).

19. Cronbach's alpha = .748 for the three-item scale, which ranges from 1 ("Never") to 5 ("More than once a week"), M = 2.56, SD = .98.

20. Delli Carpini, Cook, and Jacobs (2004, pp. 323–324). On political conversation and disagreement, see Mutz (2006) and Huckfeldt, Johnson, and Sprague (2004).

21. Cronbach's alpha = .609 with each item modestly and roughly equally correlated with each other. The scale ranges from 0 (none correct) to 5 (all correct), M = 3.20, SD = 1.43.

22. On political knowledge in the United States, see Delli Carpini and Keeter (1996). Political knowledge is not simply a reflection of one's political knowledge, but also reflects individual factors, such as political interest and intelligence (Luskin, 1990), as well as one's media environment (Jerit, Barabas, and Bolsen, 2006).

23. To get the 36 percent figure, subtract the odds ratio of .64 from 1.0 (because it is a negative effect). One explanation for this finding may be that women more readily obtain the sympathy and trust of the court than do men (on gender and trust, see Orbell, Dawes, and Schwartz-Shea 1994), perhaps because of the societal expectation that they have a greater range of responsibilities outside the courthouse, including work, caring for children, caring for elderly parents, etc. (see Gerstel and Gallagher 2001).

24. On persistent discrimination, see Equal Justice Initiative (2010). If the present study identifies any such aggrieved group in King County, it would be those prospective jurors with the highest levels of formal education, an attainment that tends to provide its own civic instruction (and elevate the educated to higher civic status). On the civic benefits and sorting effects of education, see Nie, Junn, and Stehlik-Barry (1996).

25. Losh, Wasserman, and Wasserman (2000, pp. 307–8).

26. Boatright (1998, pp. ix, 103, 205), though Boatright (1998, p. xi) also notes that King County has a total *excuse and deferral* rate of 55 percent. In one of the more inventive studies on this subject, Oliver and Wolfinger (1999) show data suggesting that at least some, albeit few, U.S. citizens cancelled or avoided voter registration to stay off the jury rolls. Now that states merge voter registration lists with registered driver lists and other data, such desperate efforts to hide from the courts are more misguided than ever.

27. For juror status (not used, dismissed, empanelled) against *voir dire* satisfaction rating, X^2 = 38.6, df = 8, $p < .001$.

28. Dwyer (2002, pp. 120–121).

29. These results, and those that follow, collapse together the experiences of jurors in our study's three courthouses, as the particular location of service played little role in shaping the quality of empanelled jurors' experiences.

30. For trial type, r = .108 ($p < .001$); for deliberation, r = −.017 (p = .540).

31. Italics added for emphasis.

32. Miller and Shanks (1996).

33. Bandura (1986).

34. Hans (1993).

35. Prior voting was unrelated to one's subjective jury experience, but younger persons and those belonging to a major party reported a more engaging, rewarding jury experience. In the case of party membership, this relationship was significant for both infrequent and frequent voters.

Chapter 5

1. The interview was conducted by research assistant Sarah Perez on February 2009.

2. The interview was conducted by research assistant Elysa Hovard on March 3, 2009.

3. For a representative example, see Burnett and Badzinski (2000). On the perils and promise of mock jury designs, see Diamond (1997).

4. These interview studies are helpful but hard to generalize from; see, for example Pettus (1990).

5. Unless stated otherwise, references to the "King County" data include all jurors, including those actually serving in the Seattle Municipal Courthouse.

6. Mize, Hannaford-Agor, and Waters (2007, p. 7).

7. If the time use measure is dichotomized between those who perceived their time as ill-used (1) versus all other jurors (0), there is a weak association, $t = 2.10$, $p = .037$ (adjusting for unequal variances). Allen (1977, pp. 252–53) found that duration of service *did* affect jury satisfaction, though at the time of his study, longer terms of service often entailed serving on multiple juries.

8. For a comparison of the political cultural orientations of Seattle residents, people living in the portions of King County beyond Seattle, and the rest of Washington, see Gastil's July 18, 2006 *Seattle Times* op-ed, "Parting the Cascade curtain: Rethinking the state's cultural fault line," available online at http://seattletimes.nwsource.com/html/opinion/2003129898_sungastil16.html.

9. Along with these small differences come many other non-effects, with work status, educational attainment, and ethnicity having no effect on diversity perceptions. Alternative regressions broke ethnicity down into a larger number of dummy codes (Asian-American, $n = 75$; Black, $n = 30$), but there were no ethnicity effects with these finer distinctions. The King County/Seattle sample's limited ethnic diversity makes investigation of those differences problematic, however, because these small subsamples compromise the statistical power of such tests.

10. Cohen (1988).

11. This adds up to 102 percent owing to rounding of each individual statistic. This happens elsewhere, with totals ranging from 98–102 percent, for the same reason.

12. Pettus (1990, p. 94).

13. Kalven and Zeisel (1966, pp. 488–89); see also Leigh (1984).

14. Thanks to Leah Sprain for collecting and characterizing these juror comments. See Sprain and Gastil (2006). Italics in this paragraph added for emphasis.

15. Ball (2001, p. B1).

16. For example, Barber (1984); Mansbridge (1983); Weithman (2005). Also see Sprain and Gastil (2006) for more on these issues.

17. Burkhalter, Gastil, and Kelshaw (2002, p. 402); also see Pearce and Littlejohn (1997).

18. Recent writings on deliberative theory and practice have noted the positive role emotion can play in deepening discussion of an issue (Mansbridge et al., 2006, pp. 19–20).

19. Far from being dismissed for juror misconduct, Henry Fonda won an Oscar for his portrayal of this character (Juror #8, a.k.a. "Mr. Davis"). A few jurors in our study referenced that film. One wrote, "Ever see the movie *12 Angry Men*? Once I had completed my jury duty, my sister recommended I watch it. My experience seems to be somewhat similar (without the aggressive behavior)." Our first author feels a kinship for the juror who misremembered the lead actor's name: "We had an interesting case and spent an entire day, as a jury, trying to come to a unanimous decision. We were unsuccessful, but it was reminiscent of Robert Duvall in the old movie (*Angry men?*)."

20. This is how Judge Dwyer (2002, p. 61) instructed his juries in federal court.

21. Dwyer (2002, pp. 72–3).

22. Jonakait (2003, p. 258).

23. Portions adapted from Sprain and Gastil (2006). Further evidence of jurors' "intuitive rules for deliberation" come from Sunwolf and Seibold (1998).

24. Gore (2007, pp. 2–3).

25. Just as Bormann (1996) identified a "public discussion model" in Western culture for how to talk about issues in public, it appears that jurors have a broadly shared cultural understanding of how to conduct jury deliberations. Those understandings should serve well civic reformers who hope to inspire the public to revitalize or renew its deliberative traditions (Leighninger and Bradley, 2006).

26. This section is adapted from Gastil, Burkhalter, and Black (2007).

27. Hastie, Penrod, and Pennington (1983); Sandys and Dillehay (1995).

28. For one of the most concise, comprehensive overviews of the subject, see Devine et al. (2001).

29. On real juries, see Kalven and Zeisel (1966) and Sandys and Dillehay (1995); on mock juries, MacCoun and Kerr (1988).

30. The general concern about jury deliberation has led some legal researchers to create guidebooks to advise jurors on how to deliberate effectively (e.g., Boatright and Murphy, 1999).

31. Diamond et al. (2003a–b).

32. Sandys and Dilehay (1995). These studies do not definitively show that jurors are engaging in respectful and egalitarian deliberation. However, the absence of early votes implies that jurors may be able to consider evidence more fully than if they had voted. As Kalven and Zeisel (1966) note, early votes very often determine the trial verdict.

33. Devine et al., (2001).

34. Hastie, Schkade, and Payne (1998).

35. Small group researchers increasingly attend to concerns about identifying the appropriate level of analysis (Kenny et al., 2002). In this study, our hypotheses and research were cast at the group level, as they discuss the composition, behavior, and outcomes of whole juries. To assess the appropriateness of aggregation and group-level analysis of data measured at the individual level, intraclass correlations (ICC) were computed for each variable. Positive correlations for all scales indicated the appropriateness of group-level analysis (e.g., for Listen, ICC = .310, p = .03). Readers who might have preferred an alternative analytic approach may be reassured to know that the results shown below were approximately equivalent to those obtained by corresponding individual-level analysis.

36. This was tested using an ANOVA analysis, which treats each outcome as a different category; the differences in mean satisfaction did not vary across the categories (F = 1.71, df = 2, 945, p = .182). If jury verdict was treated as a continuous variable, with the mixed-verdict category in the middle, its association with satisfaction remained very weak (r = .05, p = .096, n = 948).

37. t = 9.84, p < .001, equal variances not assumed.

38. Though the sample had shrunk, we remained optimistic that with these more direct measures of the character of jury deliberation, we might nonetheless find a significant effect in our data if there existed one in the larger population of jurors. In terms of statistical power (Cohen, 1988), we expected that the population effect size would be sufficiently larger that the loss in sample size resulted in no net loss in overall statistical power.

39. After the regression, we took a closer peek at the individual survey items making up the deliberation scale. We ran a partial correlation for each one, looking at its correlation with post-service voting after controlling for preservice voting and the other controls previously shown in Table 5.8. The result was that each individual correlation was significant in the expected direction (maximum p = .022), with partial correlations ranging from pr = .13 to .20. The largest of those effects was for the item asking jurors if their jury had "thoroughly discussed the relevant facts of the case."

Chapter 6

1. Technically speaking, the results shown in chapter 3 showed that a high-school civics course probably *does* have an effect comparable in size to jury service, but we do not wish to quibble.

2. Gastil, Deess, and Weiser (2002).

3. The depth of these trial related comments is suggested by one female juror who, after a mistrial, wrote that her judge offered considerable insight into what had happened: "He explained that the prosecution was not ready to proceed after opening statements because [the] police had misplaced the evidence and the witness had not arrived. He had given the prosecution a time limit for how long he would wait before dismissing the case. He was told a few minutes after he dismissed [us] that the witness had arrived. He told us about other more serious charges pending against the defendant, and

that he had thought it would have been wiser for the defendant to enter into a plea bargain, but that [the defendant] had maintained his innocence. He told us what he understood the defense would have been if the trial had proceeded. He mentioned that the defense lawyer was a public defender and that he is a very good one."

In effect, the judge offered these jurors a kind of consolation prize—a recap of what might have been, had a trial taken place. That detailed comment also reveals the aforementioned sentiment of appreciation and recognition of the jury's importance.

4. This quote is edited for clarity; the original reads, "*our* American Citizen" (italics added).

5. On the way conversation reinforces and shapes our memories and creates narrative, see Tannen (2007) and Hyman (1994). Fivush (1995) offers a brief overview on the accuracy-reinforcing character of reminiscence, versus the less common creation of false memories. In the context of political information, see Eveland (2004).

6. The few nonconversational jurors had diverse demographic backgrounds and came from a broad cross-section of trials—a mix of low and high-profile civil and criminal cases, with no two alike.

7. Theiss-Morse and Hibbing (2005). A more sanguine view of the connection between voluntary organizations and politics comes in Evans and Boyte (1992).

8. Classics in this tradition include Verba, Schlozman, and Brady (1995) and Verba and Nie (1972).

9. In particular, they discouraged questions regarding jurors' incomes and the details of their deliberations, either of which might concern an attorney in a case with any relevance to those issues. For this reason, we do not know our survey respondents' household incomes, but we also do not know their patterns of charitable or political donations, and the behavioral questions we did ask tend toward generality. We also had to limit the total length of questions because the court administrators could only spare a few minutes of jurors' time for our pre-service survey. Since our study compares changes in behavior over time, our long-term follow-up survey could only usefully include the same items contained within the brief pre-service survey.

10. Changes in jurors' behavior over the course of our study could have been due to other factors, and on the chance that those factors are, in turn, associated with one's jury experience, it is important to control for their influence. One Seattle woman in our study, for instance, noted on the back of her follow-up survey that "until recently, I was very involved in my community and other civic duties. Since a change of jobs where I travel a great deal, I feel I've lost touch with my state and local issues." Though kind of her to alert us to this, without the appropriate control variables in our analysis (i.e., we did not measure the time one spends traveling), such variations simply introduce error, which can potentially obscure the impact of jury service.

11. On the socioeconomic predictors of civic and political engagement, see Brady, Verba, and Schlozman (1995); more generally, see Verba, Schlozman, and Brady (1995).

12. On the habit-forming aspect of deliberative self-reinforcement, see Burkhalter, Gastil, and Kelshaw (2002) and chapter 2 of this volume. Were we certain of the strength of that connection in the particular case of jury deliberation, of course, we would not have conducted the present study, but that was the general expectation we brought with us to these data. For emphasizing the importance of ignorance as a motivation in research, thanks go to the fictional research "scientist" Walter Bishop on the Fox series *Fringe*.

13. Working with the small municipal sample ($N = 121$, after taking control variables into account), only larger effect sizes meet even the more modest threshold of $p < .10$ (less than 10 percent likelihood of effect appearing in the sample due to chance). In such cases, statistical protocol does not require *ignoring* a nonsignificant association, but unless it becomes part of a larger pattern, it is best to treat it as a distracting red herring in our path, thereby giving it nothing more than a passing sniff.

14. Having said that, it is important to not make *too* much of this particular finding in isolation. At the very least, one should notice that these two effects have similar sizes ($pr = .14$ vs. $.21$). Using Cohen's q-statistic (1988) for comparing effect sizes, we found these two correlations to be comparable in size. Thus, without a larger set of associations to consider, it is risky to read too much into the larger correlation over-and-above the slightly smaller one. Also, note that when the two deliberation predictors are run together in a regression equation, both correlations weaken but the gap between their sizes grows.

15. Unfortunately, we cannot translate this as concretely as we could for the voting effect because both variables in this correlation were measured on arbitrary scales; a fractional increase upward from "agree" toward "strongly agree" just does not have the heft of a specific amount of increase in voter turnout.

16. Bandura (1986); in the context of deliberation, see Burkhalter, Gastil, and Kelshaw (2002).

17. Opp (1986).

18. For relevant research reviews on spontaneous thoughts and memory, see Christoff, Gordon, and Smith (in press) and McDaniel and Einstein (2007). On cognitive engagement ("involvement") and the potential for long-term attitude change, see Petty and Cacioppo (1990) and Petty, Wegener, and Fabrigar (1997). In broader terms, see Collins and Loftus (1975).

19. Again, this relates back to the more sensible insights of behaviorism, as recast persuasively by Bandura (1986).

20. This can have a complex relationship with our preexisting levels of self-esteem. See Baumeister and Tice (2006).

21. Dillard and Backhaus (1997) provide evidence of emotion's importance at explaining the impact of a public deliberation program on its participants. In market research, emotion has often been found to be a key pathway to influencing consumer attitudes and decision-making choices; see Allen, Machleit, and Kleine (1992) and Sherman, Mathur, and Smith (1997).

22. We created this contrast by combining the "thank you," "affirmation," and "compliment" codings, liberally coding anyone as having heard praise/thank you if any of our coders detected any of these elements in the written comments.

23. Of course, some judges gave positive comments to juries in which only some of the jurors *remembered* the comment. To be clear, we are testing

the impact of recalled praise, which is surely highly correlated with *actual* praise. Moreover, whether their comments are remembered are beyond judges' control, whereas the offering of praise is not.

24. Thus, Romer, Jamieson, and Aday (2003) finds that people's fear of crime partly depends on degree of exposure to local television news, which foregrounds crime-related news.

25. We left in the sample those who never voted (5 percent of sample) and those who always voted (21 percent) because the problems recommending their removal in chapter 2 did not apply. Specifically, the dependent measures were different variables than the split variable, obviating floor and ceiling effects on our scale and the non-normal distributions they would produce. Also, because we are using longitudinal surveys rather than official records, our concerns about nonresidence do not apply, as we know these voters still reside in King County; hence, any nonvoting is just that, as opposed to out-of-date residency in the voter file.

26. This result was published in Gastil (2004), though the post-hoc explanation was developed in more detail in Gastil (1994).

27. We were not able to learn which civil jurors voted with majorities. For this analysis, all are assumed to agree with the supermajority or unanimous civil verdict.

28. Result shown is for the guilty versus not guilty dichotomy. With the three-point scale, the result is $pr = .08$, $p = .025$. In an equivalent multilevel regression model, Guilty versus Not-Guilty is marginally significant (one-tailed $p = .075$, with a coefficient of .04, SE = .029, $t = 1.44$).

29. Jay Leighter, while serving as one of our graduate research assistants, was the first to suggest that the number-of-charges effect is likely due to juries having to make more decisions, and University of Washington undergraduate James Fraser, while studying political deliberation with the first author, speculated that multiple charges make the jury's task more complex because they create the possibility of a mixed verdict. Whether or not a jury reaches a verdict is not the critical point; rather, these juries must simply consider the possibility of guilt-by-degrees, whereas a single-charge jury simply decides guilty or not guilty. That view fits the pattern found here.

30. When looking at jurors broken down by age, retirement has a clear and strong effect apart from age. Moreover, age was, as always, included in the preceding analyses as a control variable.

31. Because of the sex-composition of this group, the Female variable was removed from the set of controls for analyses.

32. Burtt (1990, pp. 24). Political participation research routinely distinguishes voting from other behaviors along similar lines (e.g., Brady, Verba, and Schlozman 1995).

Chapter 7

1. Consolini's work was backed by the same funding source we have employed, the National Science Foundation. Consolini's work can be read in more detail in her unpublished 1992 doctoral dissertation, *Learning by Doing Justice: Jury Service and Political Attitudes*.

2. Consolini (1992, pp. 184–5).

3. Consolini (1992, pp. 186).

4. Consolini (1992) refers to this variable as political efficacy, the more commonly used term for this belief.

5. For this very reason, we did not include the behavioral measures in the post-jury service questionnaire filled out days or weeks after serving.

6. On how public attitudes stabilize over time in response to new information, see Page and Shapiro (1992). On how predispositions shape the considerations underlying our attitude responses, see Zaller (1992). On how cultural orientations shape our attitudes, see Kahan et al. (2007). In the case of newly formed attitudes, see Kahan et al. (2008). On individual variation in attitude stability, see Krosnick (1991).

7. For general background, see Petty, Wegener, and Fabrigar (1997).

8. In a careful study of political efficacy versus perceived system responsiveness, the latter appears more readily subject to change; Aish and Jöreskog (1990).

9. See Figure 2.2 and accompanying text in chapter 2.

10. Portions of this section are adapted from Gall and Gastil (2006).

11. The American Judicature Society provides links to hundreds of counties around the United States to demonstrate the variety of ways courts provide orienting information to potential jurors (see http://www.ajs.org/jc/faq/jc_faq_statelinks.asp). Courts typically provide practical information (e.g., parking, attire, breaks, etc.), as well as more abstract concepts, ideas, and insights, such as the importance of the jury, essential law vocabulary, and what kinds of questions may be encountered during voir dire.

12. Davis and Kleiner (2000).

13. Wanous and Reichers (2000).

14. On the impact of prior service on juror attitudes when reporting for jury duty, see Durand, Bearden, and Gustafson (1978).

15. Contrasting newcomers ($M = 3.80$, $SD = .55$) against veterans ($M = 3.90$, $SD = .58$), $t = 4.41$ ($df = 2687$), $p < .001$.

16. Later in this chapter, we will consider what these net changes mean relative to national trends in civic attitudes over approximately the same time period.

17. Generally, see Bales (1950) and Moynihan and Peterson (2001). On deliberation, see Burkhalter, Gastil, and Kelshaw (2002). This section is adapted from Gastil et al. (2008a).

18. Quote is from Cappella, Price, and Nir (2002, p. 88).

19. Shah et al. (2005, p. 553). See also Eveland (2004), McLeod et al. (1996), and Shah et al. (2005).

20. See Finkel (1985) and Wolfsfeld (1985).

21. Almond and Verba (1963); Verba, Schlozman, and Brady (1995); and Putnam (2000).

22. For the full model, see Figure 5 in Gastil et al., (2008a). The one difference is that for this analysis, we removed the item measuring frequency of personal contributions to deliberation for the reasons discussed in chapter 5. On path analysis of panel data, see Finkel (1995).

23. For more details on this study, see Study 1 in Gastil et al. (2008a).

24. Single-item analysis of the civic faith indicators showed that the significant path was produced principally by the item, "When asked to do their part, most American citizens will make sacrifices on behalf of the nation."

25. Here, we reference the theory of planned behavior (Ajzen and Fishbein, 1980) and Ajzen's (1991) refinement of that model into the theory of reasoned action, which takes self-efficacy into account. For more on this, see Gastil and Xenos (2010).

26. On reciprocal effects and political efficacy, see Stenner-Day and Fischle (1992) and Finkel (1985).

27. Bem (1972, p. 5). For more recent research, see Albarracin and Wyer (2000).

28. See Barber (1984) and Moy and Pfau (2000).

29. Again for simplicity, the figure shows only the paths of interest, though its results are based on a full path analysis, which includes the connections among the same variables measured at different points in time (e.g., political self-confidence measured in the first, second, and their survey wave), as well as the correlations among errors. For details on such analysis, see Finkel (1995).

30. Gallup and Newport (2006, p. 202).

31 On the utility of having such a comparison group, see Cook and Campbell (1979). We anticipated a lower response rate and sent out a larger number of surveys, following as much of the advice of Dillman (1999) as was affordable.

32. The exception was civic faith, which actually went up significantly for this group ($t = 4.22$, $df = 204$, $p < .001$).

33. See Allen (1977), Cutler and Huges (2001), and Hans (2002, p. 226).

34. See Consolini (1992) and Matthews, Hancock, and Briggs (2004).

Chapter 8

1. The full text of this speech is available online at http://www.floridabar.org/DIVCOM/JN/jnnews01.nsf/8c9f13012b96736985256aa900624829/5d3d1e61610d7e5c852573150051920d.

2. Glaberson (2001, March 2).

3. Galanter (2004). For context, see Vidmar and Hans (2007), pp. 59–64. One of the stronger voices on this issue is that of University of Illinois law professor Suja Thomas (2007), who argues that the routine use of summary (judicial) judgment preempting jury trials violates the Seventh Amendment to the U.S. Constitution. This practice alone accounts for a significant portion of the decline in jury trials.

4. Optimistic notes are provided by Vidmar and Hans (2007, p. 344–46).

5. On world juries, see Hans (2008b) and Vidmar (2000). On the United States, see Dees (2001); Hans (2002); Hans and Vidmar (1986); Vidmar and Hans (2007).

6. Adler (1994).

7. For criticisms and a defense of the civil jury, see Carrington (2003) and Hans (2000). On punitive damages, see Liptak (2002a).

8. Vidmar (2000).

9. Jonakait (2003, chapters 1 and 2) provides a clear description of the criminal and civil jury in the context of U.S. constitutional law.

10. "Development in the Law, The Jury's Capacity to Decide Civil Cases" (1997, p. 1489).

11. Solove (2009).

12. Quoted in Liptak (2002a). The book-length argument is in Sunstein et al., (2002), and Sharkey (2003) provides a critique. Hans (2000) provides a full-length view to the contrary.

13. Hastie, Penrod, and Pennington (1983).

14. Hans and Vidmar (1986, p. 129).

15. Kalven and Zeisel (1966). For a review and discussion of this research, see Vidmar and Hans (2007), pp. 149–51.

16. Dwyer (2002, p. 136).

17. See, in this example, Hans (2000, pp. 70–71).

18. Myers, Reinstein and Griller (1999). More extensive overviews of the research on jury deliberation come from Devine et al. (2001) and, in a style written for use by attorneys, Sunwolf (2004).

19. Taylor v. Louisiana (1975, p. 530).

20. See, in particular, Powers. v. Ohio (1991), which we discussed in chapter 1.

21. Sobol (1995, p. 165).

22. See the *New York Times'* editorial, "Keep moving on jury reform" (1996).

23. "Keep moving on jury reform" (1996).

24. On low knowledge of public institutions generally, see Delli Carpini and Keeter (1996). On knowledge of the justice system, see the 2006 Annenberg Public Policy Center study on the subject (http://www.annenbergpublicpolicycenter.org/Downloads/Releases/Release_Courts20060928/Courts_Release_20060928.pdf).

25. For more analysis of our data in relation to these factors, see Gastil, Burkhalter, and Black (2007).

26. On class bias, see York and Cornwell (2006). On gender bias, see Mills and Bohannon (1980), Strodtbeck, James, and Hawkins (1957), and on forepersons see Kerr, Harmon, and Graves (1982).

27. See Benhabib (1996), Fraser (1997), Mendelberg (2002), Sanders (1997), and Young (1996). For a direct response, see Dahlberg (2005).

28. For more detailed analysis of our data along these lines, see Hickerson and Gastil (2008).

29. Kaye (2007).

30. The pamphlet can be found at http://www.nycourts.gov/admin/publicaffairs/democracyinaction.pdf. A number of other states have developed similar materials.

31. One of the challenges that court administrators face is juror apathy and unwillingness to participate. Although other factors, such as inadequate compensation or loss of work hours, contribute to those sentiments in ways administrators cannot address, we believe that refreshing juror orientation

materials with our study findings in mind could help combat juror indifference and bolster the public's overall confidence in both juries and judges. In addition, administrators should think about tailoring materials to the different needs and interests of novices, the returning-but-never-serving, and the experienced juror (Gall and Gastil 2006). The novice juror might be most likely to peruse additional reading material on the basic mechanics of juries and the norms of deliberation, as this group is most willing to grow in its confidence in and appreciation of juries. Those returning jurors might choose to access more contextual material on how juries fit into the larger justice system, as these jurors are already thinking about the bigger picture during orientation. Finally, special attention might be paid to those who have responded to the summons before but have never served. This group's members appear to have become numb to the motivating effects of orientation, and they might need reassurance that they are not doomed to pass their period of service in the waiting room, nor are they any more likely than other jurors to be brushed aside during *voir dire*. Such adjustments may be modest, but we expect that they will improve the overall effectiveness of the orientation process.

32. Kaye (2006, p. 841).

33. Shepard (2006, p. 1542). On a variety of jury reforms along these lines, see Hannaford and Munsterman (1997) and the compendium at the American Judicature Society website (http://www.ajs.org/jc/juries/jc_improvements_trials.asp).

34. Hans (2008a, p. 61).

35. Hans (2008a, p. 56).

36. Heuer and Penrod (1996).

37. Heuer and Penrod (1996).

38. Krauss (2005, p. 24).

39. Diamond et al. (2006, p. 1931).

40. State v. Costello (2002).

41. Mott (2003, p. 1119). See also Heuer and Penrod (1996, p. 260), "Jurors allowed to ask questions do not become advocates rather than neutrals."

42. See the ABA's "Principles for Juries & Jury Trials" online at http://www.abanet.org/juryprojectstandards/principles.pdf.

43. Hans (2008a).

44. Hans (2008a).

45. Hans (2008a).

46. Hans et al. (1999); Hannaford, Hans, and Munsterman (2000); and Diamond et al. (2003a, 2003b).

47. Hans et al. (1999, p. 371).

48. Hans (2008a).

49. United States v. Wexler (1988, p. 92 n.3).

50. United States v. Wexler (1987, p. 969–70).

51. For overviews of recent accounts, see Robinson (2009) and Schwartz (2009).

52. As we write, Wisconsin and other states are passing new laws on this subject or refining their rules for courtroom conduct (e.g., Stephen 2009).

53. Vidmar (1998, p. 849).

54. Markman v. Westview Instruments, Inc. (1996).

55. Daubert v. Merrell Dow Pharm (1993).

56. See Bertelsen (1998).

57. This also speaks to overemphasis placed on consensus in deliberative theory. See, for example, Karpowitz and Mansbridge (2005).

58. Vidmar (1998, p. 866).

59. Here, Dwyer (2002, p. 121) refers to technicalities in criminal trials. On similar issues in civil trials, see Hans (2000, 222–25).

60. Kraus (2005, p. 25).

61. Quoted from "Ninth Circuit Model Criminal Jury Instructions, Section 7.7. Deadlocked Jury" (http://207.41.19.15/web/sdocuments.nsf/dcf4f 914455891d4882564b40001f6dc/4dbfdcf2fb7d812b882564b4006ceee4?Ope nDocument).

62. On hung juries generally, see Hans et al. (2003).

63. See Carter (2005, p. 40).

64. Glaberson (2001).

65. Laville (2010a, 2010b).

66. Jonakait (2003, p. 4); see also Adler (1994) and Hans (2002).

67. To be clear, we wish to suggest that at times, juries are not used where they would have normally been put in place. We are not taking this argument to its logical extreme by calling for increased criminal arrests to increase the frequency of jury trials, though that does strike us as an amusing premise for a science fiction short story or a dystopian novel.

68. See, for instance, Bingham, Nabatchi, and O'Leary (2005), Pearce and Littlejohn (1997), and Menkel-Meadows (1995). Perusal of the membership of the National Coalition for Dialogue and Deliberation (www.thataway.org) shows the historical synergy between these movements.

69. Dugoni (2003, pp. 1–32). Thanks to Elysa Hovard for digging up this gem.

70. Quote from the masthead of the association's website (www.atra.org) on June 29, 2009.

71. See Hans (1993, 2000).

72. Vail (2008).

73. Note that there was relatively little outcry when Russian lawmakers in 2008 curtailed the authority of their nation's jury system to exclude it from hearing "serious crimes like terrorism, espionage and organizing mass demonstrations" (Agence France-Presse, 2008).

74. Though with different question wording, it is concerning that a 2008 Harris Poll found that only 58 percent of Americans believe that juries are "fair and impartial" all or at least most of the time. The same poll, however, also showed that only 23 percent would trust a judge to give a fair verdict, compared to 50 percent expecting the jury to do so. Finally, consistent with our study, that survey found that those with previous jury experience gave the jury even higher marks on those questions (http://www.harrisinteractive.com/harris_poll/index.asp?PID=861).

75. For an overview of juries across the globe, see Hans (2008b) and Vidmar (2000). Doctoral student Keri Sikich is currently conducting research on how and why countries adopt juries. Her 2009 Law and Society Association conference paper "Why Juries? Explaining the Prevalence of Criminal Juries Worldwide" is available via kwsikich@gmail.com.

76. Anderson and Nolan (2004, p. 943).

77. Quoted in Anderson and Nolan (2004, p. 943–44).

78. On the value of democratic civic education in developing countries, see Finkel (2003).

79. Dooley (2008).

80. Gastil, Lingle, and Deess (2010).

Chapter 9

1. For a history of this process, see Cronin (1989).

2. On the limited deliberative implications of conventional electoral reforms, see Gastil (2000a, chap. 4).

3. The anti-tax protests organized for April 15 were the site of the "no taxation without deliberation" slogan, which can now be found on bumper stickers and many blogs and hundreds of Web sites. The idea is that Congress is making enormous fiscal decisions without sufficient deliberation. In practice, it is hard to know whether the complaint about insufficient deliberation is a legitimate complaint or just sour grapes. By analogy, when political parties withdraw from elections in developing countries, sometimes it is clear that they are protesting what will be a rigged election, but other times, it appears they are simply avoiding an embarrassing defeat.

4. Chambers (2003, p. 308).

5. Gastil and Crosby (2003). For more context on this survey, see Gastil, Reedy, and Wells (2007).

6. For elaborations of this argument, see Fishkin (1995) and Gastil (2000a).

7. To be sure, matters referred by the legislature (generally called "referenda," rather than initiatives) are not be subject to this criticism. Moreover, some states call for judicial or other bodies to evaluate proposed ballot propositions (for example, to ensure that they address only a single subject) before allowing them to be placed on the ballot.

8. For a broad critique of initiatives along these and other lines, see Broder (2000). For a more sympathetic portrait, see Matsusaka (2004).

9. Gillette (2005, p. 852).

10. Kousser and McCubbins (2005).

11. Powers v. Ohio (1991, p. 407).

12. Barber (1984, p. 188).

13. In any society, there exist archetypal groups of this sort, often situated in longstanding institutions and always involving sets of routine cultural practices with broadly shared set of meanings, power relations, and norms. An archetypical small group is a public idealization of a particular kind of group, idealized in the sense that members of a society imagine the group in a form that has coherence and regularity in its members' behavior that exceeds the reality. When we become a member of a jury, for instance, we use social conventions to govern our behavior in the group, as evidenced by the speed with which the jurors in our study quickly adopted the jury's broadly understood deliberative norms. Any individual jury will

ultimately diverge from these regularized patterns of behavior, and any extreme deviance may earn a derogatory label, as in the case of the "runaway jury." This conception of the jury as a group archetypes is adapted from Gastil (2010).

14. Janis (1982) pioneered research on this; see Street (1997) for a useful overview. Gastil (2010) argues that it has become a negative archetype of group decision making.

15. The Western District of Virginia District Court's "Standard Jury Instructions" are available online at http://www.vawd.uscourts.gov/judges/Urbanski/StandardCivilJuryInstructions.htm.

16. On decision making, see Fishkin (1991) and Yankelovich (1991). On conflict resolution, see Gutmann and Thompson (1996) and Pearce and Littlejohn (1997).

17. See, for instance, Warren (1993) and Mathews (1994).

18. Leib (2004, p. 89).

19. See Crosby and Nethercutt (2005), Smith and Wales (1999, 2000). On the ambivalent response of interest groups to such juries, see Hendriks (2006b). Citizens' Juries is a service mark used by the Jefferson Center for New Democratic Processes (www.jefferson-center.org).

20. These examples are taken from Crosby (1995) and Crosby and Nethercutt (2005).

21. Crosby (1995, p. 164).

22. In extensive personal correspondence, Crosby has emphasized the importance of Citizens' Juries having the ability to adjust the process as it unfolds—even if that means "firing" their facilitator.

23. Fishkin (1995, p. 43). Deliberative Polling is a trademark used by the Center for Deliberative Democracy (cdd.stanford.edu). See also Fishkin (1991, 2009), Fishkin and Farrar (2005), Fishkin and Luskin (1999), and Luskin, Fishkin, and Jowell (2002). Many other conference papers and in-press publications on deliberative polling are archived at http://cdd.stanford.edu/research. Ackerman and Fishkin (2004) have applied a similar logic to the design of Deliberation Day, a proposal for a periodic national deliberative process that, like the Poll, aims to inform individual judgments rather than arrive at any collective understanding.

24. Goodin and Dryzek (2006).

25. See Fagotto and Fung (2006).

26. The complete text of the legislation is available online at http://www.leg.state.or.us/09reg/measpdf/hb2800.dir/hb2895.intro.pdf. The idea for a Citizens' Initiative Review has its origins in Crosby (2003); see also Gastil (2000a). In King County, Washington, there also exists a public discussion process written into law but supported with private funds. The portal to these Countywide Community Forums, held in small groups in living rooms and other settings, is at http://communityforums.org/web/guest/home.

27. Quote from June 29, 2009, press release by Healthy Democracy Oregon (http://www.healthydemocracyoregon.org/node/125).

28. In essence, the Review might serve as a deliberative "voting cue" for those citizens seeking guidance before voting on an initiative; see Gastil (2000a, pp. 172–75).

29. For details on the Citizens Assembly, see Warren and Pearse (2008). The official archive for the process, including documents and video, is available at http://www.citizensassembly.bc.ca/public.

30. Because of this heightened responsibility, it was likely appropriate that the Assembly was comprised of a relatively large number of citizens (160 of them selected at random, including one man and one woman from each electoral district plus two at-large Aboriginal members) and deliberated over several weekends spread across the better part of a year.

31. A revote four years later likewise failed, with support dropping down to 39 percent. For contemporary coverage of the revote, see "Change to STV system turned down again" (http://www.canada.com/Change+system+turn ed+down+again/1598336/story.html).

32. Other deliberative processes, such as Participatory Budgeting (Abers, 2000), also speak to this issue, but the focus here remains on randomly-selected citizen panels and assemblies. On the transition of participatory budgeting from Brazil to Europe, see Sintomer, Herzberg, and Röcke (2008). For a wider range of such processes, inside and outside government, see Gastil and Levine (2005).

33. For ongoing developments with Citizen Assemblies, see "J.H. snider's Citizens Assembly blog" (http://pioneerplus.ejournalism.ca/?q=aggregator/sources/6).

34. San Francisco Chronicle (2006).

35. Quote from blog posting at "Canada's World" (http://canadasworld.wordpress.com/2009/03/31/how-the-citizens-assembly-on-electoral-reform-arrived-at-bc-stv).

36. On initiative elections, see Wells et al., (2009). More generally, see Gastil (2000a, chap. 3).

37. This is an extension of a comment from Jack Blaney, who chaired the B.C. Citizens' Assembly. He commented on the distance between the Assembly's proceedings and party officials while speaking at the conference "When Citizens Decide: the Challenges of Large Scale Public Engagement," held in Vancouver May 1–2, 2008.

38. On historical examples, see Carson and Martin (1999) and Barber (1984). On California civil grand juries (and their reform), see Vitiello and Kelso (2002) and the reply by the California Grand Jurors' Association (2002).

39. On this process, see http://www.citizensparliament.org.au and Dryzek (2009).

40. For other examples of such proposals, see Callenbach and Phillips (1985), Dahl (1989, p. 340), Gastil (1993, pp. 156–59), and Threlkeld (1998).

41. Leib (2004, p. 12).

42. Leib (2004, pp. 103–4).

43. Leib (2004, p. 19). The term "policy jury" is sometimes used in parallel with Citizens' Juries (e.g., Carson and Martin, 2002).

44. O'Leary (2006). This section is adapted from Gastil (2007).

45. Twenty-five of those chosen at random would join the steering committee for two year terms. The first year of service would be learning the

ropes, and the second year would confer real authority, such as choosing which bills for the People's House to review.

46. This would wonderfully complicate the "Better Know a District" segment on The Colbert Report.

47. For a cautionary, sociological perspective on the deliberative democracy movement, per se, see Ryfe (2007).

48. See, for instance, Dwyer (2002, chapters 3 and 4), Jonakait (2003, Introduction), and Vidmar and Hans (2007, chapters 1 and 2).

49. Dwyer (2002).

50. On the design of these events, see Crosby and Nethercutt (2005) and Fishkin and Farrar (2005), respectively.

51. On the long-term impact of the National Issues Forums, see Gastil (2004).

52. Fung (2005a). On the generic principle of inclusion in democracy, see Dahl (1989).

53. Deliberative events that recruit random samples often use honoraria, per diem compensation, and other incentives to recruit participants (Crosby and Nethercutt 2005).

54. Adamic and Glance (2005).

55. On teledemocracy, see Becker and Slaton (2000). For a variety of public outreach efforts, see Gastil and Levine (2005).

56. See http://www.citizensparliament.org.au.

57. On the potential and limits of online deliberation, see Gastil (2000b), Janssen and Kies (2005), and Stromer-Galley (2002).

58. For an overview of such issues, see Levin and Nalebuff (1995).

59. Hickerson and Gastil (2008).

60. On dialogue, see Barge (2002) and Pearce and Littlejohn (1997); on the interplay of dialogue and deliberation, see Burkhalter, Gastil, and Kelshaw (2002). For a cautionary note about inserting therapy-laden "dialogue" into public processes, see Tonn (2005).

61. See Mansbridge (1983) and, in a more cautionary tone, Sanders (1997).

62. Sunstein (2002) voices this concern. Though careful deliberative theorists have long emphasized the need for majority rule resolving disputes, even when orienting deliberation toward consensus (e.g., Barber, 1984; Cohen, 1997; Gastil, 1993), the problem still arises in real-world events that give insufficient regard to dissenting voices (Karpowitz and Mansbridge, 2005).

63. Sunstein (2003, pp.164–65). Sunstein (2005) suggests additional safeguards to ensure effective deliberation.

64. Kahan et al. (2006). It is important to be mindful, however, of how people with different political-cultural orientations might approach deliberation *itself* differently (Gastil et al. 2008b).

65. This reprises Putnam (1995a–b), discussed in chapter 1.

References

Abelson, Robert P. 1995. *Statistics as Principled Argument*. Hillsdale, N.J.: LEA.

Abers, Rebecca. 2000. *Inventing Local Democracy. Grassroots Politics in Brazil*. Boulder/London: Lynne Rienner Publishers.

Abramson, Jeffrey. 1994. *We, the Jury: The Jury System and the Ideal of Democracy*. New York: Basic Books.

Ackerman, Bruce, and James S. Fishkin. 2004. *Deliberation Day*. New Haven, Conn.: Yale University Press.

Adamic, Lada A., and Natalie Glance. 2005. "The Political Blogosphere and the 2004 Election: Divided They Blog." Paper presented at the annual meeting of the International Conference on Knowledge and Discovery, Chicago, IL.

Adler, Stephan J. 1994. *The Jury: Trial and Error in the American Courtroom*. New York: New York Times Books.

Agence France-Presse. 2008. "Russia: Jury Trials Under Attack," *New York Times* (December 6), A8.

Aish, Anne-Marie, and Karl G. Jöreskog. 1990. "A Panel Model for Political Efficacy and Responsiveness: An Application of LISREL 7 with Weighted Least Squares." *Quality and Quantity* 24: 405–26.

Ajzen, Icek. 1991. "The Theory of Planned Behavior." *Organizational Behavior and Human Decision Processes* 50: 179–211.

Ajzen, Icek, and Martin Fishbein. 1980. *Understanding Attitudes and Predicting Social Behavior*. Englewood Cliffs, N.J.: Prentice-Hall.

Albarracin, Dolores, and Robert S. Wyer, Jr. 2000. "The Cognitive Impact of Past Behavior: Influences on Beliefs, Attitudes, and Future Behavioral Decisions." *Journal of Personality and Social Psychology* 79: 5–22.

Alexander, Keith L. 2008. "D.C. Arrests Residents For Missing Jury Service." *Washington Post* (July 14), B1.

Allen, James L. 1977. "Attitude Change Following Jury Duty." *Justice System Journal* 2: 246–57.

Allen, Chris T., Karen A. Machleit, and Susan Schultz Kleine. 1992. "A Comparison of Attitudes and Emotions as Predictors of Behavior at Diverse Levels of Behavioral Experience." *Journal of Consumer Research* 18: 493–504.

Almond, Gabriel A., and Sidney Verba. 1963. *The Civic Culture: Political Attitudes and Democracy in Five Nations.* Princeton: Princeton University Press.

Amar, Akhil Reed. 1997. *The Constitution and Criminal Procedure: First Principles.* New Haven: Yale University Press.

Amar, Vikram D. 1995. "Jury Service as Political Participation Akin to Voting." *Cornell Law Review* 80: 203–59.

Anderson, Kent, and Mark Nolan. 2004. "Lay Participation in the Japanese Justice System: A Few Preliminary Thoughts Regarding the Lay Assessor System (Saiban-In Seido) from Domestic and Historical and International Psychological Perspectives." *Vanderbilt Journal of Transnational Law* 37: 935–92.

Bales, Robert Freed. 1950. Interaction Process Analysis: A Method for the Study of Small Groups. Reading, Mass.: Addison-Wesley.

Ball, Andrea. 2001. "Trauma of Trials Takes Toll on Juries," *Austin American-Statesman* (December 30), B1.

Balzac v. Porto Rico, 258 U.S. 298 (1922).

Bandura, Albert. 1986. *Social Foundations of Thought and Action: A Social Cognitive Theory.* New York: Prentice-Hall.

Barber, Benjamin R. 1984. *Strong Democracy: Participatory Politics for a New Age.* Berkeley: University of California Press.

Barge, J. Kevin. 2002. "Enlarging the Meaning of Group Deliberation: From Discussion to Dialogue." In *New Directions in Group Communication*, ed. Lawrence R. Frey, 159–178. Thousand Oaks, CA: Sage.

Batson v. Kentucky, 476 U.S. 79 (1986).

Baumeister, Roy F., and Dianne M. Tice. 2006. "Self-Esteem and Responses to Success and Failure: Subsequent Performance and Intrinsic Motivation." *Journal of Personality* 53: 450–67.

Becker, Ted, and Christa Daryl Slaton. 2000. *The Future of Teledemocracy.* New York: Praeger.

Becker, Theodore L., Donald C. Hildum, and Keith Bateman. 1965. "The Influence of Jurors' Values on Their Verdicts: A Courts and Politics Experiment." *Southwestern Social Science Quarterly* 45: 130–40.

Bem, Daryl. 1972. "Self-Perception Theory." In *Advances in Experimental Social Psychology*, 6th ed. Leonard Berkowitz, 1–62. New York: Academic Press.

Benhabib, Seyla. 1996. *Democracy and Difference: Contesting the Boundaries of the Political.* Princeton: Princeton University Press.

Bennett, W. Lance. 1998. "The Uncivic Culture: Communication, Identity, and the Rise of Lifestyle Politics." *PS, Political Science & Politics* 31: 741–61.

Bentler, Peter M., and Douglas G. Bonett. 1980. "Significance Tests and Goodness-of-Fit in the Analysis of Covariance Structures." *Psychological Bulletin* 88: 588–600.

Bergman, Paul, and Michael Asimow. 2006. *Reel Justice: The Courtroom Goes to the Movies*. Riverside, NJ: Andrews McMeel Publishing.

Bertelsen, Kristy Lee. 1998. "From Specialized Courts to Specialized Juries: Calling for Professional Juries in Complex Civil Litigation." *Suffolk Journal of Trial and Appellate Advocacy* 3: 15–16.

Bessette, Joseph M. 1994. *The Mild Voice of Reason*. Chicago: University of Chicago Press.

Bingham, Lisa Blomgren, Tina Nabatchi, and Rosemary O'Leary. 2005. "The New Governance: Practices and Processes for Stakeholder and Citizen Participation in the Work of Government." *Public Administration Review* 65: 547–58.

Boatright, Robert G. 1998. *Improving Citizen Response to Jury Summonses: A Report with Recommendations*. Des Moines, IA: American Judicature Society.

Boatright, Robert. G., and Beth Murphy. 1999. "Behind Closed Doors: Assisting Jurors with Their Deliberations." *Judicature* 83: 52–58.

Bormann, Ernest G. 1996. "Symbolic Convergence Theory and Communication in Group Decision Making." In *Communication and Group Decision-Making*, Cambridge, England: Cambridge University Press. 2nd ed. Randy Y. Hirokawa and Marshall Scott Poole, 81–113. Beverly Hills: Sage.

Brady, Henry E., Sidney Verba, and Kay Lehman Schlozman. 1995. "Beyond SES: A Resource Model of Political Participation." *American Political Science Review* 189: 271–94.

Broder, David. 2000. *Democracy Derailed: Initiative Campaigns and the Power of Money*. New York: Harcourt.

Browne, Michael W., and Robert Cudeck. 1993. "Alternative Ways of Assessing Model Fit." In *Testing Structural Equation Models*, ed. Kenneth A. Bollen and J. Scott Long, 136–62. Newbury Park, California: Sage.

Burkhalter, Stephanie, John Gastil, and Todd Kelshaw. 2002. "A Conceptual Definition and Theoretical Model of Public Deliberation in Small Face-to-Face Groups." *Communication Theory* 12: 398–422.

Burnett, Ann, and Diane M. Badzinski. 2000. "An Exploratory Study of Argument in the Jury Decision-Making Process." *Communication Quarterly* 48: 380–96.

Burnheim, John. 1985. *Is Democracy Possible? The Alternative to Electoral Politics*. Los Angeles: University of California.

Burtt, Shelley. 1990. "The Good Citizen's Psyche: On the Psychology of Civic Virtue." *Polity* 23: 269–93.

Button, Mark, and Kevin Mattson. 1999. "Deliberative Democracy in Practice: Challenges and Prospects for Civic Deliberation." *Polity* 31: 609–37.

Byrne, Barbara M. 2001. *Structural Equation Modeling with AMOS: Basic Concepts, Applications, and Programming*. Mahwah, N.J.: Lawrence Erlbaum.

California Grand Jurors' Association. 2002. *Loyola Law Review* 35: 609–59. Available online at http://llr.lls.edu/volumes/v35-issue3/ccja.pdf.

Callenbach, Ernest, and Michael Phillips. 1985. *A Citizen Legislature*. Berkeley: Banyan Tree Books.

Cappella, Joseph N., Vincent Price, and Lilach Nir. 2002. "Argument Repertoire as a Reliable and Valid Measure of Opinion Quality: Electronic Dialogue During Campaign 2000." *Political Communication* 19: 73–93.

Carrington, Paul D. 2003. "The Civil Jury and American Democracy." *Duke Journal of Comparative & International Law* 13: 79–94.

Carson, Lyn, and Brian Martin. 1999. *Random Selection in Politics*. Westport, CT: Praeger.

———. 2002. "Random Selection of Citizens for Technological Decision Making." *Science and Public Policy* 29: 105–13.

Carter, Terry. 2005. "The Verdict on Juries." *ABA Journal* 91: 40–41.

Chambers, Simone. 2003. "Deliberative Democratic Theory." *Annual Review of Political Science* 6: 307–326.

Christoff, Kalina, Alan Gordon, and Rachelle Smith. (in press). "The Role of Spontaneous Thought in Human Cognition." In *Neuroscience of Decision Making*, ed. Oshin Vartanian and Denise R. Mandel. Psychology Press. Available online at http://www.christofflab.ca/pdfs/spontaneous_thought_chapter_2007.pdf.

Cohen, Jacob. 1988. *Statistical Power Analysis for the Behavioral Sciences*, 2nd Edition. Hillsdale, N.J.: Lawrence Erlbaum.

Cohen, Jacob, Patricia Cohen, Stephen G. West, and Leona S. Aiken. 2003. *Applied Multiple Regression/Correlation Analysis for the Behavioral Sciences*, 3rd Edition. Mahwah, N.J.: LEA.

Cohen, Joshua. 1997. "Deliberation and Democratic Legitimacy." In *Deliberative Democracy: Essays on Reason and Politics*, ed. James F. Bohman and William Rehg. Cambridge: MIT Press.

Cohen, Joshua, Joel Rogers. 1995. *Associations and Democracy*. London: Verso.

Collins, Allan M., and Elizabeth F. Loftus. 1975. "A Spreading Activation Theory of Semantic Processing." *Psychological Review* 82: 407–28.

Consolini, Paula. 1992. *Learning by Doing Justice: Jury Service and Political Attitudes*. Doctoral dissertation, University of California at Berkeley.

Cook, Fay Lomax, Jason Barabas, and Lawrence R. Jacobs. 1999. *Deliberative Democracy in Action: An Analysis of the Effects of Public Deliberation*. Unpublished manuscript, Northwestern University, Evanston, IL.

Cook, Thomas D., and Donald T. Campbell. 1979. *Quasi-Experimentation*. Chicago: Rand McNally.

Cooke, Maeve. 2000. "Five Arguments for Deliberative Democracy." *Political Studies* 48: 947–69.

Craig, Stephen C., Richard G. Niemi, and Glenn E. Silver. 1990. "Political Efficacy and Trust: A Report on the NES Pilot Study Items." *Political Behavior* 12: 289–314.

Cronin, Thomas E. 1989. *Direct Democracy: The Politics Of Initiative, Referendum, and Recall*. Cambridge: Harvard University Press.

Crosby, Ned. 1995. "Citizen Juries: One Solution for Difficult Environmental Questions." In *Fairness and Competence in Citizen Participation: Evaluating Models for Environmental Discourse*, ed. Ortwin Renn, Thomas Webler, and Peter Wiedemann, 157–74. Boston: Kluwer Academic.

———. 2003. *Healthy Democracy: Bringing Trustworthy Information to the Voters of America*. Minneapolis, MN: Beaver's Pond.

Crosby, Ned, and Doug Nethercutt. 2005. "Citizens Juries: Creating a Trustworthy Voice of the People." In *The Deliberative Democracy Handbook: Strategies for Effective Civic Engagement in the Twenty-First Century*, ed. John Gastil and Peter Levine, 111–19. San Francisco: Jossey-Bass.

Cutler, Brian L., and Donna M. Hughes. 2001. "Judging Jury Service: Results of the North Carolina Administrative Office of the Courts Juror Survey." *Behavioral Sciences and the Law* 19: 305–20.

Dahl, Robert A. 1989. *Democracy and Its Critics*. New Haven: Yale University Press.

———. 2002. *How Democratic Is the American Constitution?* New Haven: Yale University Press.

Dahlberg, Lincoln. 2005. "The Habermasian Public Sphere: Taking Difference Seriously." *Theory and Society* 34: 111–36.

Daubert v. Merrell Dow Pharm, 509 U.S. 579 (1993).

Davis, Valerie, and Brian Kleiner. 2000. "How to Orient Employees into New Positions Successfully." *Management Research News* 2: 44–48.

Dees, Tom M. 2001. "Juries: On the Verge of Extinction? A Discussion of Jury Reform." *Southern Methodist University Law Review* 54: 1755–812.

Deess, Perry, and John Gastil. 2009. "How Jury Service Makes Us Into Better Citizens." *The Jury Expert* 21: Available online at http://www.astcweb. org/public/publication/article.cfm/1/21/3/How-Jury-Deliberation-Makes-Us-Better-Citizens.

Delli Carpini, Michael X., and Scott Keeter. 1996. *What Americans Know and Why It Matters*. New Haven: Yale University Press.

Delli Carpini, Michael X., Fay Lomax Cook, and Lawrence R. Jacobs. 2004. "Public Deliberation, Discursive Participation, and Citizen Engagement: A Review of the Empirical Literature." *Annual Review of Political Science* 7: 315–44.

Deneen, Patrick J. 2005. *Democratic Faith*. Princeton: Princeton University Press.

Denver, David, Gordon Hands, and Bill Jones. 1995. "Fishkin and the Deliberative Opinion Poll: Lessons from a Study of the Granada 500 Television Program." *Political Communication* 12: 147–56.

"Development in the Law, The Jury's Capacity to Decide Civil Cases." 1997. *Harvard Law Review* 110: 1489–1513.

Devine, Dennis J., Laura D. Clayton, Benjamin B. Dunford, Rasmy Seying, and Jennifer Pryce. 2001. "Jury Decision Making: 45 years of Empirical Research on Deliberating Groups." *Psychology, Public Policy and Law* 7: 622–727.

Diamond, Shari Seidman. 1997. "Illuminations and Shadows from Jury Simulations." *Law and Human Behavior* 21: 561–71.

Diamond, Shari Seidman, Mary R. Rose, Beth Murphy, and Sven Smith. 2006. "Juror Questions During Trial: A Window into Juror Thinking." *Vanderbilt Law Review* 59: 1926–72.

Diamond, Shari Seidman, Neil Vidmar, Mary R. Rose, Leslie Ellis, and Beth Murphy. 2003a. "Inside the Jury Room: Evaluating Juror Discussions during Trial." *Judicature* 8: 54–58.

———. 2003b. "Jury Discussions during Civil Trials: Studying an Arizona Innovation." *Arizona Law Review* 45: 1–81.

Dillard, James P., and S. J. Backhaus. 1997. "An Exploration into Emotion and Civic Deliberation." Paper presented at the annual meeting of the National Communication Association, San Diego, CA.

Dillman, Don A. 1999. *Mail and Internet Surveys: The Tailored Design Method*. New York: Wiley.

Dooley, Laura. 2008. "National Juries for National Cases: Preserving Citizen Participation in Large-Scale Litigation." *New York University Law Review* 83: 410–49.

Dryzek, John. 2009. "The Australian Citizens' Parliament: A World First." *Journal of Public Deliberation* 5. Available online at http://services. bepress.com/cgi/viewcontent.cgi?article=1114&context=jpd.

Dugoni, Robert. 2003. *The Jury Master.* New York: Grand Central Publishing.

Durand, Richard M., William O. Bearden, and A. William Gustafson. 1978. "Previous Jury Service as a Moderating Influence on Jurors' Beliefs and Attitudes." *Psychological Reports* 42: 567–72.

Dwyer, William L. 2002. *In the Hands of the People.* New York: St. Martin's.

Edwards, Bob, Michael W. Foley, and Mario Diani. 2001. *Beyond Tocqueville: Civil Society and the Social Capital Debate in Comparative Perspective.* Hanover, NH: University Press of New England.

Elstub, Stephen. 2008. *Towards a Deliberative and Associational Democracy.* Edinburgh: Edinburgh University Press.

Equal Justice Initiative. 2010. *Illegal Racial Discrimination in Jury Selection: A Continuing Legacy.* Montgomery, Alabama: Equal Justice Initiative. Available online at http://eji.org/eji/files/Race%20and%20Jury%20Selection%20Report.pdf.

Evans, Sara M., and Harry C. Boyte. 1992. *Free Spaces: The Sources of Democratic Change in America.* Chicago: University of Chicago Press.

Eveland Jr., William P. 2004. "The Effect of Political Discussion in Producing Informed Citizens: The Roles of Information, Motivation, and Elaboration." *Political Communication* 21: 177–93.

Fagotto, Elena, and Archon Fung. 2006. "Embedded Deliberation: Entrepreneurs, Organizations, and Public Action." Report prepared for the William and Flora Hewlett Foundation. Available online at http://www.prevnet. org/ru21/common/pdf/Hewlett-Masterfile-April06.pdf.

Ferejohn, John. 2002. "Judicializing Politics, Politicizing Law." *Law and Contemporary Problems* 65: 41–68.

Finkel, Steven E. 1985. "Reciprocal Effects of Participation and Political Efficacy: A Panel Analysis." *American Journal of Political Science* 29: 891–913.

———. 1995. *Causal Analysis with Panel Data.* Thousand Oaks, California: Sage.

———. 2003. "Can Democracy Be Taught?" *Journal of Democracy* 14: 137–51.

Finkel, Steven E., Edward N. Muller, and Karl-Dieter Opp. 1989. "Personal Influence, Collective Rationality, and Mass Political Action." *American Political Science Review* 83: 885–903.

Fishkin, James S. 1991. *Democracy and Deliberation: New Directions for Democratic Reform.* New Haven: Yale University Press.

———. 1995. *The Voice of the People.* New Haven: Yale University Press.

———. 2009. *When the People Speak: Deliberative Democracy and Public Consultation.* Oxford: Oxford University Press.

Fishkin, James S., and Cynthia Farrar. 2005. "Deliberative Polling: From Experiment to Community Resource." In *The Deliberative Democracy Handbook: Strategies for Effective Civic Engagement in the Twenty-First Century,* ed. John Gastil and Peter Levine, 68–79. San Francisco: Jossey-Bass.

Fishkin, James S., and Robert C. Luskin. 1999. "Bringing Deliberation to the Democratic Dialogue: The NIC and beyond." In *The Poll with a Human Face: The National Issues Convention Experiment in Political Communication*, ed. Maxwell McCombs and Amy Reynolds. Mahwah, NJ: Lawrence Erlbaum.

Fivush, Robyn. 1995. "Language, Narrative, and Autobiography." *Consciousness and Cognition* 4: 100–3.

Franken, Harry. 1986a. "Ex-wife Tells Judge about Slaying of Pair." *Columbus Dispatch* (November 18, 1986) B5.

———. 1986b. "Holiday Delays Closing Arguments in Powers' Murder Trial." *Columbus Dispatch* (November 26), D3.

———. 1986c. "Powers Trial Now Up to Jury." *Columbus Dispatch* (December 2), D3.

———. 1986d. "Woman Describes Escape in Shootings." *Columbus Dispatch* (August 8), B3.

———. 1987a. "Psychologist Testifies for Slayer." *Columbus Dispatch* (April 30), D5.

———. 1987b. "Witnesses Call Killer a Father Figure." *Columbus Dispatch* (April 29), E3.

Fraser, Nancy. 1997. *Justice Interruptus: Critical Reflections on the "Postsocialist" Condition.* New York: Routledge.

Freie, John F. 1997. "The Effects of Campaign Participation on Political Attitudes." *Political Behavior* 19: 133–56.

Fung, Archon. 2005a. "Deliberation Before the Revolution – Toward an Ethics of Deliberative Democracy in an Unjust World." *Political Theory* 33: 397–419.

Galanter, Marc. 2004. "The Vanishing Trial: An Examination of Trials and Related Matters in Federal and State Courts." *Journal of Empirical Legal Studies* 3: 459–570.

Gall, Alevtina, and John Gastil. 2006. "The Magic of Raymond Burr: How Jury Orientation Prepares Citizens for Jury Service." *Court Manager* 21: 27–31.

Gallup, Alec M., and Frank Newport, eds. 2006. The Gallup Poll: Public Opinion 2005. Lanham, Md.: Rowman and Littlefield.

Gastil, John. 1993. *Democracy in Small Groups: Participation, Decision-Making, and Communication.* Philadelphia: New Society Publishers.

———. 1994. *Democratic Citizenship and the National Issues Forums.* Doctoral dissertation, University of Wisconsin-Madison.

———. 1999. "The Effects of Deliberation on Political Beliefs and Conversation Behavior." Paper presented at the annual meeting of the International Communication Association, San Francisco, CA.

———. 2000a. *By Popular Demand: Revitalizing Representative Democracy through Deliberative Elections.* Berkeley: University of California Press.

———. 2000b. "Is Face-to-Face Citizen Deliberation a Luxury or a Necessity?" *Political Communication* 17: 357–61.

———. 2004. "Adult Civic Education through the National Issues Forums: Developing Democratic Habits and Dispositions through Public Deliberation." *Adult Education Quarterly* 54: 308–28.

———. 2007. "Review of *Saving Democracy: A Plan for Real Representation in America* by Kevin O'Leary." *Perspectives on Politics* 5: 645–46.

———. 2008. *Political Communication and Deliberation.* Thousand Oaks, California: Sage.

———. 2010. *The Group in Society.* Thousand Oaks, California: Sage.

Gastil, John, and Ned Crosby. 2003. "Voters Need More Reliable Information." *Seattle Post-Intelligencer* (November 6). Available at http://seattlepi. nwsource.com/opinion/147013_uninformed06.htm

Gastil, John, and James P. Dillard. 1999. "Increasing Political Sophistication through Public Deliberation. *Political Communication* 16:3–23.

Gastil, John, and Peter Levine, eds. 2005. *The Deliberative Democracy Handbook: Strategies for Effective Civic Engagement in the Twenty-First Century.* San Francisco: Jossey-Bass.

Gastil, John, and Michael Xenos. (2010). "Of Attitudes and Engagement: Clarifying the Reciprocal Relationship between Civic Attitudes and Political Participation." *Journal of Communication* 60: 318–43.

Gastil, John, Stephanie Burkhalter, and Laura W. Black. 2007. "Do Juries Deliberate? A Study of Deliberation, Individual Difference, and Group Member Satisfaction at a Municipal Courthouse." *Small Group Research* 38: 337–59.

Gastil, John, E. Pierre Deess, Philip J. Weiser, and Jordan Meade. 2008. "Jury Service and Electoral Participation: A Test of the Participation Hypothesis." *Journal of Politics* 70: 1–16.

Gastil, John, E. Pierre Deess, and Phillip J. Weiser. 2002. "Civic Awakening in the Jury Room: A Test of the Connection between Jury Deliberation and Political Participation." *Journal of Politics* 64: 585–95.

Gastil, John, Colin J. Lingle, and E. Pierre Deess. (2010). "Deliberation and Global Criminal Justice: A Jury System for the International Criminal Court." *Ethics & International Affairs* 24: 69–90.

Gastil, John, Justin Reedy, and Chris Wells. 2007. "When Good Voters Make Bad Policies: Assessing and Improving the Deliberative Quality of Initiative Elections." *University of Colorado Law Review* 78: 1435–88.

Gastil, John, Jay Leighter, Laura W. Black, and E. Pierre Deess. 2008a. "From Small Group Member to Citizen: Measuring the Impact of Jury Deliberation on Citizen Identity and Civic Norms." *Human Communication Research* 34: 137–69.

Gastil, John, Justin Reedy, Don Braman, and Dan M. Kahan. 2008b. "Deliberation Across the Cultural Divide: Assessing the Potential for Reconciling Conflicting Cultural Orientations to Reproductive Technology." *George Washington Law Review* 76: 1772–97.

Gerstel, Naomi, and Gallagher, Sally K. 2001. "Men's Caregiving: Gender and the Contingent Character of Care." *Gender and Society* 15: 197–217.

Gillette, Clayton. 2005. "Voting with Your Hands: Direct Democracy in Annexation." *Southern California Law Review* 78: 835–68.

Glaberson, William. 2001. "Juries, Their Powers Under Siege, Find Their Role Is Being Eroded." *New York Times* (March 2), A1.

Goodin, Robert E. 2003. *Reflective Democracy.* Oxford: Oxford University Press.

Goodin, Robert E., and John S. Dryzek. 2006. "Deliberative Impacts: The Macro-Political Uptake of Mini-Publics." *Politics and Society* 34: 219–44.

Gore, Albert. 2007. *The Assault on Reason.* New York: Penguin Press.

Green, Donald P., and Alan S. Gerber. 2004. *Get Out the Vote: How to Increase Voter Turnout.* Washington, DC: Brookings Institution Press.

Green, Donald P., and R. Shachar. 2000. "Habit Formation and Political Behaviour: Evidence of Consuetude in Voter Turnout." *British Journal of Political Science* 30: 561–73.

Gutmann, Amy, and Dennis Thompson. 1996. *Democracy and Disagreement.* Cambridge: Harvard University Press.

Habermas, Jürgen. 1996. *Between Facts and Norms: Contributions to a Discourse Theory of Law and Democracy.* Cambridge: MIT Press.

Halperin, Morton H., Joseph T. Siegle, and Michael M. Weinstein. 2005. *The Democracy Advantage: How Democracies Promote Prosperity and Peace.* New York: Routledge.

Hannaford, Paula L., and G. Thomas Munsterman. 1977. "Beyond Note Taking: Innovations in Jury Reform." *Trial* 33:48–52.

Hannaford, Paula. L., Valerie P. Hans, and G. Thomas Munsterman. 2000. "Permitting Jury Discussions during Trial: Impact of the Arizona Reform." *Law and Human Behavior* 24: 359–82.

Hans, Valerie P. 1993. "Attitudes toward the Civil Jury: A Crisis of Confidence?" In *Verdict: Assessing the Civil Jury System,* ed. Robert E. Litan. Washington, DC: Brookings.

———. 2000. *Business on Trial: The Civil Jury and Corporate Responsibility.* New Haven: Yale University Press.

———. 2002. "U.S. Jury Reform: The Active Jury and the Adversarial Jury." *St. Louis University Public Law Review* 21: 85–97.

———. 2008a. "Empowering the Active Jury: A Genuine Tort Reform, 13 Roger Williams." *University Law Review* 13: 39–72.

———. 2008b. "Jury Systems Around the World." *Annual Review of Law and Social Science* 4: 275–97. (doi: 10.1146/annurev.lawsocsci.4.110707.172319)

Hans, Valerie P., and Neil Vidmar. 1986. *Judging the Jury.* New York: Plenum Press.

Hans, Valerie P., Paula L. Hannaford-Agor, Nicole L. Mott, and G. Thomas Munsterman. 2003. "The Hung Jury: The American Jury's Insights and Contemporary Understanding." *Criminal Law Bulletin* 39: 33–50.

Hastie, Reid, Steven D. Penrod, and Nancy Pennington. 1983. *Inside the Jury.* Cambridge: Harvard University Press.

Hastie, Reid, David A. Schkade, and John W. Payne. 1998. "A Study of Juror and Jury Judgments in Civil Cases: Deciding Liability for Punitive Damages." *Law and Human Behavior* 22: 287–314.

Hendriks, Carolyn M. 2006a. "Integrated Deliberation: Reconciling Civil Society's Dual Role in Deliberative Democracy." *Political Studies* 54: 486–508.

———. 2006b. "When the Forum Meets Interest Politics: Strategic Uses of Public Deliberation." *Politics and Society* 34: 571–602.

Hershey, Marjorie Randon. 1993. "Citizens' Groups and Political Parties in the United States." *Annals of the American Academy of Political and Social Science* 528: 142–56.

Heuer, Larry, and Steven Penrod. 1996. "Increasing Juror Participation in Trial through Note Taking and Question Asking." *Judicature* 79: 256–62.

Hickerson, Andrea, and Gastil, John. 2008. "Assessing the Difference Critique of Deliberation: Gender, Emotion and the Jury Experience." *Communication Theory* 18: 281–303.

Holbrook, Thomas M., and Scott D. McClurg. 2005. "The Mobilization of Core Supporters: Campaigns, Turnout, and Electoral Composition in United States Presidential Elections." *American Journal of Political Science*, 49: 689–703.

Holland v. Illinois, 493 U.S. 474 (1990).

Huckfeldt, Robert, Paul E. Johnson, and John Sprague. 2004. *Political Disagreement: The Survival of Diverse Opinions within Communication Networks*. New York: Cambridge University Press.

Hymanman Jr., Ira E. 1994. "Conversational Remembering: Story Recall with a Peer versus for an Experimenter." *Applied Cognitive Psychology* 8: 49–66.

Imwinkelried, Edward J. 2001. "A Minimalist Approach to the Presentation of Expert Testimony." *Stetson Law Review* 31: 105–27.

Jacobs, Lawrence R., Michael X. Delli Carpini, and Fay Lomax Cook. 2004. "How Do Americans Deliberate?" Paper presented at the Midwest Political Science Association, Chicago, IL.

Janara, Laura. 2002. *Democracy Growing Up: Authority, Autonomy and Passion in Tocqueville's Democracy in America*. Albany, NY: SUNY Press.

Janis, Irving L. 1982. *Groupthink: Psychological Studies of Policy Decision and Fiascoes*. 2nd ed. Boston: Houghton Mifflin.

Janssen, Davy, and Raphael Kies. 2005. "Online Forums and Deliberative Democracy." *Acta Politica* 40: 317–35.

Jerit, Jennifer, Jason Barabas, and Toby Bolsen. 2006. "Citizens, Knowledge, and the Information Environment." *American Journal of Political Science* 50: 266–82.

Jonakait, Randolph N. 2003. *The American Jury System*. New Haven: Yale University Press.

Kahan, Dan. M., and Donald Braman. 2008. "The Self-Defensive Cognition of Self-Defense." *American Criminal Law Review* 45: 1–65

Kahan, Dan. M., David A. Hoffman, and Donald Braman. 2009. "Whose Eyes are You Going to Believe? Scott v. Harris and the Perils of Cognitive Illiberalism." *Harvard Law Review* 122: 837–906.

Kahan, Dan, Donald Braman, John Gastil, and Paul Slovic. 2007. "Culture and Identity-Protective Cognition: Explaining the White-Male Effect in Risk Perception." *Journal of Empirical Legal Studies* 4: 465–505.

Kahan, Dan M., Paul Slovic, Donald Braman, and John Gastil. 2006. "Fear and Democracy: A Cultural Evaluation of Sunstein on Risk." *Harvard Law Review* 119: 1071–109.

Kahan, Dan M., Donald Braman, Paul Slovic, John Gastil, and Geoffrey Cohen. 2008. "Cultural Cognition of Nanotechnology Risk-Benefit Perceptions." *Nature Nanotechnology* 3: Available online at http://www.nature.com/nnano/journal/vaop/ncurrent/pdf/nnano.2008.341.pdf.

Kalven, Harry, and Hans Zeisel. 1966. *The American Jury*. Chicago: University of Chicago Press.

Karpowitz, Christopher F., and Jane Mansbridge. 2005. "Disagreement and Consensus: The Importance of Dynamic Updating in Public Deliberation." In *The Deliberative Democracy Handbook: Strategies for Effective Civic Engagement in the Twenty-First Century*, ed. John Gastil and Peter Levine, 237–53. San Francisco: Jossey-Bass.

Kaye, Judith. 2006. "Keynote Address, Symposium: Refinement or Reinvention: the State of Reform in New York." *Albany Law Review* 69: 831–49.

———. 2007. *The State of the Judiciary.* Available at http://www.courts.state.ny.us/admin/stateofjudiciary/soj2007.pdf

Kenny, David A., Lucia Manetti, Antonio Pierro, Stefano Livi, and Deborah A. Kashy. 2002. "The Statistical Analysis of Data from Small Groups." *Journal of Personality and Social Psychology* 83: 126–37.

"Keep moving on jury reform" (Editorial). 1996. *New York Times* (January 3). Available at http://www.nytimes.com/1996/01/03/opinion/keep-moving-on-jury-reform.html.

Kerr, Norbert L., Douglas L. Harmon, and James L. Graves.1982. "Independence of Multiple Verdicts by Jurors and Juries." *Journal of Applied Social Psychology* 12: 12–29.

Kerr, Norbert L, Robert S. Atkin, Garold Stasser, David Meek, Robert W. Holt, and James H. Davis. 1976. "Guilt beyond a Reasonable Doubt: Effects of Concept Definition and Assigned Decision Rule on the Judgments of Mock Jurors." *Journal of Personality and Social Psychology* 34: 282–94.

Knack, Stephen. 1993. "The Voter Participation Effects of Selecting Jurors from Registration Lists." *Journal of Law and Economics* 36: 99–114.

Knox, Malcolm. 2005. *Secrets of the Jury Room.* Milsons Point, NSW: Random House Australia.

Koniordos, Sokratis M. 2005. *Networks, Trust, and Social Capital: Theoretical and Empirical Investigations from Europe.* Aldershot, Hants, England: Ashgate.

Kousser, Thad, and Mathew D. McCubbins. 2005. "Social Choice, Crypto-Initiatives, and Policymaking by Direct Democracy." *Southern California Law Review* 78: 949–84.

Krauss, Elissa. 2005. "Jury Trial Innovations in New York State." *New York State Bar Association Journal* 77: 22–27.

Krosnick, Jon A. 1991. "The Stability of Political Preferences: Comparisons of Symbolic and Nonsymbolic Attitudes." *American Journal of Political Science* 35: 547–76.

Laville, Sandra. 2010a. "Four Jailed for £1.75m Heathrow Robbery." *Guardian.co.uk* (March 31). Available online at http://www.guardian.co.uk/uk/2010/mar/31/jury-less-trial-guilty-heathrow-robbery.

Laville, Sandra. 2010b. "Heathrow Robbery trial Breaks with 400-Year Tradition of Trial by Jury." *Guardian.co.uk* (January 10). Available online at http://www.guardian.co.uk/uk/2010/jan/10/heathrow-robbery-trial-jury-twomey.

Leib, Ethan J. 2004. *Deliberative Democracy in America: A Proposal for a Popular Branch of Government.* University Park, PA: Penn State Press.

Leigh, Lawrence J. 1984. "A Theory of Jury Trial Advocacy." *Utah Law Review* 1984: 763–806.

Leighley, Jan E. 1995. "Attitudes, Opportunities and Incentives: A Field Essay on Political Participation." *Political Research Quarterly* 48:181–209.

Leighninger, Matthew, and Bill Bradley. 2006. *The Next Form of Democracy: How Expert Rule Is Giving Way to Shared Governance-and Why Politics Will Never be the Same*. Nashville, TN: Vanderbilt University Press.

Levin, Jonathan, and Barry Nalebuff. 1995. "An Introduction to Vote-Counting Schemes." *The Journal of Economic Perspectives* 9: 3–26.

Lieberman, Joel D., and Bruce D. Sales. 2006. *Scientific Jury Selection*. Washington, DC: American Psychological Association.

Liptak, Adam. 2002a. "Debate Grows on Jury's Role in Injury Cases." *New York Times* (August 26), A1.

Liptak, Adam. 2002b. "A State Weighs Allowing Juries to Judge Laws." *New York Times* (September 22), A1.

Losh, Susan Carol, Adina W. Wasserman, and Michael A. Wasserman. 2000. "Reluctant Jurors: What Summons Responses Reveal about Jury Duty Attitudes." *Judicature* 83: 304–10.

Luskin, Robert C. 1990. "Explaining Political Sophistication." *Political Behavior* 12: 331–61.

Luskin, Robert C., James S. Fishkin, and Roger Jowell. 2002. "Considered Opinions: Deliberative Polling in Britain." *British Journal of Political Science* 32: 455–87.

MacCoun, Robert J., and Norbert L. Kerr. 1988. "Asymmetric Influence in Mock Jury Deliberation: Jurors' Bias for Leniency." *Journal of Personality and Social Psychology* 54: 21–33.

Maisel, Louis Sandy. 2007. *American Political Parties and Elections: A Very Short Introduction*. New York: Oxford University Press.

Mansbridge, Jane J. 1983. *Beyond Adversary Democracy*. Chicago: University of Chicago Press.

———. 1999. "On the Idea that participation makes better citizens. "In citizen competence and Democratic Institutions, ed. Stephen L. Elkin and Karol Edward soltan. University Park, PA: Pennsylvania State University Press.

Mansbridge, Jane J., J. Hartz-Karp, M. Amengual, and John Gastil. 2006. "Norms of Deliberation: An Inductive Study." *Journal of Public Deliberation* 2: Available online at http://services.bepress.com/jpd/vol2/iss1/art7.

Mara, Gerald M. 2001. "Thucydides and Plato on Democracy and Trust." *Journal of Politics* 63, 820–45.

Markman v. Westview Instruments, Inc., 517 U.S. 370 (1996).

Matsusaka, John G. 2004. *For the Many or the Few: The Initiative, Public Policy, and American Democracy*. Chicago: University of Chicago Press.

Mathews, Forrest David. 1994. *Politics for People: Finding a Responsible Public Voice*. Chicago: University of Illinois Press.

Matthews, Roger, Lynn Hancock, and Daniel Briggs. 2004. *Jurors' Perceptions, Understanding, Confidence and Satisfaction in the Jury System: A Study in Six Courts*. Online Report 05/04. London: Home Office. Available online at http://www.homeoffice.gov.uk/rds/pdfs2/rdsolr0504.pdf.

McDaniel, Mark A., and Gilles O. Einstein. 2007. "Spontaneous Retrieval in Prospective Memory." In *The Foundation of Remembering: Essays in Honor of Henry L. Roediger* 3rd ed. Henry L. Roediger and James D. Nairne, 227–42. Psychology Press.

McLeod, Jack M., Katie Daily, Zhongshi Guo, William P. Eveland, Jan Bayer, Seungchan Yang, and Hsu Wang. 1996. "Community Integration, Local Media Use, and Democratic Processes." *Communication Research* 23: 179–209.

Mendelberg, Tali. 2002. "The Deliberative Citizen: Theory and Evidence." *Political Decision Making, Deliberation and Participation* 6: 151–93.

Mendelberg, Tali, and John Oleske. 2000. "Race and Public Deliberation." *Political Communication* 17: 169–91.

Menkel-Meadows, Carrie. 1995 "The Many Ways of Mediation: The Transformation of Traditions, Ideologies, Paradigms, and Practices." *Negotiation Journal* 11: 217–42.

Miller, Warren E., and Merrill Shanks. 1996. *The New American Voter.* Cambridge: Harvard University Press.

Mills, Carol J., and Wayne E. Bohannon. 1980. "Juror Characteristics: To What Extent Are They Related to Jury Verdicts?" *Judicature* 64: 23–31.

Mize, Gregory E., Paula Hannaford-Agor, and Nicole L. Waters. 2007. *The State-Of-The-States Survey of Jury Improvement Efforts: A Compendium Report.* Williamsburg, VA: National Center for State Courts. Available online at http://contentdm.ncsconline.org/cgi-bin/showfile. exe?CISOROOT=/juries&CISOPTR=112.

Moraski, Bryon J., and Charles R. Shipan 1999. "The Politics of Supreme Court Nominations: A Theory of Institutional Constraints and Choices." *American Journal of Political Science* 43: 1069–95.

Mott, Nicole L. 2003. "The Current Debate on Juror Questions: 'To Ask or Not to Ask, That is the Question'." *Chicago-Kent Law Review* 78: 1099–125.

Moy, Patricia, and John Gastil. 2006. "Predicting Deliberative Conversation: The Impact of Discussion Networks, Media Use, and Political Cognitions." *Political Communication* 23: 443–60.

Moy, Patricia, and Michael Pfau. 2000. *With Malice toward All: The Media and Public Confidence in Democratic Institutions.* New York: Praeger.

Moynihan, Lisa M., and Randall S. Peterson. 2001. "A Contingent Configuration Approach to Understanding the Role of Personality in Organizational Groups." *Research in Organizational Behavior* 23: 327–78.

Mutz, Diana C. 2006. *Hearing the Other Side: Deliberative versus Participatory Democracy.* New York: Cambridge University Press.

Myers, Robert D., Ronald S. Reinstein, and Gordon M. Griller. 1999. "Complex Scientific Evidence and the Jury." *Judicature* 83: 150–56.

Nemeth, Charlan. 1977. "Interactions between Jurors as a Function of Majority versus Unanimity Decision Rules." *Journal of Applied Social Psychology* 7: 38–56.

Nie, Norman H., Jane Junn, and Kenneth Stehlik-Barry. 1996. *Education and Democratic Citizenship in America.* Chicago: University of Chicago Press.

Niemeyer, Simon. 2004. "Deliberation in the Wilderness: Displacing Symbolic Politics." *Environmental Politics* 13: 347–72.

Niemi, Richard G., Stephen C. Craig, and Franco Mattei. 1991. "Measuring Internal Political Efficacy in the 1988 National Election Study." *American Political Science Review* 85: 1407–13.

O'Leary, Kevin. 2006. *Saving Democracy: A Plan for Real Representation in America.* Stanford: Stanford University Press.

Oliver, J. Eric, and Raymond E. Wolfinger. 1999. "Jury Aversion and Voter Registration." *American Political Science Review* 93: 147–52.

Opp, Karl-Dieter. 1986. "Soft Incentives and Collective Action: Participation in the Anti-Nuclear Movement?" *British Journal of Political Science* 16: 87–112.

Orbell, J., Dawes, R., and Schwartz-Shea, P. 1994. "Trust, Social Categories, and Individuals: The Case of Gender." *Motivation and Emotion* 18: 109–28.

Page, Benjamin I., and Robert Y. Shapiro. 1992. *The Rational Public: Fifty Years of Trends in Americans' Policy Preferences.* Chicago: University of Chicago.

Pateman, Carole. 1970. *Participation and Democratic Theory.* Cambridge: Cambridge University Press.

———. 1989. *The Disorder of Women: Democracy, Feminism, and Political Theory.* Cambridge: Polity Press.

Pearce, W. Barnett, and Stephen W. Littlejohn. 1997. *Moral Conflict: When Social Worlds Collide.* Thousand Oaks, California: Sage.

Pedersen, Johannes T. 1982. "On the Educational Function of Political Participation: A Comparative Analysis of John Stuart Mill's Theory and Contemporary Survey Research Findings." *Political Studies* 30: 557–68.

Peters v. Kiff, 407 U.S. 493 (1972).

Pettus, Ann Burnett. 1990. "The Verdict Is in: A Study of Jury Decision Making Factors, Moment of Personal Decision, and Jury Deliberations—From the Juror's Point of View." *Communication Quarterly* 38: 83–97.

Petty, Richard E., and John T. Cacioppo. 1986. "The Elaboration Likelihood Model of Persuasion." In *Advances in Experimental Social Psychology, 16th* ed. Leonard Berkowitz, 123–205. New York: Academic Press.

———. 1990. "Involvement and Persuasion: Tradition versus Integration." *Psychological Bulletin* 107: 367–74.

Petty, Richard E., Duane T. Wegener, and Leandre R. Fabrigar. 1997. "Attitudes and Attitude Change." *Annual Review of Psychology* 48: 609–47.

Pope, Whitney. 1986. *Alexis de Tocqueville: His Social and Political Theory.* Beverly Hills: Sage.

Popkin, Samuel. 1994. *The Reasoning Voter: Communication and Persuasion in Presidential Campaigns.* Chicago: University of Chicago.

Posner, Richard A. 2008. *How Judges Think.* Cambridge: Harvard University Press.

Powers v. Ohio, 499 U.S. 400 (1991).

Putnam, Robert D. 1995a. "Bowling Alone: America's Declining Social Capital." *Journal of Democracy* 6: 65–78.

———. 1995b. "Tuning in, Tuning Out: The Strange Disappearance of Social Capital in America." *PS, Political Science & Politics* 28: 664–83.

———. 2000. *Bowling Alone: The Collapse and Revival of American Community.* New York: Simon and Schuster.

Reuben, J. Thomas, and Daniel A. McFarland. 2006. *Bowling Young II: How Youth Voluntary Associations Affect Voting in Early Adulthood.* Available at http://www.civicyouth.org.

Richard, F. D., Charles F. Bond Jr., and Juli J. Stokes-Zoota. 2003. "One Hundred Years of Social Psychology Quantitatively Described." *Review of General Psychology* 7: 331–63.

Richert, John P. 1977. "Jurors' Attitudes toward Jury Service." *Justice System Journal* 2: 233–45.

Robinson, Eric. 2009. May 22. "Web of Justice?: Jurors' Use of Social Media." Posted at *Citizen Media Law Project*, http://www.citmedialaw.org/blog/2009/web-justice-jurors-use-social-media.

Romer, Daniel, Kathleen Hall Jamieson, and Sean Aday. 2003. "Television News and the Cultivation of Fear of Crime." *Journal of Communication* 53: 88–104.

Rousseau, Jean-Jacques. 1761/1950. *The Social Contract and Discourses.* New York: E. Dutton.

Ryfe, David Michael. 2002. "The Practice of Deliberative Democracy: A Study of 16 Deliberative Organizations." *Political Communication* 19: 359–77.

———. 2007. "Toward a Sociology of Deliberation." *Journal of Public Deliberation* 3: 1–27.

San Francisco Chronicle. 2006. "Where Politicians Dare to Tread." *San Francisco Chronicle* (June 18), available at http://www.sfgate.com/cgi-bin/article.cgi?f=/c/a/2006/06/18/EDGS0INK791.DTL&hw=citizens+assembly&sn=001&sc=1000.

Sanders, Lynn M. 1997. "Against Deliberation." *Political Theory* 25: 347–76.

Sandys, Marla, and Ronald C. Dillehay. 1995. "First-Ballot Votes, Predeliberation Dispositions, and Final Verdicts in Jury Trials." *Law and Human Behavior* 19: 175–95.

Schwartz, John. 2009. "As Jurors Turn to Google and Twitter, Mistrials Are Popping Up." *New York Times* (March 18), available online at http://www.nytimes.com/2009/03/18/us/18juries.html.

Schwartz, Barry. 1986. *The Battle for Human Nature.* New York: W. W. Norton.

Shah, Dhavan, Jaeho Cho, William Eveland, and Nojin Kwak. 2005. "Information and Expression in a Digital Age." *Communication Research* 32: 531–65.

Sharkey, Catherine M. 2003. "Review of Punitive Damages: Should Juries Decide?" *Texas Law Review* 82: 381–412.

Shepard, Randall T. 2006. "The New Role of State Supreme Courts as Engines of Court Reform." *New York University Law* Review 81: 1535–52.

Sherman, Elaine, Anil Mathur, and Ruth Belk Smith. 1997. "Store Environment and Consumer Purchase Behavior: Mediating Role of Consumer Emotions." *Psychology & Marketing* 14: 361–78.

Sintomer, Yves, Carsten Herzberg, and Anja Röcke. 2008. "Participatory Budgeting in Europe: Potentials and Challenges." International Journal of Urban and Regional Research 32: 164–78.

Skocpol, Theda, and Morris P. Fiorina. 1999. *Civic Engagement in American Democracy. Washington* DC: Brookings Institution Press.

Smith v. Texas, 311 U. S. 128 (1940).

Smith, Graham, and Corinne Wales. 1999. "The Theory and Practice of Citizen Juries." *Policy and Politics* 27: 295–308.

———. 2000. "Citizens' Juries and Deliberative Democracy." *Political Studies* 48: 51–65.

Smith, Mark A. 2002. "Ballot Initiatives and the Democratic Citizen." *Journal of Politics* 64: 892–903.

Sobol, Joanna. 1995. "Hardship Excuses and Occupational Exemptions: The Impairment of the "Fair-Cross Section of the Community"." *Southern California Law Review* 69: 155–232.

Solove, Daniel. 2009. "Should We Have Professional Juries?" *Concurring Opinions Blog* available at http://www.concurringopinions.com/ archives/2009/03/should_we_have.html.

Sprain, Leah, and John Gastil. 2006. "What Does It Mean to Deliberate? An Interpretative Account of the Norms and Rules of Deliberation Expressed by Jurors." Unpublished manuscript, Seattle: University of Washington.

State v. Costello, 646 N.W.2d 204 (2002).

Stenner-Day, Karen, and Mark Fischle. 1992. "The Effect of Political Participation on Political Efficacy: A Simultaneous Equations Model." *Australian Journal of Political Science* 27: 282–305.

Stephen, Jessica. 2009. "The Move to Silence Juror Twittering." *Wisconsin Law Journal* April 20, http://www.wislawjournal.com/article.cfm/2009/04/20/ The-move-to-silence-juror-Twittering.

Strauder v. West Virginia, 100 U.S. 303 (1880).

Street, Marc D. 1997. "Groupthink: An Examination of Theoretical Issues, Implications, and Future Research Suggestions." *Small Group Research* 28: 72–93.

Strodtbeck, Fred L., Rita M. James and Charles Hawkins. 1957. "Social Status in Jury Deliberation." *American Sociological Review* 22: 713–19.

Stromer-Galley, Jennifer. 2002. "New Voices in the Public Sphere: A Comparative Analysis of Interpersonal and Online Political Talk." *Javnost the Public* 9: 23–42.

Sunstein, Cass R. 2002. "The Law of Group Polarization." *Journal of Political Philosophy* 10: 175–95.

———. 2003. *Why Societies Need Dissent.* Cambridge: Harvard University Press.

———. 2005. "Group Judgments: Statistical Means, Deliberation, and Information Markets." *New York University Law Review* 80: 962–1049.

Sunstein, Cass R., Reid Hastie, John W. Payne, David A. Schkade, and W. Kip Viscusi. 2002. *Punitive Damages: Should Juries Decide?* Chicago: University of Chicago Press.

Sunwolf. 2004. *Practical Jury Dynamics.* Charlottesville, VA: Lexis Nexis.

Sunwolf, and David, R. Seibold. 1998. "Jurors' Intuitive Rules for Deliberation: A Structurational Approach to Communication in Jury Decision Making." *Communication Monographs* 65: 287–307.

Swain v. Alabama, 380 U.S. 202 (1965).

Tannen, Deborah. 2007. *Talking Voices: Repetition, Dialogue, and Imagery in Conversational Discourse.* New York: Cambridge University Press.

Taylor v. Louisiana, 419 U.S. 522 (1975).

Teddlie, Charles B., and Abbas Tashakkori. 1998. *Mixed Methodology: Combining Qualitative and Quantitative Approaches.* Newbury Park, California: Sage.

Theiss-Morse, Elizabeth, and John R. Hibbing. 2005. "Citizenship and Civic Engagement." *Annual Review of Political Science* 8: 227–49.

Thomas, Suja A. 2007. "Why Summary Judgment Is Unconstitutional." *Virginia Law Review* 93: 139–80.

Thompson, Dennis F. 2008. "Deliberative Democratic Theory and Empirical Political Science." *Annual Review of Political Science* 11: 497–520.

Thompson, Leigh L., Elizabeth A. Mannix, and Max H. Bazerman. 1988. "Group Negotiation: Effects of Decision Rule, Agenda, and Aspiration." *Journal of Personality and Social Psychology* 54: 86–95.

Threlkeld, Simon. 1998. "A Blueprint for Democratic Law-Making: Give Citizen Juries the Final Say." *Social Policy* 28: 5–9.

Tjosvold, Dean, and Richard H. G. Field. 1983. "Effects of Social Context on Consensus and Majority Vote Decision Making." *Academy of Management Journal* 26: 500–6.

Tocqueville, Alexis de. 1835/2002. *Democracy in America*. Washington, DC: Gateway Editions (Trans. by Henry Reeve, 1899). Full text of this translation is available online at http://xroads.virginia.edu/ HYPER/DETOC.

Tonn, Mari Boor. 2005. "Taking Conversation, Dialogue, and Therapy Public." *Rhetoric & Public Affairs* 8: 405–30.

Toobin, Jeffrey.1994. "Juried on Trial." *New Yorker* (October 31), 42–47.

Underwood, Barbara. 1992. "Ending Race Discrimination in Jury Selection: Whose Right Is It, Anyway?" *Columbia Law Review* 92: 725–74.

United States v. Wexler, 657 F. Supp. 966 (E.D. Pa. 1987).

United States v. Wexler, 838 F.2d 88 (3d Cir. 1988).

Vail, John. 2008. "Real issue is jurors' rights." *National Law Journal*. Republished online at http://reclaimdemocracy.org/articles/2008/civil_jury_trials.php.

Verba, Sidney and Norman Nie. 1972. *Participation in America: Political Democracy and Social Equality*. New York: Harper and Row.

Verba, Sidney, Kay L. Schlozman, and Henry E. Brady. 1995. *Voice and Equality: Civic Voluntarism in American Politics*. Cambridge: Harvard University Press.

Vidmar, Neil. 1998. "The Performance of the American Jury: An Empirical Perspective." *Arizona Law Review* 40: 849–99.

———. 2000. *World Jury Systems*. Oxford: Oxford University Press.

Vidmar, Neil, and Shari Seidman Diamond. 2001. "Juries and Expert Evidence." *Brooklyn Law Review* 66: 1121–80.

Vidmar, Neil and Valerie P. Hans. 2007. *American Juries: The Verdict*. Amherst, NY: Prometheus.

Vitiello, Michael, and J. Clark Kelso. 2002. "Reform of California's Grand Jury System." *Loyola Law Review* 35: 513–607. Available online at http://llr.lls.edu/volumes/v35-issue2/vitiello.pdf.

Wanous, John, and Arnon Reichers. 2000. "New Employee Orientation Programs." *Human Resources Management Review* 10: 435–51.

Warren, Donald. 1996. "Practice Makes Perfect: Civic Education by Precept and Example." In *Educating Tomorrow's Valuable Citizen* ed. Joan N. Burstyn, 119–37. Albany, NY: State University of New York Press.

Warren, Mark E. 1992. "Democratic Theory and Self-Transformation." *American Political Science Review* 86: 8–23.

———. 1993. "Can Participatory Democracy Produce Better Selves? Psychological Dimensions of Habermas' Discursive Model of Democracy." *Political Psychology* 14: 209–34.

———. 1999. *Democracy and Trust*. Cambridge: Cambridge University Press.

———. 2000. *Democracy and Association*. Princeton: Princeton University Press.

Warren, Mark E. and Hilary Pearse. 2008. *Designing Deliberative Democracy: The British Columbia Citizens' Assembly*. Cambridge: Cambridge University Press.

Weintraub, Jeff A. 1992. "Democracy and the Market: A Marriage of Inconvenience." In *From Leninism to Freedom* ed. Margaret Latus Nugent, 47–66. Boulder, CO.: Westview Press.

———. 1997. "The Theory and Politics of the Public/Private Distinction." In *Public and Private in Thought and Practice: Perspectives on a Grand Dichotomy*, ed. Jeff A. Weintraub and Krishan Kumar, 1–42. Chicago: University of Chicago Press.

Weithman, Paul J. 2005. "Deliberative Character." *Journal of Political Philosophy* 13: 263–83.

Welborn, Larry. 2009. "Juror's Painting Memorializes Little Girl." *Orange County Register* (October 29). Available online at http://www.ocregister.com/articles/araoz-madison-painting-2627338-soto-risch.

Wells, Chris, Justin Reedy, John Gastil, and Carolyn Lee. (2009). "Information Distortion and Voting Choices: Assessing the Origins and Effects of Factual Beliefs in an Initiative Election." *Political Psychology* 30: 953–69.

Wheeler, Shannon. 2001. *Too Much Coffee Man's Amusing Musings*. Milwaukie, Oregon: Dark Horse.

Wigley, Charles J. 1995. "Disclosiveness, Willingness to Communicate, and Apprehension as Predictors of Jury Selection in Felony Trials." *Communication Quarterly* 43: 342–52.

Wilber, Del Quentin. 2008. "Stevens Juror Lied to Be Dismissed: Judge in Alaska Senator's Trial Declines to Sanction Woman." *Washington Post* (November 4, 2008), A15.

Wolfsfeld, G. 1985. "Political Efficacy and Political Action: A change in Focus Using Data from Israel." *Social Science Quarterly* 66: 617–28.

Yankelovich, Daniel. 1991. *Coming to Public Judgment*. New York: Syracuse University Press.

York, Erin, and Benjamin Cornwell. 2006. "Status on Trial: Social Characteristics and Influence in the Jury Room." *Social Forces* 85: 455–76.

Young, Iris M. 1996. "Communication and the Other: Beyond Deliberative Democracy." In *Democracy and Difference: Contesting the Boundaries of the Political*, ed. Seyla Benhabib, 120–35. Princeton: Princeton University Press.

Youniss, James, Jeffrey A. McLellan, and Miranda Yates. 1997. "What We Know about Engendering Civic Identity." *American Behavioral Scientist* 40: 620–31.

Zaller, John R. 1992. *The Nature and Origins of Mass Opinion*. Cambridge: Cambridge University Press.

About the Authors

The four authors of this book have worked on this project since 1997, when they first began collecting data on jury service and voting. Each has undertaken distinct responsibilities, with John Gastil serving as the principal author.

John Gastil is a professor in the Department of Communication at the University of Washington. Each of his previous books are relevant to the current project, including *Democracy in Small Groups* (New Society, 1993), *By Popular Demand* (University of California, 2000a), *Political Communication and Deliberation* (Sage, 2008), *The Group in Society* (Sage, 2010), and the co-edited volume, *The Deliberative Democracy Handbook* (Jossey-Bass, 2005). He has published relevant works in *Communication Theory, Political Communication, Small Group Research,* and other scholarly journals.

Perry Deess is the Director of Institutional Research and Planning at the New Jersey Institute of Technology. Throughout this project, he had primary responsibility for data processing, survey implementation, theoretical background, and editing. He has published relevant works in *Journal of Politics, Mobilization,* and other journals and has written reports on law and public opinion at the Vera Institute of Justice and the Institute for Public Policy. He also has numerous publications in the fields of institutional assessment, program evaluation, and education.

Philip J. Weiser is a professor in the School of Law at the University of Colorado. He analyzed the legal and historical context of this research and has drawn out many of its implications. He is coauthor of *Digital Crossroads: American Telecommunications Policy in the Internet Age* (MIT, 2005) and has written articles and chapters relevant to this project in *Deliberation, Democracy, and the Media* (Rowman & Littlefield, 2000), the *New York*

University Review of Law and Social Change, and the *New York University Law Review*.

Cindy Simmons teaches journalism, media law, and negotiation in the University of Washington's Department of Communication. For this book, she researched the landmark case *Powers v. Ohio* and worked with undergraduate researchers to examine the jury's place in contemporary law, journalism, and popular culture. Simmons holds a J.D. from the University of Washington School of Law and an M.A. in journalism from the University of Wisconsin-Madison. She worked as a journalist for 15 years, covering state government, the courts, and public affairs.

Index

LaVergne, TN USA
02 April 2011
222615LV00003B/16/P